FOOTSORE 1

Walks & Hikes
Around Puget Sound

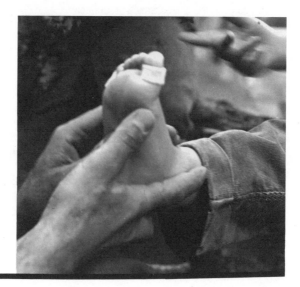

Third Edition

By Harvey Manning/Photos by Bob & Ira Spring
Maps by Gary Rands/The Mountaineers • Seattle

Whulj Trail—Tacoma to Everett • Seattle—Inland •
Lake Washington to East Sammamish Plateau •
Issaquah Alps • Cedar River • Duwamish — Green River

The Mountaineers: Organized 1906 "... to explore, study, preserve and enjoy the natural beauty of the Northwest."

Published by The Mountaineers
306 2nd Avenue West, Seattle WA 98119
The opinions expressed in this book are the author's and do not necessarily represent those of The Mountaineers.

Published simultaneously in Canada by
Douglas & McIntyre, Ltd., 1615 Venables St.,
Vancouver, British Columbia V5L 2H1

Series design by Marge Mueller; layout by Nick Gregoric
Cover photo: Cedar River Trail in Renton

Manufactured in the United States of America
First edition, December 1977; second printing November 1978
Second edition, February 1982; second printing April 1984;
    third printing August 1985; fourth printing June 1986
Third edition, May 1988

1 0
5 4 3 2

Library of Congress Cataloging in Publication Data

Manning, Harvey
    Footsore : walks & hikes around Puget Sound / by Harvey Manning ; photos by Bob & Ira Spring ; maps by Gary Rands. — 3rd ed.
        p.   cm.
    Includes index.
    ISBN 0-89886-156-X (v. 1) :
        1. Hiking — Washington (State) — Puget Sound Region — Guide-books.
    2. Puget Sound Region (Wash.) — Description and travel — Guide-books.
    I. Title.
GV199.42.W22P835 1988
917.97'79 — dc19   88-5354
                                                                                            CIP

Safety Considerations

Safety is an important concern in all outdoor activities. No guidebook can alert you to every hazard or anticipate the limitations of every reader, so the descriptions in this book are not representations that a particular trip is safe for your party. When you take a trip, you assume responsibility for your own safety. Some of the trips described in this book may require you to do no more than look both ways before crossing the street; on others, more attention to safety may be required due to terrain, traffic, weather, the capabilities of your party, or other factors. Keeping informed on current conditions and exercising common sense are the keys to a safe, enjoyable outing.

CONTENTS

4

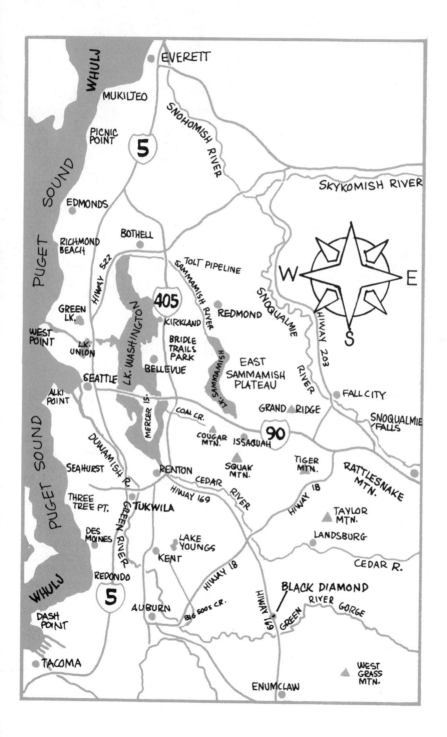

Green River Gorge near Kummer Bridge

INTRODUCTION

In the middle 1960s when we (that is, the Literary Fund Committee of which I was chairman and Tom Miller the idea man) embarked on the publication of trail guides, our initial goal was a single volume encompassing the full range of hiking that had been done by The Mountaineers since 1907, when the club took its first walk, to Seattle's West Point Lighthouse; climbed its first mountain, Si; and made its first wilderness expedition, into the heart of the Olympic Mountains. As the concept evolved under Tom's guidance we realized that the several quite different sorts of walking didn't marry very happily in a single collection. Our initial book, *100 Hikes in Western Washington,* published in 1966, focused primarily on the kind of hiking in most immediate and dire threat of being lost, in the mountain wilderness of the Cascades and Olympics. The threats to wilderness have persisted, indeed grown; in response, as well as to spread the boots around, the one book has given way to six Washington state volumes, the *100 Hikes* series. A second category of walking — at the wilderness edge on trails suitable for an hour or two (or, with families, all day) — was split off into the two-volume *Trips and Trails* series.

There remained a very large residue, containing none other than that first club hike to West Point and many other well-loved routes on beaches, lowlands, and foothills, some in wildland, some in pastoral or even urban settings. In 1969 Janice Krenmayr plugged the hole in our list with *Footloose Around Puget Sound.* The book was most timely. At the start of the decade the federal Outdoor Recreation Review Commission (ORRC) had found walking and bicycling to be the two fastest growing outdoor activities; further, it pointed to urban and near-urban trails as the most glaring deficiency in the nation's recreation system. *Footloose* showed the way. Recreation officials carried copies around the nation like so many letters to young churches. At a national workshop, a speaker held up a copy and said, "Every large city in the United States needs a book like this." Before many years virtually every large city *did* have a *Footloose*-type book.

Footloose was my special pet. I enjoyed working with Janice as her editor and following the paths she pioneered. When, after several revisions, she decided against undertaking another, I was stricken at the prospect of the book's death. Ira Spring suggested I step in as her replacement, and I did, expecting to devote a winter and spring to updating what still would basically be her good old *Footloose*. I can only say in apology that the idea ran away with me. Between Thanksgiving of 1976 and Thanksgiving of 1978 I walked 3000 miles of beaches, lowlands, and foothills and we had on our hands not a revision but a third series, the four volumes of *Footsore*.

The series is timely. As this third edition of *Footsore 1* stumbles through my non-motorized typewriter in the spring-summer-fall of 1987, another presidential commission ("Son of ORRC") has repeated the findings of a quarter-century ago and renewed the recommendation for a national system of non-motorized trails connecting cities to countryside and wilderness, city to city — and neighborhood to neighborhood. Those few whose belief in the inviolability of property rights runs to fanaticism are mobilizing their lawyers. They will have their day in court. But they will, in the long run, lose, because they must. This nation must not be hobbled by a sea-to-sea array of NO TRESPASSING signs.

"Where Man Is a Visitor"

The Wilderness Act of 1964 defines a "national wilderness" as a place where "the earth and its community of life are untrammeled by man, where man himself is a visitor who does not remain." This is the domain of the *100 Hikes* series.

The counties east of San Francisco Bay have joined in a parks and recreation district that is acclaimed nationally as a model of thoughtful planning. Among its philosophical innovations is the definition of a "regional wilderness": the minimum size is about 2500 acres; the topography should "substantially" block out and mute the sights and sounds of surrounding civilization; the land may have been trammeled in the past but the evidences either have been or can be softened by time. An example within the *Footsore* realm is the Cougar Mountain Regional Wildland Park.

We might proceed from national to regional to recognize a "community wilderness," in the hundreds of acres, sufficiently compact that the center is considerably buffered from the rumble-bang-honk-yowl of the city, the whole is fundamentally "passive," which is to say Nature is the Chief Ranger and quiet people the chief users (except for the wild creatures, who are permitted to be as noisy as they please). Examples of the "community wilderness" abound in *Footsore*. However, the coverage here is not comprehensive. A green space that is the salvation of the soul of a community, providing a refuge minutes from home, may not offer long enough walks (or, alternatively, a particularly outstanding and unusual natural feature) to attract pedestrians from a distance, and this is the test for inclusion in these volumes.

Not represented here at all is the equally invaluable "neighborhood wilderness" of the sort formerly ubiquitous in cities, the vacant lot down the block where kids explored jungles of the Dark Continent, sought the Sources of the Nile, and — in winter when the marsh filled with water — rafted into mysteries of the Sargasso Sea. Few lots are vacant anymore; some, though, have been reserved as "pocket parks," perhaps offering scarcely room to walk, only space to sit under a tree, yet none the less precious to the people — and the birds — who live nearby.

Where Man *Does* Remain

Footsore is not devoted exclusively to the wild and pristine. Indeed, it rejoices in man-trammeling, when done in good taste. *Footsore* walks railroad tracks, waterfront docks, logging roads. It traverses miles of residential neighborhoods on the Burke-Gilman, farms on the Sammamish River, shopping squares and industrial "parks" on the Green River. It looks out from the beach to the freighters and tugs and fishing boats and play boats. It boards ferries to cross the waters. It loiters on the streets of little old Coupeville and Steilacoom. It goes on tour of the wineries of the Sammamish valley and the brewery at Tumwater Falls.

In summation, *Footsore* is the bridge between "downtown" and "national wilderness." Its subject is the place where man lives. Works. Fools around. Where he trammels, yet where he also, in certain preserves, by concerted action does not. The place where he has taken pains to repair the most hideous damage done by pioneer trammelings and has permitted Nature to heal many other wounds. The place where he has settled into the landscape to become as native as the aplodontia (mountain beaver) — another creature notorious for its trammeling but with a respected role in the ecological drama and not unlovable, as beasts go.

The Two-Hour Circle

As late as the 1950s the federal ORRC Report could keep a perfectly straight face while listing "driving for pleasure" as a form of outdoor recreation. Truly enough, it was possible, then, as in the 1920s, to take the kids for a Sunday drive, poking along back roads in order to say hello to the cows, stopping to feed a deer or photograph Mount Si. A hiker living in the heart of Puget Sound City could set out for Snoqualmie Pass knowing that after a brief tussle the highway would be open, the driving easy, the eyes free to explore the scenery. However, in the era of "Son of ORRC" the driver who pokes along a back road is going to get poked in the rear end by an impatient pickup truck; to raise the eyes from the freeway to the peaks is to set the stage for a multi-vehicle chain-reaction holocaust.

Except for sadists and masochists, there is next to no driving for pleasure in the realm of *Footsore.* Every minute spent in vehicular transit to and from a trailhead must be totted up in the debit column of the day's balance sheet. This surveyor has established as a rule of thumb that few if any day walks or hikes can accrue enough in the credit column to outweigh (with a reasonable profit) more than 2 hours of driving to and from. Assuming an outing day of 8 or 10 hours, 2 hours driving leaves 6 or 8 hours on the trail, enough for a handsome profit. With 3 or 4 hours driving time, the balance is probably at the break-even level. The person might have had a richer Sunday puttering in the garden. He surely would have done better *not* to do Paradise Valley but Discovery Park instead, to substitute Tiger Mountain for Mt. Dickerman.

There being four *Footsore* volumes, reaching from Bellingham to Tenino, not all hikes in all volumes lie within the Two-Hour Circle of every hiker's home. Of course. Further, some hikes are of such exceptional "regional" appeal they justify a long trial by highway. But the general rule is, the closer to home, the better the trail day — even if the trail, per se, is of lesser appeal than one more distant.

The Two-Hour Rule will be modified in future by the inevitable tightening of the Great American Gridlock and by the inevitable $5-a-gallon gas. The complaint, now, about public transit as a way to trailheads is that the bus is slower than the private automobile. As the latter phases out of the center of our lives, we'll be only too happy to spend an extra hour on the bus. All the time on the bus can be put to good secondary use, such as reading a book. All the time driving a car is pure waste.

The text here notes walking routes reasonably accessible via public transit. For precise planning one must obtain current route maps and schedules. The notes are intended mainly to stimulate hikers to think bus — and bus managers to think hikers.

Caveat Ambulator

Each *Footsore* volume notes in its introduction the dates when the trails were surveyed. For example, *Footsore 1* was first surveyed during the winter-spring of 1976-77. Trailheads and most routes were resurveyed in the summer-fall of 1981. The material herein derives from the resurvey of the spring-summer of 1987, with a few revisions made in 1989. Comments from hikers-readers have been reviewed and embodied. Old trips that have been trammeled to death have been dropped. But — the good news — new trips have been added — less by the surveyor's increased perspicacity than by the born-again hikers-walkers in the parks departments of King County, Seattle, Bellevue, Issaquah, Kirkland, Redmond, Bothell, Kent, Auburn, and other municipalities. When Janice did her first *Footloose* in 1969, local parks departments typically provided picnic tables, playfields, privies, and maybe rose gardens. There now is no recreation more esteemed than the "passive," meaning the one that preserves wetlands and woodlands and wildlife for enjoyment by quiet humans.

For *Footsore 2, 3,* and *4* it remains as true in 1988 as in 1976 that this lived-on, worked-on, fooled-around-on, trammeled land of Puget Sound City is ever-changing, often radically and without notice, and the reader-hiker must not take for granted that he will find things as they were in the olden days. The *Footsore 1* province is stabilizing — because it's getting on toward being "built-out." Almost one can say, in 1988, that in the *Footsore 1* area what you see now is pretty much what you're always going to see. It's not going to get a whole lot worse, or better.

For the series as a whole, certain caveats must be made:

1. A great many *Footsore* trips cross private property where trespassing long has been tolerated and was at the time of survey. But a copy of this book in

your hot little hand does not serve as a license to infringe on property rights. If the "No Trespassing" signs have gone up, you must obey.

The behavior of you and other *Footsore* readers in many cases will determine whether or not trespassing continues to be tolerated. Obviously you should not foul the path with body wastes or garbage — and in fact the modern thoughtful walker picks up and carries out garbage left by others, gaining a glow of virtue plus whatever cash the glass and metal earn at the recycling station. For further discussion of trespassing see the introduction to "Whulj Trail: Seattle to Tacoma."

2. Railroad rights-of-way are private property and the owners do not invite trespassing. Walking tracks can be dangerous, as witness the annual death toll. However, tens of thousands of people annually trespass on train tracks and the trains do not object; occasionally they run over somebody, but it's nothing personal. Just keep an eye over the shoulder.

3. Not merely man transforms the terrain. Nature, too, runs amok. Many *Footsore* routes are maintained, if at all, solely by the stomping boots and brushcrashing bodies of hikers who, should their attention wander briefly, soon lose the contest to rank greenery.

How to Get Footsore

Outdoor recreation professionals distinguish between "walks," short excursions on easy paths in forgiving terrain, requiring no special clothing or equipment and no experience or training, and "hikes," longer and/or rougher, potentially somewhat dangerous, demanding stout shoes or boots, clothing for cold and wet weather, gear for routefinding and emergencies, rucksack to carry it all in, and best done in company of experienced companions or eased into gradually, conservatively.

Footsore describes short walks in and around Puget Sound City, outings suitable for a leisurely afternoon or even a spring-summer evening, as well as long walks that may keep a person hopping all day. For any walk, equipment demands no more than a passing thought; as for technique, the rule is just to pick 'em up and lay 'em down and look both ways before crossing the street.

Hikes are another matter and the novice must take care, when choosing a trip, to be aware of the difference and to make appropriate preparations. On every hike where a shout for help might not bring quick assistance to the lost or injured or ill, each person should carry the Ten Essentials:

1. Extra clothing — enough so that if a sunny-warm morning yields to rainy-windy afternoon, or if accident keeps the party out overnight, hypothermia ("exposure" or "freezing to death") will not be a threat.
2. Extra food — enough so something is left over at the planned end of the trip, in case the actual end is the next day.
3. Sunglasses — if travel on snow for more than a few minutes may be involved.
4. Knife — for first aid and emergency firebuilding (making kindling).
5. Firestarter — a candle or chemical fuel for starting a fire with wet wood.
6. First aid kit.
7. Matches — in a waterproof container.
8. Flashlight — with extra bulb and batteries.
9. Map. Travel directions herein assume the reader has the proper highway maps for driving to the trip vicinity, from where the text and sketch

Trail to beach in St. Edwards State Park

maps zero in on the trailhead. For the walks no other maps are necessary. However, for many of the hikes a person is risking not achieving
the destination — and not returning to civilization until carried there by a
search party — if he lacks the appropriate U.S. Geological Survey (or
Green Trails) maps, available at map shops and some backpacking
shops.

10. Compass — with knowledge of use.

Hiking isn't so complicated that a person needs a lot of instruction, but the
same can be said of dying. To learn how to select and use the Essentials a
novice lacking tutelage by a family member or friend may enroll in a course
offered by an outing club, youth group, church, park department or professional wilderness guide. Alternatively, one can buy a book; the surveyor is
partial to *Backpacking: One Step At A Time.*

Some words about the information summaries given for trips:

The "round trip xx miles" and "elevation gain xxxx feet" tell a person if the trip
fits his energy and ambition. Some hikers do 20 miles a day and gain 5000 feet
without a deep breath, others gasp and grunt at 5 miles and 1500 feet. The
novice will quickly learn his capacity. Note: the "elevation gain" is gross, not
net; an upsy-downsy trail can gain hundreds of feet while going along "on the
flat."

The "allow x hours" must be used with a personal conversion factor. The
figures here are based on doing 1½ miles an hour on the flat (walking at a rate
of 2 miles an hour but walking only 45 minutes in the hour) and an elevation

gain of about 700 feet an hour, with added time for slow tracks — muddy, brushy, loggy. From these figures a hiker accustomed to doing 1 mile an hour or 3, or gaining 200 feet an hour or 2000, can calculate his own approximate travel time.

"High point xxxx feet" tells the knowing much about the vegetation and views to expect, as well as the probable amount of snow in any given month. The bottom line, the "all year" or "February-December" or whatever, attempts to spell this out. It does not suggest the "best time," which is a subjective judgment based on whether one likes spring flowers or fall mushrooms or what. The intent is to tell when, in an average normal year (whatever that is) a trail is probably sufficiently snowfree for pleasure walking, meaning less than a foot of snow or only occasional deeper patches. Several factors are involved. One is elevation. Another is distance from Puget Sound, whose large volume of above-freezing water warms winter air masses. In any locality, higher is generally snowier. But also, for identical elevations the farther from saltwater is generally snowier. And mountain valleys, acting like giant iceboxes, generally are snowier than nearby lowlands outside the mountain front. Finally, though south and west slopes get as much snow as north and east, they also get more sun (and also more sun than valley flats) and thus melt out faster.

These factors are taken into account, and eked out with guesswork, in coding the trips. To explain the code:

"All year" means the trail is always open — except during intervals when the snowline drops to sea level or near it. (This is the case with the entirety of *Footsore 1,* so that in this one volume the summary "walkable all year" applies.)

"February-December" doesn't imply any prejudice against January, which may be no colder than adjacent months, but means an ordinary winter has maybe 4-8 weeks, from late December to late February, when the trail may be under more than a foot of snow. But it can be snowfree in a mid-January thaw or throughout a mild winter. And in a tough winter can be up to the knees from November to March.

"March-November" means a typical snowpack of several feet or so that begins piling up in November, early or late, and melts mostly out in March, early or late. Again, the path may be walkable in dead of winter. Or up to the crotch from October to May.

"April-November" means quite a deep snowpack that may begin accumulating in October (or December) and may melt in March (or June).

And so on. In short, the aim is to tell approximately how things usually have been, not predict what they will be.

In Feet Is the Preservation of Wildness

The least impactful use man can make of a wild place is not to be there at all, and this is mandatory for certain wildlife habitats, such as nesting areas of bald eagles and great blue herons during their season of mating and hatching and nurturing.

Walking — with a light foot and a low voice — can be virtually harmless to the land and its creatures if done on a properly placed and constructed path, and if the feet keep to the path when it traverses steep hillsides or fragile wetlands.

Jogging and running put thud-thud pressure on the land, without damage if the trail is heavy enough to withstand the pounding. However, these uses are far more "consumptive" than walking because in any given period of time they cover a great many more miles. Further, different speeds do not mix well on a crowded trail; the runner doing 10 miles an hour is furious at the loiterers doing 2, and they are as jarred from wildland calm by his hurtling body as if he were a truck-and-trailer doing 80 per on their neighborhood cul de sac.

Special provision must be made when wheels are served by the same trail as feet. Bicycles, roller skates, and skateboards confine themselves mainly to paved multi-use trails, some of which also are favorites with walkers; separate trails sometimes are the solution to conflicts, or paint lines down the blacktop. A lot of patience and consideration on both sides is a prerequisite to a nice day. (The "mountain bike" designed to go off the paved path onto rough roads and foot trails must be banned from the latter. They are specifically forbidden by the National Wilderness Preservation Act, which does not specify a ban on "motorized" vehicles, as often mistakenly stated by the U.S. Forest Service, but "mechanized" vehicles — including the mountain bike. It is also excluded from trails of all national and many state parks, county and city parks — in summary, from any trail that has a higher degree of protection than "multiple use." The objection is not noise and only to a lesser degree the rutting but the speed differential; the essence of the sport is "bombing" downhill, an essence that is not compatible with pedestrian peace.)

Sad to say, horses have little time left on most trails in Puget Sound City. The speed differential means a horse is always overtaking hikers, being impeded by them or harassing them. The impact of a horse is enormously more than that of a human, entailing horse apples and horse flies, hoof-churned morasses, hoof-destroyed tread. The impact can be withstood by heavy construction, but this is very expensive.

The conflict between feet and big feet (horses) and between quiet feet and quiet wheels (bicycles) is one of speed. The conflict between all of these and loud wheels is more fundamental. "Quiet" is as valuable a natural resource as pure water, clean air, undisturbed wildlife, pristine plant communities. A single machine-man — on dirtbike or ATV or ORV or hellroaring 4×4 — consumes more quiet than thousands of hikers. When the resource is limited (as it increasingly is) such greed is intolerable. Even were there no destruction of soils, plants, and water the hogging of the "quiet" would forbid noise machines on the trails.

Happily, with several scandalous exceptions where more education of public officials remains to be done, *motorized wheels are illegal on every walk and hike in Footsore 1.* In the terrain of *Footsore 2, 3, 4* the conflict is far from resolved. The superconsumers, supported by a network of dealers, industry-organized user groups, and bureaucrats, have ridden over the largest user of trails — the hiker. But the hiker is picking himself up, dusting the wheel tracks off his back, and beginning to tell the land-management agencies that he, the hiker, is the boss.

How does a walker-hiker throw his weight around?

1. Meeting illegal wheels, express disapproval. Stand your ground — even where wheels are legal the state law gives the pedestrian the right-of-way. Ask if the wheeler knows he is illegal. Scowl. Whip out a notepad and take down any license number that may be visible, physical description of vehicle and rider, date and time of day, exact location, and turn in this information to the lang-manager. Most scofflaws are repeaters and your report, assembled with others, may make a case in court.

2. Arriving home from a hike where illegal wheels displeasured you, write a letter to the land-manager, whether federal, state, or local. If in doubt, write a letter to *me* and I'll see that it gets where it will do some good.

Footroads

A logging road on a tree farm can be a superb walk, the quiet perhaps molested only by the occasional logging truck. It is good to be able to include in the *Footsores* (especially *2*, *3*, and *4*) a number of walking routes that are not hiker-only footpaths but *footroads.* In many a situation this book advocates that a road be closed to public wheels and deliberately converted to a footroad.

The term *wheelstops* is used to designate blockages on roads that are not technically abandoned but have "gone back to nature" through the providential action of blowdown or washout, or governmental action, or the contributed labor of citizen volunteers.

The finest footroads have perfect wheelstops that convert them to de facto trails. Generally quite acceptable are ways traveled only by the occasional logging truck or other work machine. Meeting two or three recreation vehicles an hour may not critically aggravate the hypertension. A day-long parade of razzing motorcycles — well, you'd have better stayed in bed.

The surveyor sought routes reasonably free of racket most of the time. Some routes were judged too scenicly splendid to be conceded to wheels; labeled "Never on Sunday," they are recommended for, say, stormy winter Wednesdays before school lets out. Some routes found serene by the surveyor may subsequently have been invaded, some perfect wheelstops breached by 4×4 engineers, those good-deed-a-weekend latter-day Dan'l Boones.

Rails & Trails

When Janice did *Footloose* in 1969, she didn't write up the railroad from Ballard to Bothell in the main body of the book. She walked the route but the trains were still running and she felt this ruled out description as a "trail." Instead she put it in a special section as an "oughter be." The opinion was shared. The trains quit. In no time at all the Burke-Gilman Trail ranked among the most popular urban trails in the nation.

We cannot rejoice at the abandonment of rail lines. In 1916 the United States had some 254,000 miles of rails. More than a third of those miles have been abandoned and another 4000 miles are going every year. From 1970 to 1987, the rail system of the State of Washington shrank from 5200 to 3600 miles. Are the freight-hauling needs of the state and nation less? The passenger-carrying needs? Obviously not. The monster trucks juggernaut along the freeways, their slipstreams leaving a wake of passenger cars bouncing about like leaves in a gale. The skies are so a-roaring that most of the population of America will have been in Hell or Heaven half an hour before they realize the loud noise they just heard was not merely another jet but the thunderclap of Judgment Day.

America in the era of $5 gasoline is going to have to devise a less costly transportation system. It is going to have to rebuild the rail network. The job will have to be done by the public sector, the private having demonstrated its incompetence. Pending the crystallizing of the national resolve, a program must be instituted of conserving rail routes, transferring them to public ownership as service is discontinued. Thus, when the national system begins construction, it will not be faced with astronomical costs of right-of-way acquisition.

The nation cannot accept "reversion to adjoining owners" when service is stopped. Over the years the private entrepreneurs received such considerations from the public — land grants, subsidies, favorable taxation — that the public has a vested ownership right. The considerations were given in exchange for providing services. When this is discontinued, the public has first claim on the right-of-way.

At present, speculators are snapping up properties that have been of low value because of adjacency to the railroad, expecting huge profits when the trains stop. Speculators have gone to court, won some victories — temporary victories, each one bringing closer the time when new law is made to right the wrong.

While a corridor is being held for future rails, the public can use it for other means of transport, such as bicycles and feet. When the rails return, the trail can be moved to the side of the right-of-way. The Rails to Trails Conservancy is fighting off the speculators nationally to preserve corridors. A better — socially more comprehensive — name for the campaign would be *Rails & Trails.*

Maps That Tie the Land Together

The aim of the four *Footsore* volumes is to teach how a person may tie the land together with his feet. And — when standing on open beaches or high ridges — with his eyes. Maps are indispensable aids. The sketch maps in these volumes outline the general terrain. The US Geological Survey maps give fine detail. For the big picture, however, another sort of map is invaluable — the pictorial landform.

Puget Sound Region: Washington, by Dee Molenaar, was designed and produced specifically as a companion to the *Footsore* series and covers the entire province, from Olympics to Cascades, Canada to Chehalis, permitting the hiker to obtain the grand orientation that keeps him related at all times to all horizons. Particularly helpful is a condensed textbook in the margin, a history of the geologic structures and the Pleistocene glaciers; the pictorial map of the maximum extent of the Puget Lobe of the Cordilleran Ice Sheet explains innumerable terrain features that baffle the uninformed eye.

Richard Pargeter has two similar maps of somewhat different coverage. *The Puget Sound Country: A View from the Northwest* focuses on the area of *Footsore 1,* is also excellent for *Footsore 4,* and touches on *Footsore 2.* Historical "briefs" scattered about the map add depth. His *Washington's Northwest Passages: A View from the Southwest* looks from *Footsore 1* country over the domain of *Footsore 3,* with particular emphasis on the waterways and the navigators who explored them.

The inveterate *Footsore* walker will want all of these.

Harvey Manning
Cougar Mountain

WHULJ TRAIL —
SEATTLE TO TACOMA

In this edition the name is changed from "Puget Sound Trail" to the more comprehensive and anciently authentic "Whulj Trail." The reason is that "Puget Sound," by which Vancouver designated the waters south of Point Defiance, has crept so steadily northward it threatens to annex the very Pacific Ocean. Puget Sound may extend to the south end of Whidbey Island but cannot be allowed to conquer Admiralty Inlet, Possession Sound, and the bays and straits beyond. However, a need does exist for a name to encompass the entirety of the "inland sea." Any sound judgment must veto "Puget Sound" and (ugh!) "Greater Puget Sound." The best name is the one most Salish-speakers gave "the saltwater," or "the saltwater we know." The simplest Englishing of the Salish word is "Whulj," pronounced exactly the way it's spelled. (Other renditions are *whulge, whulch, whole-itch,* and *khwulch.*) In this edition "Puget Sound Trail" has been subsumed under the larger name, "Whulj Trail," because though the portion of the route covered by *Footsore 4* and most of that in this volume follow the shore of Puget Sound, this volume reaches to Possession Sound and *Footsore 3* proceeds along many bays, ending at Bellingham Bay, whose residents deeply resent being told by Seattle newspapers that they live "on Puget Sound."

So much for that.

Informed that walkable beach connects the Queen (or Emerald) City to Second City, the ordinary walker-on-the-public-trails protests, "But it's *private.* You can't go there. I've read that in the newspapers so it must be so."

Let us leave aside for the moment the fact that in the 35 miles between the mouths of Elliott Bay and Commencement Bay there are better than 7 miles of public park beach and address the other 28 miles — as well as the thousands of other miles of beach up and down and all around Whulj. About 4000 to 5000 years ago, after millennia during which the land was rising when released from the weight of the Pleistocene ice and the water was rising as the Pleistocene glaciers melted, the beach of Whulj stabilized at just about its present location. Already living in the vicinity were the first wave of immigrants, from Asia, and though the water road was their highway, the beach was where the clams were. In the 19th century arrived the second wave of immigrants, from Europe via eastern America, and they also had frequent resort to the gray trail beside the waves, so much easier than the green jungles atop the bluffs. In summary, the Whulj Trail has been a public travel corridor for about five times longer than there have been lawyers.

When it attained statehood in 1889, Washington was given by the federal government clear title to all the tidelands — the beach between mean high tide and mean low tide. The federal government supposed it had the right to give that title. The state government supposed it had the right to sell the tidelands, and did so until the start of the 1970s when the Legislature called a halt. By then, 60 percent of the state's beaches had been sold, including perhaps 90 percent of what anybody could adapt to residential or commercial or industrial

Lighthouse on Alki Point

purposes. Many of the bluffs carved by the waves from morainal materials deposited by the Puget Lobe of the Cordilleran Ice Sheet were too tall, steep, and unstable for development, and the tidelands at their base remained in public hands or were cheaply returned there by Forward Thrust and other park-acquisition programs. However, for most of those 28 miles noted above, purchasers have paid the state or a subsequent owner good money — up to $2000 a linear foot for beach frontage with tidelands attached. They have pieces of paper showing they possess clear and absolute title to the tidelands, guaranteed by the state. They have attorneys who will defend those pieces of paper until their clients run out of money; for folks who can afford $2000 a front foot and the enormous annual property taxes, this effectively is never.

What, then, of the folks who don't have that kind of money yet feel the rhythms of Whulj in their blood, who cannot be happy without periodic visits to soothe city-battered ears with the sound of waves, to clean hydrocarbon-fouled lungs with the smell of salt, to watch sailboats and rowboats and ferry boats, to see the sun sink into the Olympics? The character of the country between the Cascades and Olympics has been shaped more by the Whulj than any other influence, including the rain. To adapt the dictum of Mr. Bumble, "If the law says the people can be walled off from Whulj, the law, sir, is *a ass*!" In Whulj country, walking beside the water is as inalienable a right as turning the eyes up to the heavens. No matter what attorneys may say who have not researched the subject, the consensus of legal scholars who have done so is that the law is perfectly clear. The millennia of continuous public use have made Whulj Trail a public highway, not in the power of the State of Washington to sell with a clear title, not in the power of any person to *completely* (note emphasis) own.

However, so much property value is at stake that if the matter ever went to the courts the litigation would continue until the return of the glacier and cost

Mud Lake, Bellefields Nature Park

more than World War III. So please, beach-owners and beachwalkers, let us vow not to go to court. Owners: Erect your NO TRESPASSING PRIVATE PROPERTY signs, "bluff signs" though they are. When rowdies carry kegs of beer into your front yard, call the cops. If addlebrains come by with sixteen children screaming and a dozen dogs "marking" your front door, instruct them in good manners. But don't make a federal case about the respectful pedestrian who passes quickly and quietly by.

For beachwalkers, the surveyor has lengthier advice.

To begin, many stretches of Whulj are so lightly populated that the residents are more than tolerant of strangers, are downright hospitable (see *Footsore 3* and *Footsore 4*). Still, the Seattle-Tacoma beach is so close and so quick for so many people that the recreational resource is too valuable not to be exploited. For most people most of the time, the 7 miles of public park beach are sufficient. However, the dedicated beachwalker is not content with pacing up and down a petty mile, wants to link the miles into a long, rich day. The surveyor has done so often, "trespassing" for miles, with no greeting from beach people except a smile and a wave. If they come down to talk, it's a friendly chat, sharing memories of great walks on the beaches. On the average, beach people have more soul than inlanders. They're much worth talking to.

Beachwalkers also are better people, on the average, than some others. They can demonstrate their excellence to the property "owners" by obeying these commandments:

Commandment One. Do unto beach residents as you would want done unto you if you were one of them.

Commandment Two. The same legal scholars who declare the inalienable right of the public to *walk across* "private" beaches go on to say that the walker has no rights to dig clams, pick oysters, gather pebbles or driftwood, camp, build a fire, have a picnic lunch, leave garbage, relieve himself, or sit down. (The prohibitions do not apply to those who have treaty rights dating from the 1850s.)

Commandment Three. Should anyone come out of a house screaming and hollering to get you off "his" beach, do so instantly, with no smart talk. Go to another beach.

Upon this foundation of Commandments has been erected a structure of Rules derived from many hours of interviewing beach people met on their home shores. Most are nature-sensitive folk; that's why they live on the beach. Most sympathize with other nature-sensitives and are apologetic about "owning" the beach. Even amid thickets of "No Trespassing" signs most say, "Oh, nobody minds if you walk their beach, as long as you don't make a nuisance." Whatever the property rights of beach residents they have human rights — the right to live in peace, not subjected to dumping of garbage in yards, to noisy picnics and night-time orgies; the right to sunbathe in privacy, not subjected to the stares of a thousand foreigners marching by.

Some of the signs say "Trespassing by Permission Only." And this is the key to the Seattle-Tacoma segment of Whulj Trail. Many owners who bristle and fume at the opinion of the legal scholars cited here nevertheless have a personal policy of tolerating what they consider to be trespassing, so long as the "trespassers" behave as follows:

Rule 1. Good days are bad. On weekends the year around and on fine evenings of spring and summer, stay away. At such times if you must go to the beach visit the public parks described here or (for reasons discussed in that chapter) walk Whulj Trail north of Seattle.

Rule 2. Crowded beaches are the worst. If you see a mob of people walking past and ignoring "No Trespassing" signs, do not suppose there is safety in numbers. The numbers will just be infuriating residents, who will be calling the police, who don't know the (real) law and will arrest the numbers.

Rule 3. Walking off the ends of public park beaches onto "private" beaches is the most inviting to the ignorant — and to residents the most irritating.

Rule 4. The "wild" beaches, those with bluffs that keep houses at a distance, are the most hospitable to foreign feet.

Rule 5. Low tide, when the "trail" lies at the water's edge far out from houses, is better than high, when you may practically be in somebody's living room.

Rule 6. On "private" beaches (well, why not on the public beaches, too?) be clean and quiet. No garbage. Carry a litterbag and use it. No shouting. Stifle the little children. Don't come in gangs but alone or in small groups. Keep moving. Don't stare at the houses, fascinated though you may be by littoral architecture; burglars also stare when casing jobs.

Rule 7. Thou shalt not trespass with thy dog, which shalt be left at home.

If you avoid built-up stretches (who wants to walk in a succession of front yards anyway?) in favor of wilder areas, and pick the off-seasons and off-days (a stormy Wednesday morning in December) you can walk from Seattle to Tacoma with the locals scarcely seeing you; when they do, they'll be smiling a welcome.

Now, for a few practical details on how to walk a beach. A full discussion of tides and techniques is presented in *Footsore 3* and will not be repeated here, since we consider all four volumes to be a single book. The main thing to keep in mind when walking from Seattle to Tacoma is the tide chart, which is not necessary when walking from Seattle (or Ballard) to Everett (see the next chapter). On a long-distance walk, start soon after high water, thus having an outgoing tide to look forward to for many hours. Alternatively, hike on a neap tide. Beware of a spring tide!

Wear sturdy boots, *not* the tenny-runners traditionally favored for beaches. Before passage of the Shorelines Protection Act, any "owner" of tidelands could build structures as he pleased. Over the years some 40,000 docks have been built on tidelands and golly knows how many miles of bulkheads. These latter so invade the gray trail that a walker striding along as happy as a clam on a strip of public highway 50 feet wide may suddenly find himself forced out, and out, until he is up to his knees in the salt. The bulkheads also, in guarding homes from waves, prevent those waves from attacking the bluff and bringing down to the beach the natural nutriments of gravel and sand that feed the longshore currents. A *starved beach* results, the surface perhaps 2 feet or more lower than before the building of the bulkheads and studded with materials the longshore currents can't carry away — cobbles, big and round and slippery. A pace of a mile an hour may be too fast on a cobble beach. Lacking good boots, a person can develop very bad miseries in the Achilles tendons.

There are all too many bulkheads and cobbles between Seattle and Tacoma. But as a result of what brought them there also is more recent history here than on any other stretch of Whulj. Many a house has been built here over the years, only to slide down to the beach on a clump of bluff, or be slid down upon. But many a house has survived and grown into the landscape. The era of the mosquito fleet, of middy blouses and straw boaters and mandolins, is recalled by boxy clapboard houses with sleeping porches and verandas, by cabins that might have been chopped up for kindling a half-century ago but instead were lovingly preserved as family memories. Sadly, a new generation has moved in from Kansas, come to Oz to see the Emerald City, and each family has more money than many a Third World nation, enough that they are enriching a new generation of architects and engineers. The old homes with the salt blown deep in their woodwork by the winds of a half-century, with wallpaper that smells of kelp and clams, are being demolished to make room for prodigies of space-age technology — technology that also attacks those wild-jungled bluffs we used to think of as the greenbelts of God.

The joys of beachwalking need no praise here. But the importance of Whulj Trail must be stressed. First, it is close to the homes of just about everybody in Puget Sound (Whulj) City. Second, it's an all-year route, never blocked by snow except during the infrequent Ice Ages. Third, due to a partial rainshadow from the Olympics, the weather is better than farther east in — say — the Issaquah Alps. Frequently when storms are chasing each others' tails over the Northwest and the mountains and foothills never free themselves of one storm's murk before the next descends, "Blue Holes" open along the beach. These interludes are superb for walking — clouds boiling around the Olympics, whitecaps flashing in the sun, surf rattling the gravel, wind nipping the nose.

Of course, when the inland weather is sunny-blue, fogs may linger long on the water. But that's not a bad time for walking either, foghorns sounding, ghost ships sliding through mists, gulls wailing at the mystery of it all.

USGS maps: Seattle South, Duwamish Head, Vashon, Des Moines, Poverty Bay, Tacoma North
Walkable all year

Mile 0–5½: Pioneer Square–Duwamish River–Duwamish Head (map — page 21)

The route south from the Skid Road and west over the Duwamish Waterways is noted purely for future reference. Good things are happening and a pedestrian corridor south from the central (Old Seattle) waterfront may be in the works. Already a number of public viewpoints are being provided to permit closeup study of the Duwamish Waterfront, the industrial and shipping guts of

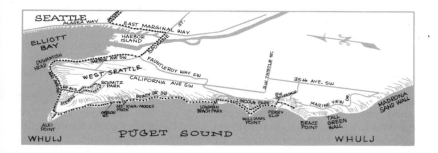

the metropolis. For these, see the Duwamish River Trail described later in these pages.

On the west shore of Elliott Bay, at Salty's, the walking route is now open and splendid; for that, too, see the Duwamish River Trail.

At the end of these 5½ miles from Pioneer Square is the logical place to start walking Whulj Trail. Duwamish Head is unsurpassed for watching marine traffic: Bainbridge Island and Bremerton ferries, ships and barges and tugs to and from Duwamish Waterways, sailboats and motorboats to and from marinas. Views too of downtown Seattle, Queen Anne Hill, Magnolia Bluff, Winslow and Eagle Harbor on Bainbridge Island, the Olympics.

Mile 5½–8: Alki Beach Park–Alki Point Lighthouse (map — page 21)

The 154-acre park with 13,000 feet of shoreline is the most popular beach walk in Seattle. A favorite time is winter storms when ocean-size breakers smash over the seawall, repeating the performance on the Five O'Clock News. The sidewalk is open at any tide, though often thronged after school lets out by boppers on roller skates. At low tide a person can stroll the beach, the seawall berming out sights and sounds of the busy street, where young males cruise up and down in pickup trucks, yearning at the promenading young females on the sidewalk. Come sundown and the residents nail up the storm shutters and call out the riot police.

The entire strip beyond Duwamish Head is Alki Beach Park. At the south end is the sandy bathing beach, where there is beach at even the highest tide, and the usual gangs of gulls and crows and pigeons and ducks and blackbirds and sandpipers whose presence the rest of the route will not be further mentioned.

A stretch of private beach intervenes between bathing beach and the Alki Point Lighthouse. (Visiting hours on weekends and holidays 1-4 P.M.)

Schmitz Park (map — page 21)

An inland sidetrip from Alki Avenue the short way up SW Stevens Street or 59 Avenue S to Alki Recreation Center, which abuts the lower end of Schmitz Park. (Alternatively, drive up SW Admiral Way and at Stevens go down the park entrance road to the small parking area.)

Started from one of three gifts of land by Ferdinand and Emma Schmitz, this 50-acre park contains one of Seattle's few bits of virgin forest — Douglas firs up to 5 feet in diameter and cedars even thicker, nurselogs supporting rows of hemlocks, and thickets of salmonberry, walls of swordfern.

The "birthplace of Seattle" monument close by (on Alki Point at 63 Avenue SW) causes one to reflect that when the schooner *Exact* landed the first group of roving real-estate speculators in 1851 (the men began to plat, the women to weep, and the natives to shake their heads) this forested ravine was just about exactly as it is now. And this was what the country looked like all the way from the Sound to the mountains.

From Alki Recreation Center walk a blockaded old street, now a path, up the ravine, complete with a creek that here is not, as are most city streams, in a storm sewer. At the parking lot old street yields to old trail continuing up the ravine, definitely not city-park-kempt but natural-wild. The trail divides and redivides in a maze of paths down to and along the creek, up tributaries, along sidehills, by sandbanks, onto knolls. To fully sample the park ascend the ravine along one side to where it's about to enter residences, swing to the far side, and loop back down. Though small, the park contains nearly 2 miles of paths.

Sample round trip from beach 2 miles, allow 1½ hours
High point and elevation gain 250 feet

Mile 8–12: Me-Kwa-Mooks Park–Lowman Beach Park–Williams Point (map — page 21)

South of Alki Point the bluff, which here has temporarily receded inland (or to put it the other way, the Alki spit has thrust out from the bluff), returns to the beach. Note one of the few outcrops of non-glacial rock in the area — sandstone ledges beneath glacial debris.

Immediately south of the point are homes on the beach. Then the beachfront drive prevents construction and permits public access for a bit. Walking is halted by pilings of Harbor West, a condominium perilously built on a dock. Cheek-by-jowl homes extend 2 miles south; even though in spitting distance of the water one can't see it.

Right in the middle, however, is a small opening. At Oregon Street is a 34-acre park, half a wooded upland on the base of the bluff, half shorelands, 2000 feet in length. Another Schmitz gift, to avoid confusion it has been renamed from Emma Schmitz Memorial Viewpoint to Me-Kwa-Mooks ("entire Alki area"). The opening permits a walker to see the view has changed. Bainbridge Island is being replaced by Blake Island and the Kitsap Peninsula. Now prominent to the south is the green-and-white ferry shuttling from Fauntleroy Cove to Vashon Island.

Private beach ends at Lowman Beach Park. A public alley-street leads behind homes to the beach at Lincoln Park. The 1 mile through the park requires separate treatment.

Lincoln Park (map — page 21)

The 130 acres and 5350 feet of shoreline in Lincoln Park place it on everybody's list of the Top Three Beach Parks in Seattle. The excellent bus service has made it a favorite for generations.

For a basic introductory loop start from the parking area off Fauntleroy Avenue SW at Cloverdale Street. Head for the water, following steps or ramp down to the bulkhead walkway, which destroys the naturalness of beach but does permit high-tide walking. (At low tide one can walk natural beach.) The bluff, partly green jungle, partly gray sand cliff, rises 175 very vertical feet, topped by magnificent madrona groves. Smackdab on climactic Williams Point is Colman Pool, a good thing in the wrong place, reminding us that a sewage plant was built on West Point — and an aquarium was not built on Meadow Point, Seattle by then having learned to leave spits alone.

Having walked 1 splendid mile north to homes, retreat to the first of three good (safe) paths that climb the bluff to the top. Walk the rim path, lawns and groves left, wild bluff right. Views over the water to Vashon ferry, Bainbridge ferry, Olympics.

Basic loop trip 2 miles, allow 1½ hours
High point and elevation gain 175 feet

Puget Sound and Olympic Mountains from Lincoln Park

Mile 12–16½: Fauntleroy Cove–Brace Point (map — page 21)

The south boundary of Lincoln Park is Fauntleroy Cove. A walker who is fond of water transport will have to pause here to watch the Vashon ferry come in. Once a procedure as routine as the sun rising and setting, nowadays there is always the possibility of excitement. Electronics having replaced the brain, a glitch in the circuits may take out the dock, as used to happen only when the captain was hitting the bottle or flirting with his lady. Needless to point out, on any long-distance walk an excellent rest stop is a trip over to the island and back.

The only practical way to get on the beach at Fauntleroy Cove is from Lincoln Park, walking (low tide) under the ferry dock, south of which the "privates" have formed ranks shoulder to shoulder to repulse the "publics." The most interesting feature of the shore here is the history of waterside architecture, 1890 to 1988. A scattered few examples remain of the clapboard-and-shingle, veranda-and-sleeping-porch homes from the turn of the century, and even some "beach shacks" whose innards date to the 1920s. However, history is doomed to be destroyed by modern technology — the glass-and-cedar boxes perched atop steel pilings pounded deep in the beach, with timber connections to the bluff so designed that when the bluff slides down to the beach the timbers will go with it, beneath the box on the stilts.

The flats of Brace Point, another in the series of destroyed spits, contrast with the Tall Green Wall a short way south. Here, ¼ mile of beach is kept wild by a bluff rising 300 steep and unstable feet from the beach to the top, a feature of the shoreline that catches the eye from far south. In years past such steepnesses were judged "unbuildable" and complacently supposed by the government and citizenry to be greenbelts decreed by nature. However, today's engineers can build anything anywhere, and the "permanent" strips of green in the bluffs south of Seattle increasingly are being "engineered." This is the case with the Tall Green Wall.

To its south is a minor spit, long since trammeled; old piling stubs thrust out in the waves, remnant of a dock. The bluff has been deeply scooped by some unnatural agency, presumably an ancient gravel mine. At its base are the houses of Arroyo Beach, connected by switchback road to Arroyo Heights; one supposes "arroyo" is what the developer decided to call the gravel pit, much more salable than "Gravel Pit Estates."

Next south of the gravel mine (and the homes of Seola Beach) is one of the most magnificent madrona groves on Whulj, half covering one of the finest walls of sand in the area. But, engineers and princes are ripping up trees and sand for their castles.

The first neat and easy and no-hassle put-in of public feet on the beach south of Lincoln Park is Seahurst Park.

Seahurst (Ed Munro) Park (map — page 26)

Seahurst (King County) Park, 185 acres of woods and 5000 feet of beach, is reached from Ambaum Boulevard in Burien via SW 144 Street. Like most beach parks, this one consists of a creek valley so difficult for profiteering that it remained wild until King County bought it in the 1960s.

The parking area by the creek mouth gives access to a unique combination of an upper concrete seawall protecting a picnic-area path usable at highest tides, a lower gabion wall atop which is beach walkable at middle tides, and the outside natural beach open at low tides. All this eventually ends, and in ½ mile north so does the park, at a row of homes. All the way is a fine high bluff. Park beach also extends a scant ½ mile south from the creek; wild beach continues south.

To beach the park adds wildwoods. On the south side of the creek, by the bridge, an unmarked path climbs the bluff, then contours steep slopes, crossing above the large inland parking lot and diverging up a roadless tributary valley. The gulch is wild, the firs big, the bushes a green snarl. The way swings around the valley, crossing creeks, sidepaths branch this way and that, permitting quite a long trip. In the park are about 3 miles of trail, ranging from primitive to downright mean. For the introduction, loop down to the entry road and return on it to the beach.

Basic woods-walk loop trip 2 miles, allow 1½ hours
High point and elevation gain 300 feet

Mile 16½–23½: Three Tree Point–Indian Trail (map — page 26)

The ¼ mile south from Seahurst Park is below a tall wild sliding bluff, houses unseen atop, slumping trees hanging boughs over the sand. Homes begin and continue 2 miles to Three Tree Point (Point Pully).

Maplewild Avenue SW leads to the beach just south of Three Tree Point. The light is on private property and cannot be visited. There is no parking beside the short piece of public beach.

The Indian Trail. Said to be part of an old Indian route, this 4-foot-wide public walkway extends about 1 mile north from the point. To find it (unmarked) turn off Maplewild at SW 170 Street, just by Three Tree Point Store. A street-end (which goes to the beach, providing public access) has parking for two or three cars. Off it, north, stairs lead up a path. The only signing is to forbid public use between sunset and sunrise. (Middle-of-the-night orgies by the Wild and Crazy Guys were ruining the neighborhood.) The path goes north in back-yards along the steep bluff, giving intimate glimpses of bluff-suited architecture and views through firs and madronas to the water and the Olympics. The trail ends at Maplewild — no parking at this end. A short bit south of the north end a public path drops to the beach, permitting a waterside return for a 2-mile loop. Don't do the Indian Trail on weekends or summer evenings; come on a winter morning. Don't park stupidly; park on a shoulder somewhere in the neighborhood in such a manner as not to block a street or driveway; if you can't find a good place, go away and return some other day.

Three Tree Point is a landmark visible for miles; once beyond it, the walker has new vistas south, including Rainier. For 1 mile the road is close by the beach, house-lined most of the way. There is then a broad valley with few houses and a seemingly public road to the beach. A walker, passing by, asks of a picnicking family, "Is this a park?" They reply, "Yes, Normandy Park." He cries, "Aha! Let the public rejoice!" Their eyes glaze and they say, "Well, the park is public if you live in Normandy Park — but you see, Normandy Park is not a park, it's a city — a private city."

South from the broad valley of the beach road the shore is solid houses for ½ mile. Then the bluff leaps up to 100 feet, 200 feet, in one stretch even 300 feet, and stays up for 2½ miles, the lonesomest long stretch of beach between Seattle and Tacoma. Three little valleys break the wall of vertical wildness. On the first survey for this book, in 1977, they held a total of some half-dozen unpretentious homes. Returning for purposes of this edition, the surveyor just about had a fit of the apoplexy upon passing the northernmost valley, where three inter-related houses were being finished, together with an array of outbuildings suitable for a baronial estate, and roading and landscaping to match — more money than the old pedestrian's eyes ever had seen spent on so small a piece of landscape all at once, an amount he estimated in the many millions. The second valley is a marvelous large marsh behind a baymouth bar. On the first survey it sheltered a cozy cottage and a gracious old house, both carefully avoiding trespass on the bar. Now, a row of spiffy houses belly up along the bar. The marsh — surpassed hereabouts only by that of Dumas Bay — remains intact (or did on the most recent survey) and may have some form of official protection. The southernmost of the three valleys, formerly containing two small houses, now is chock-a-block.

On his first trip the surveyor innocently supposed these valleys were in whole or part being held for a major park. They were, of course, merely being held while land values rose high enough to maximize developers' profits.

Just south of the series of valleys there *is* a park — none other than Normandy Park Park! (See below.)

South of the Park Park wilderness a driveway manages to snake down the bluff to homes in a little rumple in the bluff, the mini-valley of "Fancy Houses Creek." Beyond lies one of the more interesting neighborhoods of Puget Sound City — a row built on pilings at the foot of the bluff, having access only by trail at high tide, by vehicles only at low tide, driving the beach from the south. Pass by here on a weekday morning and you will be joined on your journey by the whole neighborhood of dogs.

The final ½ mile of this segment is the huge pier (and public parking area) of Des Moines Marina, close by the town, where the highway nears the water after a long absence. At the north end of the marina is the access to the beach north, via Covenant Beach Park (see below).

Normandy Park Park (map — page 26)

When projects were being chosen for the Forward Thrust bond issue, King County Parks alertly put its finger on every available chunk of undeveloped shore south of Seattle. One of these was a scant ½ mile of pristine beach defended by a formidable 200 feet of forest bluff. Upon purchase of the property, located within the City of Normandy Park, the good people of that municipality expressed consternation at the prospect of "county" folk traipsing through their sanctum. King County therefore turned the park over to the city. The feared invasion of unwashed outlanders has not occurred because the park is not marked and the only trail down the precipice is mainly used by 10-year-old boys who don't want to become 11. Ah, but what wild delights await the doughty mountaineer-beachwalker!

From 1st Avenue S turn west on S 208 Street, then south on Marine View Drive. In the one and only short stretch without houses spot a woods road that in several hundred feet ends on the brink of the bluff, elevation 225 feet.

Don't expect to necessarily get to the beach in one unbroken piece. And getting back up the bluff in any condition whatsoever may prove impossible. Engineering a safe and easy trail down the glacial drift will take a bit of money and as of 1988 the City hasn't got it.

The obvious old woods road that sets out amiably over the brink soon ends. The main trail down from there has three stretches that can abrade and confuse and a final drop to the beach that could kill. An alternative path off the end of the woods road tours splendid madrona groves and magnificent old-growth Douglas fir snagtops, snags, and stumps, mortally wounded by a fire of a century-odd ago but some likely to survive another century or more, alive or dead, as eagle perches.

Don't take the children on this walk — not until the City builds a genuine trail in its only genuine park. It says it hopes to do that, someday, and may have done so by the time you arrive.

Round trip to big fir snagtops ½ mile, allow 1 hour
High point and elevation gain 225 feet

Covenant Beach Park–Des Moines Park (map — page 26)

Des Moines Creek flows some 3 miles from the south end of Seattle-Tacoma Airport, through a greenbelt, down into a green gorge, exiting on the beach at the north end of Des Moines Marina. The final stretch of gorge long was occupied by Covenant Beach Bible Camp. Abandoned for that purpose, in 1987 it was bought by King County Parks.

Plans for development are in preparation. The possibility exists of a trail extension beyond the existing 1 mile, perhaps a total of 2 or more miles, upstream through the existing (undeveloped) Des Moines County Park. In any event, acquisition by the county removes any qualms pedestrians formerly had about walking off the marina onto the beach. Feel free.

Round trip up the creek 2 miles, allow 1 hour
High point and elevation gain 100 feet

Mile 23½–25½: Des Moines (map — page 31)

The Des Moines Marina is not — repeat not — an access to the beach south. Yacht clubs and homeowners have fenced off the beach and locked the gate. A long-distance walker seeking to link the north and the south must do a lot of skulking to find a way through the defenses. Take it from an expert: the closer you get to the Marina, the more watchful the sentries. The beach, however, is readily accessible from the south end of this segment.

From the marina the first ¾ mile is beach houses, there being virtually no bluff in the broad Des Moines valley. But the next 1 mile is something else — the bluff abruptly leaps up 150 feet and though homes are on top and some paths come down, the beach is quite wild because the bluff is exceptionally vertical, formed here of hard sandstones-shales and, atop an unconformity, 90-degree gravels. This fine long stretch of naked cliff is striking from miles away. Imbedded in river gravels are large granite erratics dropped from icebergs. Layers of black, partly carbonized wood are an early step toward coal. Tree clumps from the top of the bluff have slid to the bottom, there growing on the sand — until the next big storm makes driftwood of them.

The final ¼ mile of this segment is in Saltwater State Park, whose north end has a great big fence signed against trespassing.

Clay bluff near Saltwater State Park

Saltwater State Park (map — page 31)

Because of the disproportion between public beaches and public here-abouts, Saltwater State Park gets some 1,000,000 visitations a year. Quite a lot for 88 acres with just 1445 feet of public beach.

Reach the park from Marine View Drive SW, Highway 509, the route having many twists and turns but guided by signs leading to the park.

In addition to beach there is forest in the valley of Smith Creek. For the basic introductory loop, park near the beach. By the restroom on the south side of the parking lot, find the unmarked trail switchbacking up the bluff, then con-touring the sidehill in big firs and hemlocks and maples, crossing little creeks. Pass under the highway bridge and climb to the plateau top, with views down to the creek. Amid a rather confusing maze of paths choose a route that turns up a tributary ravine nearly to private homes, contours past privies and campsites of the Youth Camp, then drops to the campground area, where two valleys join.

To do the loop, cross the two bridges over the two creeks just above their union, switchback to the plateau, hike through a fine conifer grove, descend to the valley, find a path ascending a tributary, pass under the highway bridge, on the opposite side of the valley from before, and hit the entrance road.

For a sidetrip, cross the road and walk out to a superb blufftop viewpoint. Then return to the entry road and walk it down to the car.

Basic introductory loop trip 1½ miles, allow 1 hour
High point and elevation gain 125 feet

Mile 25½–27: Poverty Bay–Redondo Beach (map — page 31)

A handful of homes abut Saltwater State Park to the south and signs sternly forbid trespassing. But in a very short distance begins a long stretch of mostly empty beach. For ½ mile a 125-foot cliff keeps houses respectfully at a vertical distance. Then there is a short strip of homes reached via a piling-protected road along the water from Woodmont Beach on the south. At Woodmont a public road comes to the beach and a little public picnic area. Open a can of beer here after sunset and the police will arrive before you've crunched up your first potato chip.

The bluff is low, scarcely more than a bank, and houses are solid and water-close the final scant 1 mile to Redondo Waterfront Park.

Redondo Waterfront Park (map — page 31)

In the 1920s Redondo Beach was a jumping resort, a summer-long carnival, with two dance halls, a bowling alley, merry-go-round and ferris wheel, games of skill and chance, cotton candy and hot dogs and ice cream sodas. Steamers of the mosquito fleet came south from Seattle, north from Tacoma, on weekends bringing together as many as 5000 fun-seekers at a time. The action never gets quite that frantic nowadays but the King County Park's 1060 feet of public beach draw considerable throngs. You can still buy fish and chips or, at the grocery store, an ice cream bar and a six-pack of cold root beer.

From Highway 509 just off Highway 99 in Federal Way, take Redondo Way down the ravine to Redondo Beach Drive, the marina, and the park.

The beach is the park. (The total upland area is 2.3 acres!) The way north to Saltwater is enticing. The way south (actually, more west) to Dash Point is arguably the nicest shore walk between Seattle and Tacoma.

The long-distance walker coming from the north now finds that the views are over the water to Maury Island, Vashon falling away to the rear. Puget Sound is narrow here in its East Passage, the bluffs across the water seeming very close. To the southwest appears Point Defiance and the tall stack of the ASARCO smelter, now closed; south winds no longer bring to the nose the sharp bite of sulfur dioxide. They still, however, waft the aromas of the nearby pulpmills.

Round trip 2120 feet, allow ½ hour

Mile 27–31½: Redondo Beach–Dash Point (map — page 31)

Three parks. And many wild bits, many delights of bluff and beach, creeks and marshes.

For 1 mile south from Redondo Beach houses are at waterside, and half that distance the road is there too before veering uphill and away. After ½ mile of high bluff and wild beach, the ¼ mile of Adelaide valley is inhabited. A

street-end gives public access to the beach; from 21 Avenue SW (see Lakota beach, below) turn right on 20 Place SW to very limited parking at the driftwood.

There is then ½ mile of wild bluff, partly occupied by undeveloped Lakota Beach or Poverty Bay (King County) Park, discussed below.

The wild bluff ends in a low bank and valley of densely-dwelt-in Lakota Beach, extending ½ mile to a point featuring huge granite boulders, houses on bulkheads, and the north boundary point of Dumas Bay.

Dumas Bay, about 1 long mile by shoreline from point to point, is very unlike any other part of the Trail. At low tide the bay empties and the wide flat permits a shortcut across the mouth, far from shore. Three creeks enter, one through a deep green ravine where two red houses catch the eye.

The main show is Dumas Bay (King County) Wildlife Sanctuary, discussed below.

Dumas Bay ends in a bluff at the west point. Houses are atop at first but soon yield to wildwoods. In the next 1 mile are notably large granite erratics on the beach, the hulk of a beached barge, the *Biltgood,* and non-public paths to the top of the bluff. Humanity then intrudes in the form of a dozen houses at the bluff base, accessible solely by trails hacked in the 150-foot cliff.

At the end of this intriguing neighborhood is Dash Point State Park and its long ½ mile of beach.

Lakota Beach (Poverty Bay) Park (map — page 31)

A half-mile long by a quarter-mile wide and 300 feet from bottom to top, this undeveloped King County park has naught to offer funseekers but a maze of trails through wildland forest, a cathedral choir of birds and squirrels, and a half-mile strip of lonesome beach in broad view of the Gravel Coast of Maury Island.

The turnoff from SW Dash Point Road is at a confusing intersection. Where SW 312th intersects Dash Point Road at a stoplight just south of a shopping center, turn west on 21 Place SW, unsigned at the intersection. It bends north as 21 Avenue SW. In a scant 0.7 mile turn left on unsigned SW 304 Street, which bends right as 24 Avenue. Turn left on 301 Street, which at a jog becomes 25 Avenue. The "25 Avenue" sign points across the street into the woods. Room at the deadend stub for a couple of cars to park. Step over the pile of neighborhood lawn-clippings and hedge-trimmings and find a very decent trail descending a scant ½ mile to the beach. Other trails meander about the bluff in excellent mixed forest.

Round trip to beach 1 mile, allow 1 hour
High point and elevation gain 275 feet

Dumas Bay Wildlife Sanctuary (map — page 32)

Yes, it's a public access to the beach, and that's appreciated. But the glory of this King County park — or rather, wildlife sanctuary, planned never to have any development — is the birding. Most of the park (23 acres, 450 feet of shore) is a vast lagoon marsh cut off from the saltwater by a baymouth bar. From the edge of the driftwood an impenetrable wilderness of cattails and reeds extends inland ¼ mile to the foot of the bluff; in season there's such a racket of redwing blackbirds and frogs one can hardly hear the crows and the gulls. As for the shallow little bay, its seaweeds and mucks (and two creeks) nourish such a rich assortment of tasty bites that at times one can hardly see the water. A fine April afternoon the surveyor found fleets of black brant, terns, mallard, and goldeneyes, the motley mob dominated by a solitary white-fronted goose. Mergansers and surf scoters patrolled offshore, cormorants posed on rocks, the sands were alive with killdeer and peep, and kingfishers scolded. — Not to mention the great blue herons standing in the water pretending to be driftwood: the park contains a 50-nest heronry (nesting area) whose existence in an urban area testifies to the natural defenses of the wetland.

From Dash Point Drive turn on 44 Avenue SW for 0.25 mile. At the only gap in houses, at SW 310 Street, is the parking area, elevation 80 feet. Walk the trail ¼ mile down through alder forest, beside the creek that feeds the marsh, to a little meadow by the driftwood.

Round trip ½ mile, allow hours
High point and elevation gain 80 feet

Dash Point State Park (map — page 32)

The 297-acre park has 3500 feet of sandy beach beneath a 225-foot bluff of vertical clay and sand topped by forests. It also has, de rigeur, a ravine.

From Federal Way drive via SW 320 Street, then right on 47th and finally left on Dash Point Road, south to the park entrance. Descend the ravine to the parking lot upstream a bit from the beach.

One trail leads through a tunnel under the entry road to the beach. There, on the east side of the valley, look for a broad path ascending the bluff to a viewpoint and a second picnic area.

For the main trail, the boundary loop, find the path at the upstream end of the parking lot, going up the gorgeous valley in ferns and alders. Passing under the highway bridge and by a massive cedar stump, the way crosses the creek in a wide maple-alder flat, at ¼ mile from the parking lot reaching a Y.

Dumas Bay Wildlife Sanctuary

Take the right fork, switchbacking to the plateau and park boundary. The trail proceeds across the upland in fir forest and alder-maple, marshes, delightful ravines, no sights or sounds of residences in the wildland. Ignoring minor sidepaths, at a major intersection with a road-trail turn left, soon joining the paved campground road. Turn left down the campground loop road to the bottom end of the camp and a sign, "Trail to Beach." Drop to the valley-floor Y, completing the loop, and return to the parking lot.

Boundary trail loop 2½ miles, allow 1½ hours
High point and elevation gain 250 feet

Mile 31½–40: Dash Point County Park–Browns Point County Park–Commencement Bay (map — page 32)

Some ¾ mile along the beach from the state park is Dash Point proper. The absolute tip is a private home but short of it is Dash Point (Pierce County) Park, with the Lobster House, parking, a public beach, and a long fishing pier the hiker should walk out on for northward views nearly to Three Tree Point (Point Robinson on Maury Island blocks it out), but mainly across the mouth of Commencement Bay (not yet quite seen) to Point Defiance — and the tall

Artist at work at Browns Point County Park

stack of the smelter. Also look across East Passage to points on Vashon-Maury Islands and into Dalco Passage, leading to the west side.

Beachside homes continue past the point ¼ mile; then a 175-foot cliff leaps up from the water, atop it being Marine View Drive, protecting wildness of the beach for ½ mile. At the outward bulge of Browns Point (yet another devastated spit) the bluff retreats inland, allowing solid houses the next 1½ miles around the point.

The road off the boulevard down to the lighthouse on Browns Point leads to the adjacent Browns Bay Improvement Club and Library, with public parking. Enclosing the lighthouse (beach access via the lawns) is Browns Point (Pierce County) Park. Picturesque lighthouse. Nice views, variations on those from Dash Point.

The shore swings around Browns Point to turn easterly into Commencement Bay. Here is the hiker's first look directly into the bay and across open waters to downtown Tacoma.

Now comes a long ¼ mile of homes on beach and bluff. But just as one expects increased urbanization, wildness rules. (The beach, not the view.) For nearly 1 mile the beach is guarded by a tall bluff atop which is Marine View Drive with many splendid viewpoints but apparently no paths down. For a bit the bluff is an amazingly vertical 160-foot gravel wall atop which is perched a restaurant. Other entertainments are an old beached barge, newer barges moored offshore, driftwood and dune lines and even a tiny lagoon marsh, and views to ships and directly across to Ruston and its smelter stack and, farther out, Point Defiance.

The beach becomes industrial-trashy and ends in a marina. The unsigned road down from Marine View Drive to the marina parking lot gives access to this beach, which offers the unusual combination of lonesome beachwalking in full view of the metropolis.

Past the marina the beachwalking is difficult but Marine View Drive is beside the water, with many turnouts, and the next 1 mile of shore cottages is picturesque, as are log rafts and gray and rusting Navy escort vessels.

The Trail leaves the bluffs for a final 3 miles on 11 Street E across waterways of the Puyallup River flat. The scene is crudely industrial, workaday-grimy, where the world makes its money so it can afford time off for beachwalking; rows of ships berthed along waterways; lumber yards and factories; a pulpmill belching clouds of steam. Here too is the combined flow of the Puyallup-Carbon-White Rivers, three of the major streams flowing from Rainier glaciers.

Whulj Trail enters Tacoma. To end? By no means. Tacoma has some of the best parts. But those and the way south are for *Footsore 4.*

Bus: Duwamish Head-Alki Point, 37 and 15; Lincoln Park, 18 and 34; Seahurst Park, 136 to Ambaum and SW 144, walk a few blocks to park; Three Tree Point, 136 to Marine View Drive at SW 170, walk to point; Des Moines, 130 and 132; Saltwater State Park, 130 to Marine View Drive at S 248, walk ¼ mile to park

Waterfront Park, Seattle

WHULJ TRAIL —
SEATTLE TO EVERETT

The Whulj Trail north from Seattle has three very different segments. First and shortest is the central waterfront from the Skid Road to Smith Cove — the pioneer waterfront, the Gold Rush waterfront, the tall-ship and mosquito-fleet waterfront, the city's chief history feast.

Next is Magnolia Bluff, from Smith Cove to Salmon Bay, the longest stretch of natural (mainly) beach between Tacoma and Everett, climaxing in the noble spit of West Point, which over the years has been taken for granted and ignored, then desecrated, but eventually (if not sooner) must be restored to primeval purity, to be recognized as a treasure of the whole of Puget Sound (better Whulj) City — of the entire Northwest — of the nation.

Third and finally, most of the route is the steel trail provided nigh on to a century ago by James J. Hill, the Empire Builder. Keep in mind that the Great Northern Railway (or, as it is now, the Burlington Northern) was not intended as a convenience for hoboes, tramps, and bums. The railroad tracks are not a public walkway, they are private property. How is it, then, that they have been walked from the time they were laid and hardly anybody ever has been hauled off to jail or even yelled at? Because all over America, all over the world, from their beginnings early in the 19th century railroads have been de facto public roads, and to render them securely private would require more fencing and more policing than ever could be justified to save a few pedestrians from getting hamburgered. For liability reasons, the railroad never will tell you it's okay by them if you walk the tracks, always will proclaim the sanctity of private property. Sometimes, when armies of addled youth are reeling along the rails, the police come a-chasing, even arresting. Should you ever be told to "Scat!" you be sure to SCAT. Forever remember you technically are a trespasser, possibly tolerated but never encouraged. Realize, too, that you need not be stoned or deaf to get squashed; with winter wind blowing by the ears and winter surf pounding, one may not hear trains creeping up behind; to avoid being crushed or — nearly as bad — being impelled on a leap into outer space by a train horn blowing in your ear, keep looking over your shoulder. Unless of course, it's low tide and you're down on the beach, enjoying that other and parallel trail.

The "railroad beach" isn't all that great — mainly because there isn't all that much of it. An environmental impact statement for construction of the Great Northern Railway along the shore from Ballard to Everett would bear comparison with those for the barbarian invasion of the Roman Empire and the A-bombing of Hiroshima. In the 1890s, of course, what we now call "impact" was known as "progress." The beachwalker of today belatedly files his complaint that the handsome seawall of granite blocks was erected at very nearly the line of mean low tide. Saving where a spit or a delta pushes out in the water, there is no beach whatsoever except at low water. Natural beaches of the North Sound generally have a walkable lane in calm weather at any level of the tide below 10 feet or so. On the Jim Hill Trail, the lane doesn't open until the level drops below 5 or 3 feet.

To look at the bright side, the Rail Trail is never closed. At the highest tides, in the most violent storms, the path atop the seawall is open. The best time to be here, in fact, is when ocean-size surf is booming against the wall, washing up onto the tracks, hurling spindrift into the bluff forest.

If the Jim Hill Trail is open in the worst of weather, it also is free to the feet in the best. On those balmy summer Sundays when people who live on the beach south of Seattle are exercising what they believe to be their property rights and are chasing the public off the beaches, nobody bothers the trackwalkers.

As characteristic of the Whulj Trail North as the railroad is the bluff, lifting an abrupt 200 to 400 feet above the shore — and constantly slumping down to the shore. Composed partly of concrete-like glacial till, partly of bedded sand and gravel and varved blue clay, it ranges from quite to extremely unstable. Homes are built on top by people gambling the bluff edge will not, in their lifetimes, retreat to the point occupied by their houses. Sometimes homes even are built on terraces formed by chunks of the bluff slumping off the top, the hope then being the slump terrace will descend at a rate no faster than inches a year. Sometimes homes are built below the bluffs, the residents sleeping restlessly on wet winter nights. But mainly the bluff is given up as a lost cause, permitted to remain houseless. Extending nearly the full length of the Trail is thus a strip wilderness, houses pretty much out of sight at the top, the steep, wooded, vine-tangled slope harboring a thriving population of birds and small beasts, the water-side walker for hours at a time "away from it all" while right in the middle of it all, strolling along in the heart of Whulj City.

And deeply sliced into the bluffs are numerous creeks, some in slot canyons, others in wide-bottomed, steep-walled valleys. From the shore wildland these short-to-long fingers of wildland poke into urbs and suburbs. Many (more than have been noted in the following route description) have trails inland; due to private property or lack of parking, they generally are not good accesses to the beach except for local residents, but for a hiker on the beach they provide a change of beauties, walking up a trail into a cool canyon of tangled greenery and splashing waterfalls.

So much for the land side of the Trail. What about the water side? Well, it's just your standard, routine, Whulj mix: waves on the beach, shorebirds on the sands and waterfowl swimming and gulls and crows above, the changing panorama across the waters to islands, Kitsap Peninsula, and Olympics, the parade of tugs and lografts and barges and freighters and ferries and fishing boats and sailboats, and memories of the water traffic that was, the old pilings, remnants of docks last used half a century ago, ghosts of the vanished mosquito fleet.

Special hot tip for carfree walkers: A *Footsore* reader who gets to all her trailheads by bus reports a really gaudy way to do the Trail North, in 2 days. One morning take Metro 306 from Seattle to Everett, hit the tracks south, and in the afternoon, at Edmonds, catch the 316 or 376 back to Seattle. Another morning ride 305 to Richmond Beach and walk south to West Point and the gaggle of Metro lines that serve Discovery Park.

USGS maps: Seattle South, Seattle North, Shilshole Bay, Edmonds West, Edmonds East, Mukilteo, Everett
Walkable all year

Mile 0–1½: King Street Station–Klondike Gold Rush National Historic Park–Skid Road–Central Waterfront (map — page 41)

Seattle's central waterfront has undergone many a transformation since Henry Yesler built his sawmill, the logs supplied by oxen hauling them along a skid road, and his wharf, which brought loggers and fishermen and lonesome settlers from all over Whulj by steamer, by sailboat, by rowboat, by canoe, to frolic in Madam Damnable's establishment. Elliott Bay's excellent shelter from southerly blows and the closeness of solid land to deep water quickly made it the premiere port of the region, and so it remained through the Gold Rush and World War II. However, larger ships and cargos began to demand the large, flat expanses of "made" land on the Duwamish Waterways; dredging deepened these channels to float ships. The central waterfront became an amiable slum, most of the old pier buildings empty, few of the slips ever seeing a ship. Even in decay, however, it remained Seattle's most exciting scene, refusing to be elbowed aside in the affection of the populace (and of the tourists) by such artifices as the Seattle Center. After musing upon the matter a good long while, the Movers & Shakers recognized there was as much money to be made from play as work. The central waterfront was transformed into a place of fun. Plans for further changes are being bruited about. One can only hope that Alaskan

Way (nee Railroad Avenue) is not entirely converted to a row of boutiques and fancy eateries. What some planners see as "dilapidation," others of us see as history. What the hoity-toity view as industrial grime, namely ships and trucks, the old settler considers to be the *meaning* of waterfront. Office buildings, hotels, condos, and even cruise ships (the *Love Boat*?) are no substitute for the lingering workaday traffic which reminds why Seattle came to be here in the first place.

This opening segment of Whulj Trail North is the best lowdown, downtown waterfront walk in the West — and most likely, the East as well.

Begin inside the King Street Station on South Jackson Street. (The close-by Union Station survives architecturally but not railroad-functionally.) Within the echoing vaults listen for conspiratorial whispers of ghosts plotting how to bribe the Congresses of Heaven and Hell into giving them land grants (alternate sections in a 40-mile strip either side of the tracks) for the Great Heaven Railroad, the Northern Hell, and the Union Eternal. Are you wondering how the trains arrive here from the north? In June of 1893 the first Great Northern passenger train arrived — via Railroad Avenue — that is, the waterfront. What with ships loading and unloading, the congestion was fierce. A bypass tunnel 5141.5 feet long, 25.8 feet high, and 30 feet wide (the widest tunnel in the world, then!) was completed in 1904 under 4th Avenue, the tracks leading into the Union Depot, opened in May of 1906. Walk east from King Street Station and look down from the street to the tunnel mouth.

(*Note:* While the Movers & Shakers are jazzing up the waterfront, they ought to take thought about hooking it on either end to a Seattle-Whulj Trail System. From King Street Station the air distance to Jose Rizal Park on Beacon Hill is ¾ mile. A walking route of about 1 mile easily could be devised. From Rizal Park a hiking route could lead through the Beacon Greenbelt to Beacon Ridge (which see). By adding a connection to the existing City of Renton Trail System, the way could be opened to walk from the Seattle Waterfront to the Cedar River and Snoqualmie Pass and — perhaps by hitching a ride on a wagon train — to Independence, Missouri.)

But, to the water: From Jackson turn right on 2nd Avenue S to S Main and turn left to Pioneer Square, Klondike Gold Rush National Historic Park, benches, bricks, trees, and bistros of Occidental and Pioneer Place Parks, and guided tours of Underground Seattle. Via Main or Yesler or King, cross under the highway viaduct to Alaskan Way.

(*Note:* The preceding chapter notes the scheming being done for Whulj Trail South. Parallel to this water-near route but farther inland is the line of the Seattle & Walla Walla Railroad, Seattle's first, designation now being sought as a National Historic District, with a walking route to Georgetown, Black River Junction, Renton, and north to old Newcastle, connecting to trails to Bellevue and Issaquah and Snoqualmie Falls. Pay attention, Movers & Shakers.)

By using King Street as the way to the waterfront, a pedestrian will come out at the site of the King Street coal bunkers and dock, where for many a decade the coals from Newcastle (and Black Diamond and all) were transferred from the Seattle & Walla Walla (later, after several changes in name, the Pacific Coast Coal Company Railroad) to sailing ships, then steamers, for transport to San Francisco, Australia, and South Africa. The site now is occupied by Pier 46, a container-ship terminal fenced off from public entry.

As examples of what fine things may be offered by Whulj Trail South, at Pier 36, another container terminal, is the Coast Guard Visual Traffic Center and

Coast Guard Museum, with ship models and marine memorabilia (free parking, open 1-5 weekends and Wednesdays and holidays).

Turning to the Trail North, the Washington Street Public Boat Landing has been that for generations and still is. During Fleet Week in the 1920s-30s the liberty parties from the battlewagons and cruisers debarked here. Seattle had the reputation as "the best liberty town on the Coast" and many bluejackets embarked here in custody of the Shore Patrol.

Pier 48 is the terminal of the blue-and-white Alaska ferries. Walk aboard with a sleeping bag and rucksackful of groceries and take deck passage to Haines. Also here is the Working Waterfront Viewpoint, with periscopes. Across the railroad tracks is the Underground Antique Mall.

From Pier 48 north to Pier 70 there is an alternative to walking — the green-and-cream waterfront trolley, old-timey and not obnoxiously quaint, 60¢ the ride. Cheap.

Pier 51 is the Washington State Ferries Terminal, on the site of the historic Colman Dock. The green-and-white Washington ferries will take you over the waters to Bainbridge Island or beyond it to Bremerton. Unlike the ghastly expense of automobile passage, pedestrian fares are really cheap, the biggest bargain in Seattle. Don't miss the Tsutakawa fountain at the street entrance to the terminal.

Pier 54 is Ivar's Acres of Clams, one of scores of eateries, deserving note here because it occupies the remnant of the Galbraith Dock which was the chief base of the mosquito fleet during its final several decades. In summer the *Emerald Princess,* a reconditioned sternwheeler, sets out from here on tours of the waterfront. Also here is Ye Olde Curiosity Shop, famous for scrimshaw, stuffed frogs, mummies, and tourist kitsch.

Pier 56 is headquarters of Seattle Harbor Tours, operator of the *Good Times* fleet, contemporary "mosquitoes" which not only tour the harbor, including the Duwamish Waterways, permitting close-up looks at the working waterfront as well as the historic waterfront, but voyage to Blake Island State Park. There, at Tillicum Village, descendants of the original (12,000 years ago) settlers serve baked salmon and display examples of traditional arts and crafts. Moreover, the 4-mile circuit of the island beach and the dozen-odd miles of island trails are the best beach-and-forest hiking so near Seattle. The route is described in *Footsore 3* but all a hiker really needs to know is when the next *Good Times* leaves; look in the phone book and call the number.

The ferries and the modern mosquitoes give the best perspective on the skyline of downtown Seattle. Not entirely submerged by its giant new neighbors is the Alaska Building, its name giving away its age. At 14 stories, this was the city's first "skyscraper" and the first constructed with steel reinforcing. The Smith Tower, opened to the public on the 4th of July of 1914, was hailed as the "Queen City's noblest monument of steel," the tallest building outside New York City. With its 1929 companion, the Northern Life Tower, it dominated the downtown sky until the 1970s brought the Sea-First Building, whose summit stands 714 feet above sea level, and the mid-1980s brought the tallest building west of Chicago and north of Houston, 76 stories, topping out at 1409 feet above sea level. Designed to withstand most earthquakes and nearly all winds, Mt. Selig (Columbia Center) goes as high as a person afoot can get in King County west of Cougar Mountain (1595 feet).

Pier 57 has Water Link, a maritime interpretive center open in summer, and another contemporary mosquito, the Gray Line *Sightseer,* which tours the

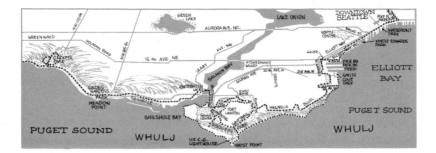

waterfront and continues around West Point and into Shilshole Bay to the Ballard Locks.

All this, and shops, and restaurants, and fireboats and fishing boats and even a few cargo ships. A nice thing about the waterfront is you don't have to be neat or even clean — the scene is casual and the whole place reeks anyway. If all the fish and chips consumed here on a fine summer Sunday were laid end to end a person would need a very long stick to shake at them. If all the ivory carvings sold here in a season weren't, the Eskimos of Hong Kong would be destitute.

Piers 58 to 60 are the city's pride, the Waterfront Park and Aquarium. The one has benches to lounge on while viewing water traffic and sipping clam nectar. The other has a model tidal basin, fish ladder, underwater viewing room, and examples of marine life indigenous to local waters. Across Alaskan Way the moving stairway lifts a person to the Pike Place Market, a whole other story.

Big plans are being made in the Piers 62 to 66 area, including the *Love Boat* terminal, a nice idea but no substitute for the Canadian Pacific *Princess* boats which until recently would whisk you in a day to and from a foreign nation and the city named for Queen Victoria. (Incidentally, the *Princess* boats were reputed to be no slouch in the love department themselves.)

Plaques along the way note historic spots, such as the first *maru* to arrive from Japan, marking the advent of Seattle as a world port; arrival of the "ton of gold" from Alaska; and the landing used by sailors of the Great White Fleet. Thirteen battleships of the Atlantic Fleet anchored in Elliott Bay four days in 1908. The ships lit up the sky at night with a searchlight show. The Alaska Building was draped with more than 500 flags. On the last day of the celebration, May 26, a military parade through Seattle was 3 miles long.

Mile 1½–3: Myrtle Edwards Park–Elliott Bay Park (map — page 41)

At Broad Street, Alaskan Way ends and Myrtle Edwards Park begins. A large metered area extending to Bay Street permits parking long enough for a leisurely walk north to Smith Cove and back. The 1200-foot length of Myrtle Edwards Park (City of Seattle) is succeeded by 4000-foot-long Elliott Bay Park (Port of Seattle).

In the whole of its green-lawn 1¼ (walking distance) miles through the two parks the path is close by the seawall; at low tide the beach can be walked instead. Trees are beginning to offer stretches of shady strolling. Train-watching (adjacent tracks are fenced off) is superb, and ferry-watching and general ship-watching. Also available for watching are ducks, gulls, crows, joggers, bicyclers (most of the way on a separate path), Elliott Bay, and the Olympics. The 200 tons of granite and concrete arranged in a sculpture have caused remark. So too, notably among residents of Queen Anne Hill, has the huge grain terminal at Pier 86, next to which a fishing (viewing, too) pier juts 100 feet out from shore.

The path ends at Pier 89 on Smith Cove. A large parking lot (free) on 16th W (¼ mile from Elliott Avenue and reached via W Galer Street) permits the walk to be done from this end.

Mile 3–3½: The Smith Cove Lacuna

Attention, Movers & Shakers. While hitching the central waterfront to trails on the south end, please jab the Port of Seattle in the ribs or wherever else will catch its attention. There is no good reason to let Piers 90 and 91 block the route from the central waterfront to Magnolia Bluff tidelands that lead around the corner to West Point.

At present a person bent on connecting Elliott Bay Park to Discovery Park must walk from West Galer on railroad tracks to the stairway up to Garfield Street Bridge, then follow Magnolia Boulevard (glorious blufftop views over Elliott Bay and Seattle) to 32 Avenue, which descends a gulch to a deadend at the beach. Or, if the tide is high and there is no beach, stay with Magnolia Boulevard (more stupendous views) to Emerson Street and the South Gate of Discovery Park and use the Loop Trail (see below) to attain West Point.

Mile 3½–7: Smith Cove Park–Magnolia Bluff–West Point
(map — page 41)

The first scheduled walk taken by The Mountaineers, weeks after founding of the club, was from Smith Cove to West Point Lighthouse. The connection to those footsteps of 1907 (as well as those of the preceding 4000 to 5000 years) deepens the historical richness.

The Port of Seattle's Smith Cove Park (also called simply "Public Viewpoint") provides a put-in. From 15 Avenue W turn west on W Dravus, turn south on 20 Avenue W, which bends right to become Thorndyke. Pass a sign that leads left to "Pier 91, trucks only," and turn left on 21 Avenue W, marked "Pier 91 — Port of Seattle — Public Viewpoint." Miles of Datsuns and Toyotas, the largest parking lot in the West, end at the little park at the mouth of Smith Cove. A stone's throw across a slip ships are docked at Pier 91, unloading Datsuns and Toyotas. Ferries shuttle through Elliott Bay. Views extend to Alki Point, Blake and Vashon Islands, Restoration Point on Bainbridge Island, the Green and Gold (Blue) Mountains on the Kitsap Peninsula. It's a nice spot to sit and look. But also it lets the feet down the riprap onto the beach — the first natural beach of the Trail and the only natural shoreline on Elliott Bay.

The situation hereabouts is confused. A while back the City of Seattle wisely decided it ought to acquire all the tidelands from Smith Cove around the curve of Magnolia Bluff. Unfortunately, a good many years earlier the city had stupidly permitted the platting not only of the tidelands but the underwater shelf below mean low tide. In modern times there could not, of course, be any actual development of the plat — the era of filling Elliott Bay is distinctly over. Therefore the city expected to pick up the beach for peanuts. Ah, but the

West Point Lighthouse and Olympic Mountains

American Way is that the public must always pay for its stupidities. A speculator who had acquired the underwater shelf informed the city that this was the case and demanded an exorbitant price. The city should have swallowed its pride and paid up.

There is now in the works a stinkpot harbor that will have some 1200 to 1500 slips behind a rubble breakwater some ½ mile long. The last significant kelp bed in Elliott Bay is at risk. So are the sea lions who hang out there. The birds and the fish? Let 'em sue. The "amelioration" will include a public beach access, shoreline walkway and observation deck on the rubble-mound breakwater where the visitor may enjoy watching 1000 trips a day, in and out, or may not. The birds and the fish aren't making a fuss, but the Muckleshoot and Suquamish and Tulalip tribes are (as of this writing in 1987).

Ah, well, on with the walk.

Particularly in the first 2 miles from Smith Cove the major attraction is the "working bay" — the parade of ships and ferries and other boats to and from the downtown waterfront and the industrial Duwamish Waterways. Other views are to Four Mile Rock and across the mouth of Elliott Bay to Alki Point where it all began. Look up the vertical till bluff to the line of madronas (when that fellow gave the bluff the name he thought they were magnolias). Gamblers

Row, where Perkins Lane follows slump terraces down the very face of the bluff and where residents so value the combination of nearness to city and distance of mood they are willing to risk losing homes in a slippery spell, intrigues the passerby who has no stake in the game. Old pilings at the bluff foot and litters of boards on the slope speak of gambles lost over the decades.

The way swings from westerly to northwesterly to northerly, Seattle and its towers lost around the corner, the view now over the water to Bainbridge Island and the Olympics. At low tide the beach is a broad tideflat, the walker at such distance from the bluff he is scarcely aware of houses tucked in the trees. A sign announces "End of Public Beach" — or, coming from Smith Cove, the start. This means that all the way to this spot people clutch pieces of legal paper saying they own the tidelands. As the preceding chapter explains, your feet nevertheless have free right-of-way below the line of mean high tide.

The sign does have a grander significance: this is the boundary of Discovery Park. Now the bluff is a tall wilderness of trees and bushes, the greenery broken on high by the famous sand cliffs and at the bluff base by vertical walls of blue clay.

Then, West Point, the finest spit on the entire inner Whulj and more "valuable" than competitors elsewhere because it is in the very middle of Whulj City, accessible by public transit to every citizen in the Metro service area. Further, it is at the crossroads of "Main Street," where ships from far seas turn this way into Elliott Bay, that way toward Bremerton, or continue south to Tacoma and other ports; where ferries shuttle from the bay and from Fauntleroy Cove to four landings across the waters; and where fishing boats, tugs and barges, and play boats ceaselessly go every which way.

Until 1966 West Point also was the most pristine large spit on the inner Whulj, disturbed to a relatively minor extent by a century of the West Point Lighthouse, two-thirds of a century of Fort Lawton, and a raw-sewage outlet installed by the city soon after the Army arrived. Then came that most Worthy Cause, Metro, which in the process of cleaning up Lake Washington dirtied up West Point with a sewage plant.

Because the Army had been there so long, blocking easy access, comparatively few people stood up to defend West Point. At present, the hiker must avert his gaze from the horrendous structures squatting where the tidal lagoon used to be, must hold his nose while walking by to attain the clean winds at the lighthouse.

This was bad enough, but then Metro proposed to install a secondary-treatment facility that would make 1987 look like the good old days. To its everlasting credit, the City of Seattle, led by its mayor, supported by the Friends of Discovery Park, cried "It must not happen! Metro must get off the point!" Members of the Metro Council protested, "It's Seattle's park! Let Seattle pay for it!" This sort of vision, able to make out objects on the tip of the nose but no farther, would pronounce Mt. Rainier to be "Tacoma's volcano."

Seattle will prevail. King County — and all the provinces of Whulj — will have their West Point. Man's blasphemies will be removed, nature will be permitted to restore a complete and natural beach — the waves throwing up a driftwood line, the winds blowing up a dune line, the waters filling up a lagoon marsh, and the reeds growing and the blackbirds scolding birdwatchers. All will be as it was before and folks will come from the world around to praise Seattle for its soul. The grandchildren of the Metro Councilors will apologize for their grandfathers and grandmothers.

Discovery Park (map — page 47)

Seattle's largest park, 535 acres above high tide and several hundred more of state tidelands assigned to the city for park use. Seattle's oniy all-natural park and its largest open space. To quote the 1972 master plan, "The primary role of this park in the life of the city is dictated by its incomparable site. That role should be to provide an open space of quiet and tranquility for the citizens of this city — a sanctuary where they might escape the turmoil of the city and enjoy the rejuvenation which quiet and solitude and an intimate contact with nature can bring."

Add: The grandest sand spit of Inner Whulj. The finest natural beach of Greater Seattle. The noblest wave-cut bluffs. A wildlife sanctuary ringed around by the megalopolis.

Since its establishment in 1972 the park has been in a continuing process of un-development. The military is being gently urged to complete its evacuation. The Metro stinkplant is earning infamy for its supporters. Unnecessary structures are being removed, new or retained ones made as unobtrusive as possible. Old roads are being demolished. The exotic species imported by a century of civilization are being weeded out, native species re-introduced. A trail system samples the diversity of the bluff uplands, meadows and forests alike; of the precipitous bluff itself; and of the beaches below the bluff.

A newcomer ought first to stop by the visitor center at the East Gate, off W Government Way and 36 Avenue W, to pick up a map showing the latest un-developments and the newest trails. The walking can begin from there, served by Metro bus 24; or the South Gate, Metro 19; or the North Gate, Metro 33.

The principal car access is the very large North Parking Area, by the North Gate. Drive west from 15 Avenue NW on Dravus, north on 20 Avenue which becomes Gilman Avenue which becomes Government Way and leads to the East Gate. At the East Gate follow signs to the North Gate.

Wolf Tree Nature Trail

A self-guided nature trail sets out from the North Parking Area and circles through mixed forest and swamp, along the sidehill and over Sheuerman Creek; the latter is named for the Christian who bought the land in 1887 and with his Native American wife, Rebecca, lived in a log cabin with their ten children. We learn this from the pamphlet available at the trailhead, and much more, including explanations of sights along the trail: "dog hair stand," "witches broom," and the "wolf tree."

Loop trip ½ mile, allow 1 hour

Loop Trail

This is the basic introduction to park uplands and the core of the trail system, connecting to all paths. The loop roughly circles the periphery, passing all park entrances and Metro bus stops.

From the North Parking ascend the hill on any of several paths ¼ mile to intersect the Loop. In the counterclockwise direction it soon passes the sidepath to the North Bluff, with views north out over Puget Sound, and the North Beach Trail and the access to the Indian Cultural Center.

Crossing the service road-trail to West Point, it passes the South Beach Trail and at South Bluff, atop the famous sand cliffs, provides glorious Sound views. Inland is the South Meadow, with old dunes dating from a drier climate of the past.

Up and down through woods and past old Army buildings, the Loop Trail self-completes in 2¾ miles. On the way it samples the bluffs, as much as 250 feet high, the meadows which top out at 360 feet above sea level, the mixed-species second-growth forests, and gives access to the structured open spaces, including the Fort Lawton Parade Ground in the park's Historic District and the Indian Cultural Center.

Through the generations of military maneuvering the soldiers largely converted the vegetation to species from the East, Europe, Macedonia, and the domains of Cyrus the Great. However, citizen volunteers are patiently eliminating invasive foreigners and making the area safe for plants which belong. The trail and park are getting better and better, year by year.

Loop trip 3 miles, allow 2 hours
High point 300 feet, elevation gain 500 feet

North Bluff–North Beach Trail
From the north arm of the Loop Trail a sidepath leads off to the North Bluff and the Indian Cultural Center and the Shilshole Overlook, a panorama including Shilshole Bay, Bainbridge Island, the Olympics, and Mt. Baker.

The North Beach Trail drops down to isolated North Beach — a delightful little stretch of fully natural beach between the homes of Lawtonwood and Metro's riprap monstrosity.

One way ½ mile

West Point Trail
The Hmongs from the hills of Laos rehabilitated this old trail in 1982, building bridges and wooden stairways and surfacing the trail to make it a safe and lovable path in any season. The bluff terrain is steep but the trail permits relaxed enjoyment of the superb forest, which includes enormous bigleaf maples at least 130 years old, their bark draped with fern moss, branches hung with licorice fern. Old! Green! Serene!

The path takes off from the North Bluff and in ½ mile ends at the West Point service road just across from the South Beach-South Bluff Trail.

One way ½ mile

South Bluff–South Beach Trail
The especially nice thing about this trail is that it permits a person to descend from the Loop Trail to the beach avoiding the reeking and rumbling Metro service road.

The way takes off from the Loop near the South Bluff promontory. Views are grand over the water to the Olympics. Watch for canine tracks; the park is Old Coyote's favorite lair within the megalopolis.

One way ½ mile

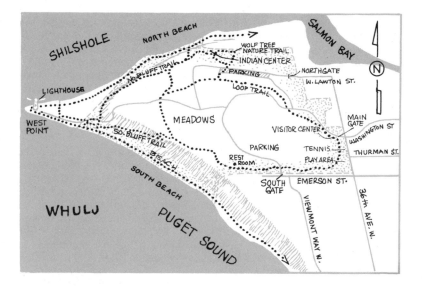

Indian Cultural Center (including Daybreak Star Arts Center)

The military began pulling out in 1972 after three-quarters of a century in residence. Seattle's sewers arrived shortly after the soldiers; this, too, will pass. The West Point Lighthouse, marking the tip of the magnificent spit since 1872, likely will be encouraged to remain, to recall the tall ships it used to guide through the night, and the steamers, and even a few canoes. The second-growth forest reminds of the tidewater loggers of the 1860s. The park's name evokes the voyage of George Vancouver, in 1792, in H.M.S. *Discovery.*

The earliest settlers arrived ten or a dozen millennia ago. David Buerge, in *Naming the Land,* says there were eight or nine peoples in the Greater Seattle area, speaking dialects of a common language and sharing a single "nationality," as do the Scots, Welsh, Cornish, and English who consider themselves jointly British.

The Duwamish lived in Seattle and Renton and along the river; the Suquamish branch of the family produced the most famous local leader, Sealth. The largest village, Dziszilalich, was at Pioneer Square.

Lake Washington was the home of the Hatchuabsh, the "big lake people"; Lake Sammamish, of the Hat-hatchuabsh, the "second lake people," and also the Issquoabsh; Lake Union, the H-atschubsh, the "small lake people."

Known to their neighbors, who feared them, as the "people of the Moon," the Snoqualmies lived at Fall City and Carnation, from which they hunted, traded, and raided.

The major saltwater people were the Shilsholabsh or Sheel-shol-ashbush, a word meaning "threading the bend" (with a canoe to Lake Union). Their domain extended from Smith Cove to Mukilteo, north of which lived the Snohomish. The largest village was at Salmon Bay, to catch salmon headed for Lake Union. Other camping spots lay along the shore to the north; Whulj walkers will guess them. The saltmarsh of south Edmonds, cut off by a baymouth bar, likely held a second major village.

The Shilshole people seem to have suffered a great catastrophe along about 1800, perhaps an especially destructive raid from the north. Subsequently, of course, they suffered the onslaught of the European plagues. Early European visitors saw three longhouses at Salmon Bay. By 1853 the population was reduced to a dozen families; by the late 1880s, two families. "Indian Charlie" (Hwulch'teed) lived in a cedar shack on the site 50 years, to the turn of the century. He was the last of his people. The U.S. Army Corps of Engineers dredged the site for the Ship Canal.

The Beach

The Discovery Park beach has a number of claims to being (or having been) the very best on the entire Whulj Trail: There is no railroad. The bluff offers not only the usual tills and gravels but some of the tallest walls of sand. The parade of ships and boats and cockleshells makes it hard to get a nap, so much is always going on. Are birds your game? Clouds? Waves? Storms?

Moreover, you get here afoot. From the North Parking Area it's 1 mile via Loop Trail and service road, or North Beach Trail or West Point Trail or South Beach Trail, and another ¼ mile past the stinkplant to the lighthouse.

Aside from the spit, the once and future greatest on Inner Whulj, there is the beach with no picture-window voyeurs intruding on your communion with the clams and the gulls. South to Smith Cove is 3½ miles. North to Salmon Bay, 2 miles. The bad news, of course, is Metro: the North Beach has ½ mile of joyless riprap leading to the little bit of natural beach; the South Beach has been fixed up to repair some atrocities, but still does not become truly natural until the spit is left completely behind.

Total round-trip beach walk 12 miles, allow two tides

Mile 7–9½: Commodore Park–Chittenden Locks (map — page 41)

At low tide the beach can be walked all the way around the shore of Shilshole Bay into Salmon Bay. At high tide, go inland. From West Point climb the service road-trail to the Loop Trail, which leads to the North Parking Area. From there exit through the North Gate onto 40 Avenue, turn on Commodore to Commodore Park, where the beach route joins. This over-the-hill way is about 2 miles, about the same as the beach, but with more elevation gain.

Commodore Park is a jimdandy. Look out saltwater Salmon Bay past railroad bridge and jetties to Shilshole Bay and Puget Sound. On a sunny day admire the parade of vessels lined up to go through the Big Lock or the Little Lock into freshwater Salmon Bay.

Follow the promenade path through the park to the pedestrian walkway over Chittenden Locks.

Pause to examine the fish ladder which salmon and trout ascend on their way to spawning grounds in the Lake Washington basin. A below-ground viewing gallery gives the best close looks at big fish available outside a fish market. (After studying the fish you may wish to study fishing boats, another endangered species. For a sidetrip, walk east on Commodore 1 mile to the fleet based at Salmon Bay Terminal, "Fishermen's Wharf.")

Hiram M. Chittenden Locks ("Ballard Locks") are the key component of a navigation system dedicated in 1917. A channel was dredged from Puget Sound through Shilshole Bay to Salmon Bay, joining this body of water via the Fremont Cut to Lake Union, and that body via the Montlake Cut to Lake

Breakwater at Golden Gardens Park

Washington. The latter was lowered from the natural elevation above sea level of 29-33 feet to the level of Lake Union, 21 feet, and Salmon Bay was raised by the dam at the locks. Lake Washington, which formerly emptied via the Black River to the Duwamish River, thence to Elliott Bay, now drains through the Lake Washington Ship Canal to Shilshole Bay. The Black River virtually ceased to be. The Cedar River, which flowed into the Black and thus the Duwamish, was diverted into Lake Washington, which it thus furnishes a constant source of flushing water from the mountains, the uncelebrated other half of the clean-up-the-lake success story for which Metro is always given full credit. Aware-ness of all this fooling around with Mother Nature adds interest to watching ships and boats being lowered or raised through the locks. (Footnote: the Ship Canal never made Lake Washington, as everyone imagined would happen, a great seaport.)

Adjoining the locks are the 7 acres of Carl English Botanical Gardens, displaying plants from lands all over the world.

Mile 9½–13½: Golden Gardens Park–Meadow Point (map — page 41)

At Chittenden Locks begins a connection on streets to the Burke-Gilman Trail (which see).

49

The Whulj Trail proceeds westward from the locks on the north shore of Salmon Bay. Staying close to the water on sidewalks and dirt paths, in 1 mile a walker leaves Salmon Bay for Shilshole Bay and its enormous jetty-protected moorage for hundreds (or is it thousands?) of pleasure boats. The Port of Seattle has decorated the way with Leif Ericson's statue, a monster 19th-century wrought-iron anchor, and other marine artifacts.

The moorage at last yields to the 95 acres of Golden Gardens Park, dating from 1923 and with bathing beach and unobstructed Sound views. Meadow Point is the last spit in Seattle retaining all elements of a complete beach: driftwood line, dune line, lagoon. It does not have a swimming pool (as does Colman) or a sewage plant (as does West). There was a plot to decorate it with an aquarium but saner heads squelched that dizzy idea; the aquarium was put on Seattle's central waterfront, where it belongs.

The railroad tracks having joined the route at Chittenden Locks, from Meadow Point on north to Everett they constitute the high-tide lane.

The bank above the tracks is not high and is quite solidly built-up through the Blue Ridge area and what used to be called North Beach.

Then the bluff suddenly rears up 200 feet from the water, tall and steep and unstable. From now on a common feature of the route is the sensor wire at the base of the bluff; when chunks of bluff slide over the tracks, as they do every winter, all winter, a light blinks on in a control room and trains are signalled to watch out.

Carkeek Park (map — page 52)

Along about 1880, soon after the giant cedars were felled, skidded to the beach, and rafted to shingle mills in Ballard, a Bavarian-born baker and confectioner, A. W. Piper, cleared land for a farm. He died in 1904 and in 1927 the land was bought by Seattle to replace a Carkeek Park that had been condemned by the U.S. Navy for the Sand Point Naval Air Station. In 1981 volunteers of the Carkeek Watershed Community Action Project experienced a rush of nostalgia for Bavarian apple pies. Hacking away ivy and hellberries and brush, they found gnarled, mossy survivors of Piper's orchard — some 30 apple trees, two pear, two cherry, and a huge sweet chestnut. The volunteers sat in the grass sampling archaic varieties of apples, appreciated, as one of them put it, "by the same kind of people with a taste for baroque music."

Piper farmed the plateau upland and the valley bottom. Near the mouth of Piper's Creek, on the south side, a brickyard turned blue glacial clay into the basic building block of pre-concrete America. In the era of World War I the surveyor's mother and friends used to walk after Sunday school north from Ballard along the Great Northern tracks to "the brickyard."

The 1930s brought the CCC and the first development, including trails. However, when the surveyor made his initial visit in the spring of 1938, hiking with Troop 324 from the Scout Lodge next to Ronald School to attend the overnight Camporall of the North Shore District, the park was mainly under nature's management. It remains so today, one of the two largest wildlands on the Whulj Trail between Ballard and Everett.

The park of today — the 193 upland acres of bluff and canyon and the 23 acres of Piper's Creek tideland delta — was shaped to present form in 1953 and 1976. In the latter year the Viking Council of the Boy Scouts developed the major trail, 1.3 miles from the railroad tracks up Piper's Creek, ascending the

Beach at Carkeek Park

canyon floor in lush mixed forest, passing a dozen basalt-boulder "energy dissipators" that reduce erosion. Crossing and recrossing the sandy creek, the trail climbs the narrowing canyon, at last leaving it to ascend steeply to a small parking area at the street-end of 6th Avenue NW, which leads to a bus stop on NW 100 Place close to Holman Road NW.

For a loop return, find one of the several paths climbing into wildwoods south of the canyon and wander along the hillside to a bluff 175 steep feet above the tracks and beach, giving fine views over the water and south to Meadow Point.

In the 1980s came the CWCAP, a citizen group working with public agencies to "turn Carkeek into a model urban watershed, purged of fecal pollution and abandoned rusted bedsteads." Recovering Piper's Orchard has been one project. Another is the Salmon-to-Sound Trail, to restore the coho salmon run to Venema Creek, which empties to Piper's Creek downstream of the Worthy Cause stinkplant. (A 1980 plant of coho fry had limited success. A 1984 plant of chum fry brought, in November 1987, a spectacular return of mature chum salmon.) At a scant ½ mile from the mouth of Piper's Creek the route diverges from the Piper's Creek Trail, north up Venema Creek to the spawning grounds — used, too, by native cutthroat trout.

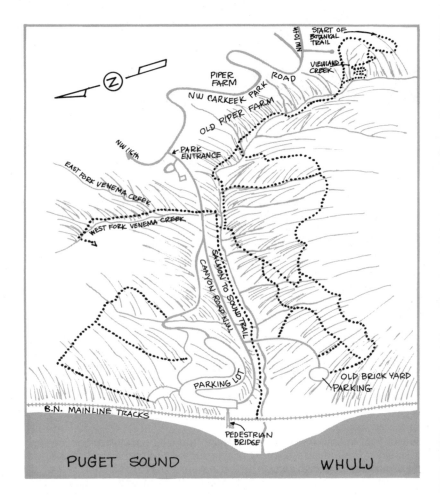

One reason the water quality here is excellent is that parts of the West Fork Venema forest appear to be virgin, with standing trees up to 4 feet in diameter and no sawn stumps.

The CWCAP also is properly proud of its Viewlands Botanical Trail, looping around Viewlands Creek and upper Piper's Creek. Exotic plants are being cleared out, natives planted, and a teaching path established for use by Seattle schools.

As the map in these pages suggests, there are miles and miles of other paths in the park. For the wildest walk of all, climb from the beach parking area north along the bluff edge to a high flat and follow the path along the rim in woods ⅓ mile to the unmarked park edge. For a loop return, take a path inland and descend to the parking area on a path whose red rubble recalls the brickyard. To go really wild, watch for a slippery path dropping to a skimpy trail contouring the tanglewood bluff halfway between rim and beach.

**Total park sampler loop trips 5-8 miles, allow 3-6 hours
High point and elevation gain 275 feet**

Mile 13½–18: Boeing Creek–Richmond Beach Park (map — page 54)

From Carkeek Park northward the bluff wildland-and-wildlife-refuge is a near-constant presence. Beside the high-tide lane atop the seawall are alders and maples, flowers in season, frogs croaking in marshy ditches, creeks tumbling down little gorges. One scarcely believes houses are at blufftop, usually set back from the lip a goodly distance as they are.

North 1 mile from Carkeek Park is a canyon in clay and sand; generations of local kids have worked away at eroding the deposit while trying to break their necks climbing the vertical walls.

At 2 miles from the park (and all this way no houses by the beach, presence of a city seeming impossible) is Highlands Point and the wide valley of Boeing Creek, named for the logger-aircraft manufacturer who kept this section of forest as a private retreat; not until World War II was the magnificent virgin Douglas fir of the "Boeing Tract" logged. The newspapers enjoyed reporting 19th-century-style logging so near the city so late in history; only a few people mourned the loss of the equivalent of a dozen Seward Parks.

On the south side of Boeing Creek a private road ascends the wild creek, in big trees that weren't worth logging (snagtops and the like) to The Highlands residential park. On the north side a road-trail with greenbelt easement but gated on the upper, inland side to keep out vehicles, ascends ½ mile to Innis Arden Way at NW 166 (very limited shoulder parking). A footpath goes around

Richmond Beach Park

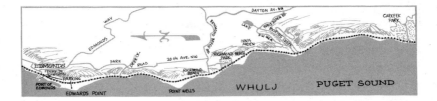

the gate, permitting beach access. In the valley bottom at NW 166 is a wide flat through which the creek meanders; until a flood took out the dam, this was Hidden Lake, Boeing's private fishing pond. King County owns half the lake-site and is considering a plan to rebuild the dam.

North from Boeing Creek is more wild bluff. Approaching Richmond Beach, keep a sharp eye for a path up a gulch to Innis Arden; this neighborhood trail makes an interesting sidetrip ½ mile up to a road.

At 4 miles from Carkeek Park is a sand hill that formerly was the site of shipwrecking; wooden ships were stripped of metal fittings and then set afire, the clouds of black smoke attracting throngs from all over the north Seattle area. Here is Richmond Beach (King County) Park. A skybridge crosses the railroad tracks to the parking area in a great amphitheater that until a third of a century ago was a gravel mine and another favorite spot for local kids to get bruises and contusions and minor fractures. From the top of the park, elevation 200 feet, the view across the Sound is superb.

To reach Richmond Beach Park, on Aurora Avenue at 185 Street turn west on the Richmond Beach Road and follow it down the steps of wave-cut bluffs, each representing a different former level of the water. When nearing the water, only one more bluff to go, turn left at a sign directing to the park.

Mile 18–22: Point Wells–Edwards Point–Edmonds Ferry Dock–Sunset Beach Park (map — page 54)

The Whulj Trail proceeds from the park through the old community of Richmond Beach, past the site of the vanished steamer dock, the site of the vanished railroad station, to Point Wells. In its pristinity this spit was a fit companion of West Point, in *its* pristinity. However, only by examining old maps can one guess what there was here to be devastated by Standard Oil for a tanker terminal, oil storage tanks, and asphalt refinery.

Wild bluff resumes at the complex, at whose north end, nearly 2 miles from the park, is a survival of the pristine spit — a tiny strip of natural beach, trees growing to the driftwood line. Guess what Worthy Cause has identified this as "one of the two best sites for a major new sewage-treatment plant"? To paraphrase Robinson Jeffers, "It's only a little beach, but oh so beautiful."

Among those who know are the local folk who come down by trail (unsurveyed) along the ravine of Deer Creek. At the palatial blufftop estates of Woodway Park begins one of the most spectacular slide areas of the route, the naked muck slopes in motion from an elevation of 220 feet down to the tracks, which often are blocked by chunks of former palatial estate. But except for the kempt-looking bluff rim giving away the existence of lawns up there, one would never suspect homes, here or anywhere from Point Wells to Edmonds.

This metropolis is entered, 3 miles from the park, at Edwards Point, site of another tanker terminal (Union), storage tanks, and small refinery. But a considerable portion of the natural beach at the point is undisturbed.

At Edwards Point begins a 1-mile breach in the bluffs; the cavity is a broad marshy valley, formerly a principal settlement of the Shilshole people, then the site of the steamer landing that grew into Edmonds.

The large parking lot at the point is accessible via shoreline streets from the ferry dock to the north. At the public beach begins the Port of Edmonds, the long breakwater-protected yacht basin offering a display of boats comparable to that of Shilshole Bay. A public observation pier and a public (city) beach enliven the walk.

The best thing about Edmonds is the ferry. For a lunch stop and an incomparable viewpoint, take the voyage to Kingston on the Kitsap Peninsula and back. At least pause to watch the ferry ease in to the slip, unload, and load.

Adjoining the dock on the north is Edmonds Underwater Park, sunken ships providing homes for marine life that scuba divers can look at but mustn't touch. Sea lions have adopted the divers' floats for off-season siestas. Connecting to the underwater park is the abovewater Sunset Beach Park, located at historic Brackett's Landing.

To reach the park follow signs from I-5 to the Edmonds-Kingston Ferry and cross the ferry lane into the park, where cars may be parked for 4 hours maximum, enough for short walks. If using this as a base for a longer trip, park south of the ferry dock in the vast free lots of the Port of Edmonds.

Another feature to note here is the only Amtrak station between Seattle and Everett.

Mile 22–26½: Browns Bay (map — page 57)

For many years one of the favorite stretches of the Whulj Trail has been from Edmonds to Meadowdale (and onward to Picnic Point). The overwater views become distinctly and dramatically different. The north-of-Seattle shore and Bainbridge Island fade south in haze, the vista now being across to the Kitsap Peninsula. But one sees out northwest between the peninsula and the white cliffs of Whidbey Island to Admiralty Inlet, the route to the ocean. For the first time, and only briefly, there is a water horizon.

Immediately north of Edmonds there's no bluff and houses crowd the way. Then the wilderness wall rises again, cut by gulches and a sand canyon, offering a series of trails inland — doubtless to private property and thus not public accesses to the beach.

At about 3 miles the shore bends in to Browns Bay. In a lovely gulch is Lynnwood's sewage-treatment plant (the old story) and the first road access to the beach since Edmonds, via a sideroad off 76 Avenue W (see Meadowdale).

At 4 miles a structure juts out on the waterside of the tracks — Haines Fishing Wharf. On slumping hillsides above is the village of Meadowdale. To the north ½ mile is the fine broad sandy Meadowdale Beach at the mouth of Lunds Gulch.

Meadowdale Beach Park (map — page 57)

The delta-point thrusting far out in the waves, views up and down Whulj virtually the full length of the Trail, the large creek gushing from wide Lunds Gulch and rippling over the beach, these are the features most famed in this undeveloped Snohomish County Park. In addition, Lunds Gulch is one of the two largest chunks of wildland (Carkeek Park the other) on the shore between Seattle and Everett.

The village of Meadowdale is reached from Olympic View Drive (known from logging days of the 19th century as the Snake Trail, so sinuous is the route) via 76 Avenue W.

Parking on the historic Haines Fishing Wharf is strictly for customers. Parking elsewhere in Meadowdale, entirely on road shoulders, is extremely limited. The public is an obvious pain to residents, who barely have room on their ever-sliding hillside for houses and streets much less visitors. This therefore is not a place to go on weekends and summer evenings.

Park with care wherever possible on a road shoulder, not blocking traffic or driveways. The best route is north on the beach the ½ mile to the gulch. Another is 75 Place W, barricaded at the edge of residences but as a foot trail continuing, the grade partly slid out, across the face of the bluff in woods, and descending to the valley bottom; however, the Wild and Crazy Guys have forced the government to put up signs and send out the police; you may feel unwelcome.

Meadowdale Country Club, it once was, a good long while ago. Nature is reclaiming foundations and charred timbers of the burned lodge, fields of what must have been a rather minute golf course, and valley roads.

To explore the wildland, walk upvalley on an old road that dwindles to trail. The creek flows over sandbars and little waterfalls. The valley walls, rising steeply to the plateau top at 450 feet, are massed alders, fern-hung maples, hemlocks growing from huge cedar stumps notched for the fallers' spring-boards, and appropriate other vegetation. At 1 mile from the beach the trail, still ½ mile from the head of the gulch, comes to a Y, the two branches scrambling up mossy-lush, black-mucky slopes on either side of the gulch to suburbia. Downvalley from the Y several other paths similarly climb the walls. A trail system built at various levels of the gulch on both sides could have a total length of up to 10 miles.

Sample gulch round trip 3 miles, allow 1½ hours
High point and elevation gain 450 feet

Mile 26½–28: Norma Beach (map — page 57)
Just around the corner, ½ mile north of Lunds Gulch, is another fishing wharf; this one at Norma Beach shows its half-century age, seeming about to sag to the sands. Public cars have little space to park but the public feet easily can gain the beach via the railroad tracks.

A high sand cliff catches the eye, and a trail to the blufftop; there's another way there (see below). Then, on a slump terrace above the beach, appears a row of homes (see below).

Ghosts crowd the beach — lines of old pilings, remnants of docks, visions of the vessels of the mosquito fleet that steamed up and down the water road until the 1920s. More ghosts — concrete foundations of beach cabins. Are those mandolins we hear in the summer twilight?

All this, 1 mile from Norma Beach, is none other than far-famed Picnic Point, a great sandy spit (actually, a cuspate hybrid) at the mouth of a superb valley, a lovely creek rushing across the beach.

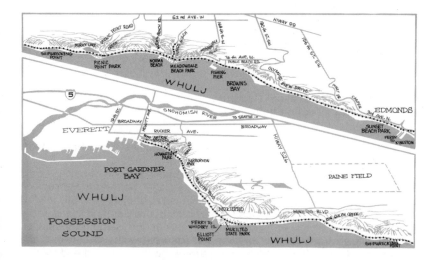

Picnic Point Park (map — page 57)

Candidate for honors as one of the best places on the whole Whulj Trail, Picnic Point does not have a sewage plant, swimming pool, or aquarium. But it almost had a refinery. When the oilers realized they'd better seek a more cooperative county to the north, they decided to turn a profit another way. Chevron Land Development Co. is building a city on the uplands.

It has leased (not sold) an itty-bitty piece of land to Snohomish County for a park which essentially is just a parking lot and an access to the beach, via a skybridge over the railroad.

But what a beach!

Take the Paine Field exit from I-5. Drive west to Highway 99 and turn south to the Mukilteo Road, Highway 525. Turn northwest (right) to the Beverly Park-Edmonds Road. Turn southwest (left) to a red blinker. Turn northwest (right) on the Picnic Point Road and descend a forested, undeveloped, beautiful, wild, parkless gulch (passing the Alderwood Manor wastewater treatment plant, that the valley should not be a total loss) to the beach parking area.

There's no park to put a trail system in but there is a nice bluff walk from here. Maps still show Puget Sound Boulevard contouring the bluff face south to Norma Beach. But it doesn't make it all the way and hasn't since about 1960. Don't drive south of Picnic Point on what road remains; the residents on the slump terrace need every bit of single-lane pavement. From the parking area walk ¾ mile along the row of houses (that are, seen from the geologist's vantage, riding the sliding hill down to the waves), to the road-end (no parking). Trail continues on the remnant grade (haunted by ghosts of Model Ts) across the bluff. The sand cliff admired from the beach (see above) is what finally discouraged the highway department; not a scrap of grade lingers here. (That is, none will linger after a temporary 1986 reopening of a road across the sand, strictly for construction access to a local project.)

Here on the vanished section a hiker can sit in the woods, high above the beach, far below the blufftop, protected on every side from the 20th century.

Gazing over the broad waters, one feels as remote from civilization as anywhere on the Whulj Trail.

It's not a large sanctuary — in ⅓ mile from drivable road is the edge of inhabited Norma Beach. But as one sits in the wild spot it grows in the direction of infinity.

Round trip 2½ miles, allow 1½ hours
High point and elevation gain 100 feet

Mile 28–33: Shipwrecking Point–Big Gulch–Mukilteo State Park–Elliott Point–Mukilteo Ferry (map — page 57)

The hiker who started the journey in Seattle now is aware of having come very far north. Indeed the route here leaves Puget Sound for Possession Sound, across whose relatively narrow width is Whidbey Island. Still in view are the Olympics but now very close to the north, above Camano Island, is the white volcano of Baker. At hiker's start the Bainbridge Island ferry shuttled back and forth from Seattle to Winslow. Then came the shuttling of the Edmonds-Kingston ferry, which now retreats southward in the distance; meanwhile to the north become more prominent the green-and-white vessels ceaselessly voyaging between Mukilteo and Columbia Beach on Whidbey.

Just north of Picnic Point the way passes a murky lake dammed by the railroad fill; homes line the inland shore, leaders of flycasters festoon the telephone wires.

At 1 mile is "Shipwrecking Point," a spit once used for stripping and burning wooden ships; a carcass and some ribcages remain to be seen but not explored — on the privately owned point is an inhabited house. A footpath of steps cut in clay ascends the bluff to a waterfall (in hard rock, a rare exposure of non-glacial materials) and, atop the plateau, a path along the creek in wildwoods to Marine View Drive at 116 Street SW.

In ¼ mile more is a substantial ravine up which goes a trail. Homes of so-called Chenault Beach (named for the Flying Tiger famous in World War II, and having no beach) then are seen atop the bluff. In the past decade some houses have been built on the water, and there goes the neighborhood.

In 1 mile more (2¼ miles from Picnic Point) is a point with a very wide beach at low tide, the mouth of the wild valley of Big Gulch. Not a park. In fact, it once was degraded to an open ditch down which ran raw sewage from Paine Field Air Force Base. Cleaned up and looking nice, it now harbors a Worthy Cause — the Olympus Terrace Sewage Treatment Plant. No public access. Thus lonesome country. The solitary plant operator frequently sights deer and bear and weasels and seals, eagles perched in favorite snags, fleets of thousands upon thousands of waterfowl swimming by. — Or let us say "used to." Construction of the treatment plant permitted the land-developers to shift into high gear and the scene is becoming steadily more human and less humane.

North ½ mile is the first close house in a long while, in a creek valley on a flat beside the tracks; the road access is private. Shortly a public road descends a slump terrace to within 50 feet of the tracks but is not recommended as a public beach access, having very little parking. An interesting portion of this community is built outside the railroad tracks on a bulkheaded invasion of the beach; the dozen cottages have walk-in trail access only; the residents tend not to buy new refrigerators very often.

Elliott Point Lighthouse and Mukilteo ferry

After this ½ mile of scattered dwellings, in the final 1¾ miles mankind retreats from the beach, up to the top of the tall, wild bluff. The way features a tangled-green slot of a gorge, a great vertical cliff of white glacial till, another creek tumbling out of a gulch.

Rounding Elliott Point the railway swings inland and is fenced off through Mukilteo. The Trail thus follows the beach to small Mukilteo State Park. On the tip is Elliott Point Lighthouse, the first since West Point, a dandy. Adjacent is the ferry dock, suggesting a sidetrip over the water to Columbia Beach, a nice rest stop after the 5 miles from Picnic Point, before starting back.

Mukilteo is reached from I-5 via Highway 526-525.

Mile 33–38: Powder Mill Gulch–Merrill and Ring Creek–Harborview Park–Howarth Park–Pigeon Creeks No. 2 and 1–Port Gardner–Everett Amtrak Station (map — page 57)

Gazing from Mukilteo to the industrial sprawl of Port Gardner, the hiker may ask, "Who needs it?" But the wild bluff continues to guard the beach and the assemblage of wild ravines is arguably the best on the entire Whulj Trail.

The shore, previously trending north, bends sharply eastward at Elliott Point. The view thus is across Possession Sound past little Gedney (Hat) Island to Saratoga Passage between Whidbey and Camano Islands and to Port Susan between the latter island and the mainland. No longer is there a parade of ships to and from the ocean and various ports of Puget Sound, but there is considerable traffic along Possession Sound to Everett.

Easterly for a scant 1 mile from the Mukilteo ferry dock the beach is blocked by another oil terminal and a series of storage tanks. A public road extends along the fence to a public parking area and beach at the far end, a good start for walking to Everett.

Howarth Park trail

Passing a ravine and a trail-staircase up the bluff to a viewpoint, then the prettiest exposure of varved blue clay on the route, in 1 scant mile of continuous vertical cliff is the first of the exceptional wildland valleys, Powder Mill Gulch, with a large creek, a broad delta-point, and a path up the gulch an unsurveyed distance inland.

In ½ mile is a nameless but noble creek and in ¼ mile more is larger and superb Merrill and Ring Creek whose prominent delta pushes far out in the waves and supports a driftwood line and dunes.

The bluff lowers and houses creep near the next ¼ mile to a small creek and little Harborview (Everett) Park, located on Mukilteo Boulevard at Dover Street. An excellent view of the harbor. At the north edge, a deep green ravine.

In a scant ½ mile (3 miles from Mukilteo ferry dock) is Howarth Park, for which be praised and congratulated the Everett Park Department. The park is reached from Mukilteo Boulevard at Seahurst Avenue; parking is provided at the upper, blufftop level and, via Olympic Boulevard which descends to the floor of Pigeon Creek No. 2, at the beach level by the railroad tracks. Extending from Pigeon 2 south to a nameless ravine, the park has enough paths — on blufftop and in gulch depths and on sidehills, on wide-view lawns and in wildwoods — to permit 2 miles of walking with scarcely any repetition. Access to the beach is via a skybridge over the tracks. On the beach side a stairway

Snohomish River at Everett

winds around and down a wooden tower resembling a donjon keep but actually serving utilitarian needs for stairs and restrooms.

The final 2 miles of the Trail have a different appeal. Or to some tastes, perhaps none. Port Gardner is entered and Everett Junction reached. Here is Pigeon Creek No. 1, which in another location surely would have been a park but here is a truck road to the Port of Everett. From the Junction the tracks lie between surprisingly wild bluff and the onetime site of a mammoth Weyerhaeuser pulpmill complex. Then comes Port of Everett Pier 1 and the Amtrak Rail Passenger Station, at Bond Street off Hewitt Avenue. Plentiful parking.

Bus: Seattle waterfront, in walking distance of a bushel of routes; Magnolia Park, Metro 19, 24, and 33; Discovery Park, 19 to South Gate, 24 to East Gate, 33 to North Gate; Chittenden Locks, 17 and 30; Golden Gardens Park, 17, 30, and 48; Carkeek Park, 28 (to trail at upper end of Piper's Canyon); Richmond Beach, 305; Edmonds, Metro 316 and 376; Everett, Metro 306.

SEATTLE — INLAND

The Whulj Trail from Tacoma to Everett is some 80 miles in length, mostly pleasantly walkable, in considerable part within city and county and state parks. More than any other feature, this is what gives Puget Sound City its personality. However, Whulj isn't the whole. There are lakes, there are hills, there are forests. The "core neighborhood" of Puget Sound City, Seattle, treasures them all.

In 1984 Seattle celebrated the hundredth anniversary of the founding of its park system, the donation of five acres at Denny Way and Dexter Avenue N by David and Louise Denny. "Park" then, and for many years after, meant lawns and formal gardens for strolling, benches for sitting. There wasn't much call for "walking" trails, not in an era when everybody got enough of *that* on the way to catch the streetcar or steamer, nor for preserves of "wilderness," not when plenty of *that* was available at the ends of the streetcar lines and handy to the steamer docks across the water.

In the 1890s the bicycle craze swept across America to Seattle; the city's street engineer, George Cotterill, responded by laying out a system of bike paths. Whether the machine was built for two or one, Daisy did indeed look sweet upon the seat. Every fine Sunday was a Bicycle Sunday for young and old. Starting from Cotterill's system, in 1903 John and Frederick Olmsted, sons of the Frederick Law Olmsted who designed New York's Central Park, proposed a network of scenic boulevards, "emerald necklaces strung with playgrounds and parks" that would be placed within a half-mile of every residence in the city. "An ideal system," they told the City Council, "would involve taking all the borders of the different bodies of water, except such as are needed for commerce, and (enlarging) these fringes ... so as to include considerable bodies of woodland as well as some fairly level land, which can be cleared and covered with grass for field sports and for the enjoyment of meadow scenery." In the Olmsted philosophy, "Civilization can't thrive in the absence of fresh air and green, open spaces" that preserve the "good and wholesome" environment of the country within the city. Far from being frivolities and luxuries, urban parks are essential to keep cities civil and humane, to keep them livable.

The Olmsteds served Seattle as consultants and mentors until the 1930s, and thanks to them and their allies and supporters, the adolescent city grew toward adulthood with green ganglia threading through a flesh of residential and commercial wood and brick and concrete. Then, into incipient Eden, slithered the serpent — or better say, rolled and honked and backfired, disguised as the Tin Lizzie, the Merry Oldsmobile, the Buick and Plymouth and Chevvy. The Sunday walk in the park and bike along the boulevard yielded to the drive in the country. Picnics shifted to Lake Wilderness and Lake Serene, Flaming Geyser and Green River Gorge, Maloney's Grove and Snoqualmie Falls, and—incredibly to those who in less than a decade lived from Model T to Model A to V-8 — Paradise Valley.

A glorious party it was, it was, a stupendous half-century binge. Then Seattle awoke. With a terrible hangover. The jug of cheap gas was empty. The nearby countryside had been filled overnight by new cities. The farther countryside was receding behind freeways clogged by mobs of cars. For quick

Seattle from Dr. Jose P. Rizal Park

and easy getaways Seattle of 1970 had to stay home — in a park system admirably suited to 1910.

Except, it wasn't as good as in 1910. Aurora Avenue had been trenched through Woodland Park, splitting a fine unity into two so-so halves. The Evergeen Point Floating Bridge violated the quietest corner of Washington Park. Ravenna Park was logged. Whenever a Worthy Cause — museum, street, sewer — was looking for a site the City Fathers generously contributed "free" land — park land.

In the 1960s a civic realization dawned that the serpent had stolen Seattle's soul, condemned it to a perdition that with each decade was going to get hotter. A great big city-wide revival meeting was held and amid much born-again clapping and hallelujahing and speaking in tongues the Washington Park Arboretum and Union Bay were saved from the threatened R. H. Thomson Expressway — appropriatedly named for "Seattle's Engineer," the man who destroyed Denny Hill by sluicing it to the bay, piped raw sewage to West Point, and committed many other barbarisms for which he was revered. To the born-again Olmsteders, however, he was the Great Beast. In 1968 they (the voters of King County) approved the Forward Thrust bond issue which provided funds to buy up lands for parks in Seattle and throughout the county. In 1972 the Army, short of ready cash to fight the war in Southeast Asia, dumped surplus land which was snapped up to become Seattle's greatest park, Discovery Park. In 1977 the Navy similarly unloaded what became Sand Point Park. Also in the 1970s the Burke-Gilman railroad was abandoned by the Burlington Northern and became one of the most-used urban trails in the nation.

All in all, it was a decade that pious Greens think of as the Second Coming of the Olmsteds. In that spirit, in 1977 an Urban Greenbelt Plan proposed 14 areas for preservation either by purchase or regulatory measures (most greenbelts are bluffs of unstable glacial drift or wetlands that shouldn't be built on). Acquisition of the Southwest Queen Anne Greenbelt began in 1980. Some others on the list are Duwamish Head, East Duwamish, East Duwamish-South (Beacon Hill), Northeast Queen Anne, St. Mark's, and West Duwamish (Highland Park).

A greenbelt doesn't have to "do" anything. It serves by simply lying there making no noise (but soaking up a lot), polluting no air or water (but always cleaning), being looked at (to quote Rea Tufts, as "part of the urban fabric"), and being lived in (not by thee and me but by squirrels, rabbits, weasels, muskrats, raccoons, and beaver, and by red-tailed hawks, great blue herons, gulls, nighthawks, horned owls, screech owls, geese, jaegers, ducks, and grebes, and by moles, voles, mice, and rats, and by pigeons, wrens, and warblers, and by those sly old coyotes that everybody in the neighborhoods assumes are just plain dogs).

It was a wise and good plan, the unfulfillment of which will be remembered as the Second Coming of R. H. Thomson. Forward Thrust had provided $1,000,000 to buy 200 greenbelt acres and in 1977 fourteen parcels, 919 acres, were identified as worthy to be kept in a natural state. However, by the end of 1983 only some 150-odd acres had been purchased. The reason? Thomson's successors had devised new techniques of drainage and anchoring which they claimed made much of the slide terrain "buildable." Speculators exploited one last chance to make fortunes from raw land in Seattle. When the city imposed new zoning controls on greenbelts, the speculators' attorneys promised to spend the next 100 years in court. The city gave up.

A saving grace of Seattle is that as an Old City (that is, built by humans before the automobile set about building New Cities) it has hundreds and hundreds of miles of what in the New Cities are called "trails" but in the Old, *sidewalks*. People from Overlake City and Big Valley City (the eastern and southern appendages of Central City) come on Sundays to park on quiet residential streets of Madrona, Beacon Hill, Capitol Hill, Queen Anne Hill, and Phinney Ridge and go strolling under the trees, beside lovingly tended gardens, through a century and a quarter of history. They marvel that this Old City was built by the same nation that built their New Cities. They wonder if Progress truly is, as the prophets proclaim, a rocket ride up to Heaven. What, they ask, is the destination of the rocket if it burns out, falls short?

In addition to sidewalks, the Old Cities have *alleys*. A *Seattle Times* columnist, Carole Beers, has written: "We have hiking trails. We have biking trails. We have official parks and official beaches.... Where, however, are the undisturbed rambles? The secret byways that beckon amblers out not so much for exercise as for an hour's vacation from madding crowds and prying eyes?

Look around. They're alleys. They're all over. There may even be some in your neighborhood.... Wandering along an alley, you get a glimpse of America — Americana through the decades, if you look closely. You get a feeling for how folks *really* live...."

As a last word of praise for the born-again Old City, when in 1979 the original proposal was made for what became the Cougar Mountain Regional Wildland Park, "wilderness on the Metro 210," the first government official to express public support was the Mayor of Seattle.

USGS maps: Edmonds East, Seattle North, Kirkland, Shilshole Bay, Seattle South, Mercer Island
Walkable all year

Olmsted Trail–Seward Park to Woodland Park (maps — pages 66 and 70)

For 30-odd years the Olmsted brothers, carrying on the family tradition rooted in New York's Central Park, played a major part in shaping a livable Seattle. Among their greatest contributions was Lake Washington Boulevard, designed to be the grand entrance to the Alaska-Yukon-Pacific Exposition of 1909, staged on the University of Washington campus. In 1916 the lowering of Lake Washington by 10 feet, preparatory to the next year's opening of the Lake Washington Ship Canal, made possible an enlargement of the park strip along

Seward Park trail

the lake's shore. Before that, in 1911, the lowering of Green Lake widened a narrow park strip to the spaciousness we know today.

Most people walk the Olmsted Trail in bits and pieces for an hour or an afternoon. However, the inveterate pedestrian ought to do the whole thing at a single go, at least once, to experience the unity of the Trail, linking the city's three major lakes, kempt-lawn parks, an arboretum containing thousands of native and exotic plants, a magnificent wildland marsh, and a forest ravine; offering beaches, creeks, birds, sailboats on blue waters, and broad mountain views.

To do the trip as the surveyor did, park the car at East Green Lake (or travel to that point by Metro bus). Ride three Metro buses (one at a time) to Seward Park; total trip time, 1½ hours. Then walk back to Green Lake, comfortably aware that should ambition falter or rain crush the umbrella, always close by and ready to rescue is Metro.

Mile 0–2½: Seward Park (map — page 66)

Park at the entrance, just off Lake Washington Boulevard S at Juneau Street.

The Olmsted Trail, done correctly, begins by looping around Bailey Peninsula, which until the lowering of the lake was an island. Walk the shore in either direction, past fish hatchery and fishing piers, bathing beaches, and views across the water to Mercer Island and south to Mt. Rainier.

Lake Washington's trough was gouged by the Canadian glacier which on its most recent of several visits arrived hereabouts some 15,000 years ago and left 13,500 years ago, at the maximum heaping 4000 feet thick. The lake's greatest depth is 205 to 210 feet. The water level varies between 20.00 and 21.85 feet above the mean low tide of the saltwater. It was lowered nearly 10 feet in 1916 to avoid having to install a system of locks between it and Lake Union for the Lake Washington Ship Canal, whose Ballard Locks between Lake Union and the saltwater were opened in 1917. The lowering made dry land of marshes and marshes of bays; the results are seen along much of the Olmsted Trail. Needless to say, nowadays such a tampering with nature would have as much chance of passing the Environmental Impact Statement test as Jim Hill's railroad along the shore from Everett to Seattle.

Primevally, Lake Washington's only major tributary was the Sammamish River, though in flood time some of the Cedar River spilled in through the marshes. The outlet was the Black River, which joined the Cedar River in the Renton vicinity and entered the Green River, the union of waters changing name to the Duwamish River for the final stretch to Elliott Bay. To keep floodwaters of the Cedar River from drowning cows in the pastures of Allentown and Georgetown, the stream was diverted into Lake Washington, becoming its second major tributary and its solitary source of pure water from the Cascade Mountains. To conclude the lake-fact summary: its outlet now is the Ship Canal.

The shore is not the sole attraction of 278-acre Seward Park. The peninsula spine features Seattle's largest virgin forest, close to 1 mile long and averaging ¼ mile wide. The old-growth Douglas firs are dazzlers, the maples are huge, and the supporting cast of native trees and shrubs forms a fine wild tangle. The forest trail system has entries around the peninsula; paths range from broad-flat to narrow-primitive. No map required. Just plunge in and explore. If lucky, get lost, thus making the wildland seem all the larger.

A basic introduction to Seward Park requires a 2½-mile shore loop plus a tour up and down the 1-mile-long peninsula; 4½ miles, 3 hours. For hikers intending to reach far points by day's end the short introduction is up either shore to the peninsula tip and back down the spine, a 2½-mile opening segment in the Olmsted Trail.

Mile 2½–9: Lake Washington Park and Parkway (map — page 66)

Parking is plentiful (not summer Sundays) the whole route.

The entire length is along streets, but most of the walking path is on "made land" (from the lake lowering) at a decent distance from car lanes, traversing this or that pocket park; machines are easy to ignore if eyes are pointed over the water to the mountains.

Lake Washington Parkway

The first 3½ walking miles are trees and lawns and wall-to-wall ducks and coots and, in the reeds, redwing blackbirds. Some attractions, in order: pretty little Andrews Bay, enclosed by Bailey Peninsula; Japanese cherry trees; yacht moorage at Ohler's Island; dismal pits of Sayres Memorial Park; bathing beach at Mt. Baker Park, adjoined on the north by Colman Park; mountain views from Baker to Pilchuck to Index to Si to Issaquah Alps to Rainier.

For the next 1 mile the street changes name to Lakeside Avenue and is lined by private homes. But under Mercer Island Floating Bridge is public access to the water. For perhaps the best mountain views of the whole trip, walk up to the plaza and out on the bridge. See Glacier Peak.

At Leschi business district and yacht harbor the boulevard resumes. Leschi Park on the shore and Frink Park on the bluff demand their due. Here in the pre-bridge era was the landing for the Mercer Island and Bellevue ferries, convenient to the eastern terminus of the cable car that came over the hill from Yesler Way, connecting on the edge of the Skid Road to the northern terminus of the Seattle & Tacoma Interurban Railway. Paths ascend the lawns, past such exotics as a giant sequoia whose cones have seeded throngs of offspring in the Seattle area, to trails that climb past mysterious masses of very ancient concrete into the wildwoods. Poke about in springtime and you'll stumble amazed into a glory of rhododendrons in bloom, a plantation long ago allowed to go wild, and doing so very nicely.

Beginning at Leschi the path is on the shore a scant 1 mile, passing the bathing beach of Madrona Park. Private homes then violate the Olmsted Precept and hog the water.

The final 1 mile leaves the lake and climbs the hill in a forest of private trees, plus the public trees of boulevard-side Howell and Viretta Parks. Not yet lost is the lake. Just down a deadend street is tiny Denny-Blaine Park. Note the handsome granite-block bulkhead, wonder why it is so high above the water — and realize that when built that's where the waves lapped. Above here the boulevard switchbacks through little Lakeview Park; dodge off the street in a secluded grassy hollow and climb a greensward knoll with a tree-screened look over the lake. Thence it's not far to East Madison Street and the Arboretum.

Mile 9–10: Washington Park Arboretum (map — page 70)

Parking at Madison Playground at the south end, in several lots along the boulevard and Upper Road, and at the north Broadmoor entrance at the north end.

The full official name is University of Washington Arboretum in Washington Park. In the 200 acres of city park managed by the University as a scientific arboretum are thousands of shrubs and trees and other plants, native and from all over the world, arranged in logical groupings, placed in artful landscapings to exploit the natural terrain of ridges and valleys, marshes and ponds and creeks. A half-century of loving care and artistry is represented.

The Arboretum needs to be visited plant by plant from one end to the other. When the tour is complete it's another season and the whole job has to be done over. The most cursory introduction requires four walk-throughs: along the valley of Lake Washington Boulevard (the main road), sidetripping in the Japanese Garden; along Arboretum Drive (Upper Road) on the ridge east of the valley; along the broad green valley-bottom lawn of Azalea Way; and along the hillside trails between Azalea Way and Arboretum Drive, passing the

Diving feet first from unused viaduct in Arboretum

Lookout, a shelter (refuge in the rain) with views down Azalea Way and out the valley north to the University District. Before starting, visit the Arboretum offices at the northeast corner, by the north Broadmoor entrance, for a brochure describing the flowering seasons and the plant groupings. Total cursory introduction 4 miles, 4 hours.

A lifetime is too short. The only justification for treating the Arboretum as a mere 1 mile of the Olmsted Trail is to stress its connection to the good things elsewhere along the route.

Mile 10–11½: Foster's Island–Arboretum Waterfront Trail–Montlake Bridge (map — page 70)

One of which is coming right up.

Parking on the south at the north Broadmoor entrance, on the north at the Museum of History and Industry.

The concrete-and-thunder Evergreen Point Floating Bridge ripped off a fifth of the former acreage of the Arboretum, brutalizing Foster's Island and Union

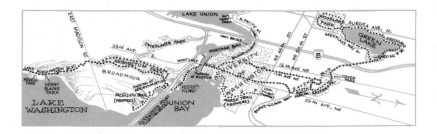

Bay marshes. But even the remnant is a wonderland. The damage could have been worse, and would have been, had not the "Save the Arboretum" campaign of the early 1960s halted the Thomson Expressway planned to blast down the middle of the Arboretum and across (or under) Union Bay; in Seattle, this battle — this victory — was the start of something new.

From the parking lot at north Broadmoor entrance the path crosses a slough to Foster's Island. Lakeshore. Groves of water-loving trees. A passage under the concrete span of the bridge approach. Views of University stadium and campus, sailboats on Union Bay, Laurelhurst homes on the far shore, and mountains.

(Note: As of 1988 plans are being noodled for a possible ½-mile McGilvra Trail from Foster's Island around the north boundary of Broadmoor Golf Club to Madison Park.)

At Foster's Island begins the Arboretum Waterfront Trail built in 1968, restored and rebuilt in 1986. The marsh traversed by the trail is not "primeval" but "new," formed from open lake when the level was lowered. "Never mind," says the wildlife, "It *feels* primeval." And it truly does, another example of Mother Nature's power to renew her virginity if only man will let her alone. Cottonwoods and willows, cattails and horsetails and bulrushes. Mammals from mice to muskrats. At times, as neighbors learn to their sorrow, beavers with a taste for tender young trees. An estimated 100,000 bird visits a year, for a day in passing, for nesting, for all-year handout-gobbling, as with the miscegenations of mallards and Muscovy and other ducks. Partly a floating walkway, partly a spongy lane of cedar chips overlying floating mats of peat, the route weaves out to what would be open water were it not for the floating lily pads (the white-flowering species here is exotic, sorry to say, having driven out the native yellow-flowerer), in through thickets of head-high hardhack to observation platforms. Fifteen benches provide spots to sit and reflect. Joggers have been banned — the posted speed limit is 1 mph (too fast!).

Competing for attention with marsh texture is freeway geometry. Temporarily. On at least three occasions the Evergreen Point Floating Bridge has come within minutes of sinking. It will go down. (*Note:* This surveyor publicly predicted the sinking of Hood Canal Bridge No. 1. The volume containing the prediction, *Footsore 3,* had barely gotten into the bookstores when, sure enough, Davey Jones opened his Locker.)

The Waterfront Trail ends at the Museum of History and Industry parking lot. (Incidentally, this museum was such a Worthy Cause when promoted by the Movers & Shakers that the City of Seattle gratefully sacrificed a lovely little park to make room for the building. Now that the M&S are seeking a bigger building, the moment has arrived to restore the green.)

The trail carries on without a break as the Lake Washington Ship Canal Waterside Trail, a project of the U.S. Army Corps of Engineers and Seattle Garden Club, rounding the corner to Montlake Cut, connecting Portage Bay of Lake Union and Union Bay of Lake Washington. Ships pass through, and yachts, and racing-shell crews. The trail goes under quaint old Montlake Bridge, built in 1925.

Before climbing steps to the bridge, sidetrip ¼ mile west to the end of the cut and the public park at the Seattle Yacht Club. Fine view of Portage Bay. Some Lake Union facts: maximum depth 50 feet; due to filling and building, present size is about half the original.

Mile 11½–13½: University of Washington (map — page 70)

Parking, for a reasonable fee, on campus.

Montlake Bridge has grand views west and east over the lakes, down to water traffic. On the north side is another waterside walkway.

Pause for the history. Primevally, the marshes at the west end of Union Bay seeped a certain amount of Lake Washington down to Lake Union's Portage Bay. In 1861 Harvey I. Pike set to work, alone, with pick, shovel, and wheelbarrow to dig a ditch to join the lakes. There wasn't much call for it at the time. However, in 1883 those paradigmatic Movers & Shakers, Messrs. Denny, Burke, & Company hired Chinese laborers to deepen the channel in order to float logs through the marsh to a timber flume into Portage Bay, to be rafted to mills on Lake Union. In 1899 a band of (masked?) farmers from the Duwamish River valley came (at night?) and dynamited the canal, hoping to lower Lake Washington with a "whoosh!" and save their pastures from the spring overflow floodings of the Black and the Cedar. In 1916 the U.S. Army completed the task begun by Pike, though the Montlake Cut in its present form wasn't tidied up until 1921.

Before proceeding to the University of Washington central campus, take a sidetrip right, from the Montlake Bridge along the waterside path and around the massive blockage of sky and horizons where awesome religious ceremonies are performed on autumn Saturday afternoons. Here is the route of the proposed Union Bay Trail, an extension of the Arboretum Waterfront Trail that would lead to respectful viewpoints of wildlife sanctuaries. When Lake Washington was lowered, 610 acres of Union Bay became marsh; for decades Seattle dumped and burned household garbage here, the expectation being that ultimately the University would be provided a new east campus. When it was discovered in the 1960s that the garbage and the underlying peat generated enough methane to make any building a potential bomb, the old marsh/former lake was dedicated to permanent parking lots. An outer 55 acres, however, was preserved from blacktop as the Center for Urban Horticulture. About 20 acres are to be developed — gardens, greenhouses, research plots, and buildings. The remainder will be left undisturbed, a pond-studded grassland fringed by marsh, a permanent wildlife refuge.

The quickest route through the University to Ravenna Park is to cross Montlake Boulevard, intersect the Burke-Gilman Trail (which see), follow it north 1½ miles to the vicinity of 25 Avenue, and cut left to the outlet of the park ravine.

The route directly up through the central campus has so much of interest that some pedestrians don't get enough of it in four years. Stop at the entrance kiosk (or call the University Information Center) and ask for copies of the two tour map-brochures, both titled "The U is for You."

One of these, subtitled "Go Take a Walk on Campus," describes a walking tour of the 346-acre central campus that covers over 3½ miles, averages about 2½ hours. Features along the way (marked on the tour map) include: Thomas Burke Memorial-Washington State Museum (10 A.M. to 4:30 P.M. Tuesday through Saturday, 1 to 4:30 P.M. Sunday); the Observatory (7 to 9 P.M. Thursday); the 58 sycamores of Memorial Way honoring the 57 University men and one woman killed in World War I; Denny Hall, built in 1894; the Washington Elm, scion of the tree beneath which George Washington stood as he assumed command of the Continental Army, and in its own right, nowadays, frequently stood under by Sons and Daughters of the American Revolution; the Student Union Building; a bronze bust of James J. Hill commemorating the completion of the Great Northern Railway to Seattle in 1893; the Sylvan Theater, featuring the four columns that once graced the Grecian facade of the University Building, where now is the Olympic Four Seasons Hotel; Frosh Pond, into which students are thrown by other students; the Herb Garden, a place to get down on hands and knees and sniff (but no nibbling); Red Square, where students of the 1960s massed to hurl insults at the gargoyles atop the Administration Building and in the Pentagon; the bronze statue of George Washington, where the Daughters of the American Revolution gather to honor Washington's birthday and where the Keep Washington Green Society comes by night on the eve of St. Patrick's Day; Henry Art Gallery; Suzzallo Library; Broken Obelisk; the magnificent fountain sculpted in 1967 by George Tsutakawa; and Parrington Hall, from the roof of which in 1943 the surveyor, as on a peak in Darien, first espied the Issaquah Alps.

The second brochure-map, subtitled "Let's Tour the Trees on the UW Campus," was prepared by C. Frank Brockman, former professor of forest resources, who also was responsible for placing many of the 200 species of trees on campus, serving forestry students as an outdoor classroom and their professors as a research facility. The suggested tour (to obtain a copy of the wheelchair alternative tour, call the University Information Center) covers 7 miles. Some of the 81 species you'll see that likely are not in your backyard: little-leaf linden, shingle oak, bristlecone pine, corkscrew willow, katsura, cypress, shagbark hickory, monkey puzzle tree, yoshino cherry, Spanish chestnut, Atlas cedar, Japanese silk tree, cork oak, slippery elm, dawn redwood, ginkgo, cucumber tree, northern catalpa, London plane, Chinese fan palm, Japanese umbrella pine, tree-of-heaven, Dombey false beech.

The 2 miles arbitrarily stipulated at the start of this section are the straight and hasty way. Ascend Rainier Vista (named for the view of The Mountain which the Olmsteds laid out to be the central axis of the campus) past Frosh Pond and Red Square to Memorial Way and exit from campus at NE 45 Street. Turn right and descend the east slope of the campus to the Burke-Gilman Trail. Alternatively, proceed north through Greek Row to Ravenna Boulevard and follow it right, downhill, to the lower end of the Ravenna Park ravine.

Mile 13½–15½: Ravenna Park (map — page 70)

Street parking all around and at the lower end of the ravine, in Ravenna Playground.

A person can drive the bridges over the deep gulch and scarcely know the park exists. But in the dark, dank hole beside the creek in the big firs and

Cherry blossoms, University of Washington

maples, the racket of the city passes back and forth overhead, little of it leaking down. The walker almost feels in the late 1880s, when the Reverend and Mrs. William W. Beck bought the ravine and nurtured it to a park named after the town in Italy which was the last home of Dante. Ravenna Creek then was a large stream, full of trout, flowing in the open from Green Lake to Lake Washington. The Becks built paths, waterfalls, a music pavilion, and a gate with a 25-cent admission fee — paid gladly in 1902 by 10,000 visitors. The Becks named the old-growth Douglas firs. Paderewski was honored, as were assorted local politicians. The tallest, some 400 feet, was Robert E. Lee. The one with the largest girth was Teddy Roosevelt — who visited the park and gave approval to his namesake tree, calling it "the big stick."

In 1911 Seattle acquired the park by condemnation in order to divert Ravenna Creek (the large original) into the new North Trunk Sewer, dug deep in the ground under the ravine, wreaking great havoc. In 1929 Clarence Bagley described the park in his history book as "a dark, damp, dismal hole in the ground," a phrase later echoed by a governor of Washington in discussing why the Hoh Rain Forest of Olympic National Park ought to be clearcut. Incredibly, in the 1930s Seattle did indeed log Ravenna Park. The site of the Roosevelt Tree now is a tennis court.

There still are a pretty (little) creek, fed by springs and rain, semi-wild areas of native plants, and trees that may be puny beside the memory of the ancient giants but in their own place and time are big enough to provide a semblance of the virgin forest. The ravine can be traversed along the bottom, on either sidehill, or by combinations of the several interlacing trails.

For 1 (walking) mile the ravine ascends from the level of Lake Washington to that of Brooklyn Avenue. At Brooklyn take the tree-lined Ravenna Boulevard, former course of the creek, under I-5 (which destroyed Cowen Park), by Boehm's Candy Kitchen, 1 mile to Green Lake, reached near the East Green Lake business district.

Mile 15½–18½: Green Lake (map — page 70)

Parking on streets and lots all around (though not much on Sundays).

At the urging of W. D. Wood, a settler-promoter who in the 1890s had joined with two companions in building the Green Lake Circle Railroad loop around the lake and up from the Fremont streetcar line, in 1911 Seattle purchased Green Lake and lowered it 7 feet to expose hundreds of acres for use as park, streets, and sundry civic purposes. More of the lake was destroyed by filling, the last of the dirt coming in 1932 from the big ditch dug by Aurora Avenue through Woodland Park. Now encompassing 260 acres, the lake has a maximum depth of 29 feet and is in so advanced a state of eutrophication that at any season after early summer and before the fall rains swimmers routinely contract the "Green Lake crud." Seattle City Water used to help keep the lake clean by flushing in surplus drinking water; nowadays, though, there isn't much surplus, Seattle makes so much money selling it to the New Cities across Lake Washington. Walkers are safe from the crud so long as they don't touch the water.

The attractions of Green Lake (lawns and trees, views of surrounding ridges and Rainier, mobs of resident and migratory waterfowl, who have their own sanctuary, Swan — or Duck — Island) need little praise. On a single summer day as many as 10,000 people visit the park and as many as 1000 people an hour take to the paths — the 2.8-mile interior path (10 feet wide) near the shore and the 3.2-mile outer path near the streets. Some 29 percent walk, 26 percent rollerskate, 46 percent bicycle or jog or run. There also are skateboards and baby strollers; in 1987 arrived the newest wheel craze, the giant tricycle.

The "courtesy code" (almost universally ignored) asks that walkers-joggers go clockwise, using the interior path, staying in the lane closest to the lake (sharing this with wheelchairs), or take the outer path; that bikers and skaters go counterclockwise on the outside lane of the interior path. Several explanations have been made for the lack of "courtesy" (half the trail travelers go the wrong way). One has to do with the mathematical sophistication of those familiar with the Moebius strip, a plane surface with only one side and thus no "inside-outside." Another is the digital watch, which has resulted in a total ignorance of the meaning of "clockwise." Finally, you meet a lot of interesting people when you run into them.

A study has shown that fewer visitors come to do the trail, by whatever means, than to sit and watch. The recommendation is to come to Green Lake on a brilliant summer Sunday and film a movie; your friends subsequently will flock to your parties, shunning the world-travelers who invite everyone to a slide show of their most recent trek to Everest basecamp.

Solitude-seeking walkers of the Olmsted Trail are permitted to skip Green Lake, and no demerits.

2–3 more miles: Woodland Park (map — page 70)

Guy Phinney, promoter-benefactor, established Woodland Park in 1891, providing a hotel, dance pavilion, boathouse, shooting lodge, and other amenities, including woodland trails that were — for folks not wealthy enough to go on safari with The Mountaineers to wilderness of the Olympics and Cascades — "wilderness on the trolley line."

In 1899 Seattle bought the park and civilized it with rose gardens, a zoo, playfields, picnic tables, and — in the 1930s — a concrete trench down the middle to let Aurora Avenue — Highway 99 — ram through, splitting the park in two.

Among Seattle's largest parks even so, it is entirely kempt. However, at certain hours of certain days of certain seasons it can give miles of serene strolling. For a basic introduction, do a 2-mile perimeter loop, no guidebook or map required. Do not feed the bears.

One-way trip 18½ miles, allow 12 hours
High point 250 feet, elevation gain 1000 feet
Bus: Metro 39 to Seward Park; 10 to Colman Park; 27 to Mercer Island
Floating Bridge and Leschi Park; 2 to Madrona Park; 11, 48, and 4 to
Arboretum; 4, 7, 8, 25, 30, 48, 76, and 77 to University; 7 and 8 to
Ravenna Park; 16, 26, and 48 to East Green Lake; 6 to West Green Lake

Burke-Gilman Trail (maps — pages 76 and 80)

No list of America's great urban trails omits the Burke-Gilman, traversing scenes industrial, marine, commercial, academic, residential, and natural, with views to ships and boats, over Salmon Bay and Lake Union to Seattle, over Lake Washington to the Cascades, and across the Sammamish River to fields and forests, with sidetrips abounding to parks and historic sites. When extended to its ultimate 19-mile length (as described herein) it will further serve as a central artery in the pedestrian system of Puget Sound City, linking the Whulj Trail, the Olmsted Trail, the Tolt Pipeline Trail, and the Sammamish River Trail. As discussed elsewhere in these pages, those trails connect (or will) to the Seattle & Walla Walla Railroad Trail, the Beacon Ridge-Renton-Cedar River Trail, the Lake Sammamish Trail and Issaquah-Snoqualmie Falls Trail, and the Snoqualmie River Trail (*see Footsore 2*). Considered as a segment of the Sound-to-Mountains Trail, here is the start from the tidewater toward the Cascade Crest.

When Judge Thomas Burke and Daniel Gilman and fellow townboomers set out in 1885 to build the Seattle, Lake Shore & Eastern Railroad, their intent was to outwit Eastern financiers who controlled the American transcontinental railway lines by making an end run to the East via the Canadian transcontinental line. After appropriate chicanery these locals and the Easterners struck a deal and got rich. In the 1970s, however, the business of operating railroads became too much of a bother for the "railroad companies" that were energetically logging, mining, farming, and subdividing ill-gotten grant lands; the Burlington Northern, mergerized product of a century of bamboozles, abandoned the Burke-Gilman line — which shortly was busier than ever with feet walking, jogging, and running, and bicycles. (No horses or motorized vehicles permitted.)

The official trail as of 1988 starts at Gasworks Park and ends at Logboom Park, a distance of about 13 miles, representing the cooperative effort of the City of Seattle, King County Parks, the University of Washington, and the City

of Bothell. To be completed in perhaps 1989 from Logboom Park to Blyth Park, there it changes name to Sammamish River Trail and keeps on going. Eventually it will be extended to Chittenden Locks and thus this section is described here.

Paved the entire official 13 miles, the trail is an easy day's up-and-back by bike. Hikers usually do as much as feels good and double back to the start. However, good bus service over the entire de facto 19 miles permits any number of ingenuities. For example, the car can be parked at Gasworks Park and the walk ended in Bothell, 15 miles; a Metro bus (with one transfer) whisks the body back to square one.

Chittenden Locks to Gasworks Park, 3¾ miles (map — page 76)

While watching ships and boats pass through Chittenden Locks, find idle amusement by mentally preparing the EIS this project, famed of yore as one of the Seven Wonders of Seattle, would require if undertaken today. Consider, for example, the consequences if the "closure device" failed, as it surely would if a large ship entered the locks a bit too fast, skippered by the sort of fellow whose ship took out the Duwamish River bridge, or directed by the sort of sophisticated computer that periodically causes one of the *Issaquah*-class ferries to splinter a dock. A wall of water 11 to 12 feet high, depending on the stage of the tide, would burst from Lake Union to Puget Sound, taking everything and everybody in its path to watery burial in Shilshole Bay. In an estimated 80 hours, Lake Washington would drop to the level of Puget Sound, the tides coming in and going out for the estimated 8 months required for repairs. Even if the floating bridges did not collapse, as is likely, they could not be used at low tide due to the danger. Play boats would be stranded in marinas, industrial barges stuck in the mud, Fishermen's Terminal in Ballard landlocked. The exposed lakebed would stink something dreadful, forcing the evacuation of the silk-stocking communities of the shore, wiping out the billions of dollars in real estate values that were saved in the nick of time by the Great Metro Cleanup.

Think of the railroad tracks (along much of this stretch, still in place) merely as the link between sidetrips. The grade runs through grimy industrial backyards but at countless spots are close-by vista points that make this the most exciting working-waterfront walk in Seattle. (The Alaskan Way waterfront is mainly for play and the Duwamish Waterways, where the really heavy work is done, are only just starting to be made gawker-accessible.)

The first 1¼ miles from Chittenden Locks by the Ballard Bridge offer many short trips to docks and shipyards and every sort of craft from funky houseboats to fishing boats to medium-size freighters that serve the North — ships with such evocative names as *Pribiloff, Silver Clipper, Polar Merchant*. On the other side of the tracks lies Old Ballard, restored and revived and full of historic

Shipyard on the north shore of Lake Union

fun. Finish off this stretch by climbing the pedestrian stairway to Ballard Bridge for views west out Salmon Bay to the locks and east to the Fremont Cut.

The next 1¾ miles to Fremont Bridge start with more ships (*Trident, North Sea, Orion*) and views over the bay to Queen Anne Hill. After a dull mile inland, the tracks return to the water at Canal Street, just off Leary Way on 2nd SW, and pass Fremont Canal Park. Here where a creek used to flow from Lake Union to Salmon Bay now is the Fremont Cut, poplar-lined on both banks, ships and boats and canoes and ducks passing to and fro. Industry preempts the shore the final bit to Fremont Bridge.

Climb from the tracks to tour the Fremont District, platted in 1875 (or was it 1888?) and site of a major mill from 1888; a successor was still there in 1946, when the surveyor worked as a helper on a planer. The reason for a town at this particular point was the outlet of Lake Union into the creek that flowed to Salmon Bay. In 1887 the Seattle, Lakeshore & Eastern Railroad (the Burke-Gilman line) came through, 6 years before Jim Hill brought his Great Northern rails in from the north to cross Salmon Bay. By 1890 electric trolleys were speeding along a timber trestle over the waters at 20 mph; a couple of decades later the surveyor's grandfather became a conductor on the cars. In 1891 the town of Fremont was incorporated into the city of Seattle and in 1917 was described as "the geographical center of Seattle."

Spend some time with the Fremont Bridge. Successor to a low timber bridge over "the creek," this handsome bascule bridge opened in 1917 to serve the Lake Washington Ship Canal. It is said to be the nation's most-opening bridge, about every 10 minutes on a summer day, or 1600 times a year, or an estimated half-million times in the first 60 years, letting through 100,000 boats a year.

When Seattle got soul, it painted the bridge a festive blue and orange to suit the mood of the Fremont District, which had fallen into decline after the opening in 1933 of the higher Aurora Bridge on the brandnew Highway 99. Upon the coming of the History Revival of the 1960s the old storefronts and brick buildings stood unmolested in their decayed grandeur, ready to be swabbed out and tidied up and converted to Fat City Tavern, Deluxe Junk, Fremont Recycling Center, The Tin Man, Dusty Springs, Guess Where, Daily Planet Antiques, Futon Frames, Happy Trails, Across the Street Cafe, Simply Desserts, Costas Opas Greek Restaurant, Pizza Art. The centerpiece is the most famous sculpture in the Northwest, Richard Beyer's *Waiting for the Interurban,* a group of life-size figures; in chill weather these are provided by local residents with wool sweaters and hats, in springtime, flowers in the hair; bowls of dogfood are set out for the dog in the group. Annually on the second weekend in June a famous festival has been held since 1971.

The final ¾ mile to Gasworks Park is near Lake Union shores, passing a succession of marinas, rows of sailboats, stinkpots, fishing boats, and now and then a rusty old bucket of a freighter that has the look of the one Lord Jim abandoned.

Gasworks Park to north end of University of Washington campus (NE 45th), 2¾ miles (map — page 76)

Gasworks Park demands a tour. Inspect machinery of the plant which for 50 years, starting in 1906 or so, generated gas from coal that was barged from the mines of Newcastle, in the Issaquah Alps. The original plant buildings were partially demolished, partially rehabilitated, made children-safe and painted festive colors, to open as a park in 1975. Walk the ¼ mile of frontage path on Lake Union. See tugboats, sailboats, police boats. Climb the manmade knoll for a view of downtown Seattle towering at the other end of the lake. Gulls, ducks, coots, crows, pigeons.

The official 1988 route begins here, following the Northlake Bikeway, a blufftop foot path separated from automobiles, to Latona Avenue NE, and turning up the bluff a block to NE Pacific Street and "Start" of Burke-Gilman Trail, ¾ mile from Gasworks Park.

On abandoned railroad grade the Burke-Gilman crosses under the Freeway Bridge and University Bridge over the ship canal and passes through the new west campus to the old central campus beginning at 15 Avenue NE. Metro bus stops make this a good place for hikers-busriders to start.

The campus is among the best parts of the whole route. Views to Lake Union and Portage Bay, up Rainier Vista to the campus center and out to The Mountain, and over Union Bay to Lake Washington and the Cascades. Plentiful parking east of Montlake Boulevard. An intersection with the Olmsted Trail (which see) offers sidetrips to campus and Arboretum.

Gasworks Park on Lake Union

At NE 45 Street the trail passes the Bob Pyle Wilderness (named for the now-famous butterfly man for his ecological activities while a UW student), crosses under the viaduct, and leaves campus. The traffic of students, professors, joggers, runners, strollers, bicyclers lessens.

University campus to Sand Point (NE 65th), 3 miles (map — page 76)

From campus the way passes close to University Village (parking, Metro buses, food, restrooms), swinging inland from the present lakeshore to curve around the former bay. Mostly residential, partly commercial, the way blooms in season with park plantings and private gardens. Urban birds sing.

The trail returns to lake views at Sand Point. (For a sidetrip on NE 65 Street to Lake Washington beaches, see Warren G. Magnuson Park.)

At Princeton Bridge, just off Sand Point Way, a hillside gazebo is a neat spot to get out of the rain.

Sand Point to Seattle city limits (NE 145th), 4½ miles (map — page 80)

Past Sand Point views are good over Lake Washington. At Thornton Creek are a Metro pumping station and a valley wildland of hellberries penetrated by a path climbing the hill to a lake panorama.

A bit beyond is Matthews Beach Park. A sidetrip is mandatory out on the forested grassy knoll and down lawns to the shore to look over the waters to sailboats and mountains and fend off ducks and coots and gulls and crows that want your lunch.

A final 3 miles through residential neighborhoods on the water conclude at Seattle city limits.

City limits to Logboom Park, 2½ miles (map — page 80)

With no change except in style of signs and that the city's foot-saving lane of crushed rock beside the hard blacktop ceases, the trail enters King County jurisdiction, proceeding by more lakeside homes (Sheridan Beach, Lake Forest Park) to Logboom Park. Access is via 61 Avenue NE off Bothell Way.

The park's groves of cottonwood, willow, maple, and alder are an isle of cool peace on a hot day. The shore, mostly marshy-natural, provides refuge for myriad birds. The resident colony of ducks includes mallards, domestic whites, and weird exotics from China, gone wild (tame-wild). The park's chief glory is the the long concrete pier, located where railroad cars once dumped logs in a "booming ground" where rafts were organized for towing to the mills. The pier provides splendid views down Lake Washington and across a stinkpot harbor to the mouth of Sammamish River.

Logboom Park to Blyth Park, 2½ miles (map — page 80)

The Burke-Gilman Trail was vigorously opposed by people along the right-of-way who feared a parade of public feet and bicycles would ruin their neighborhoods. So wrong were they that within a few years homes along the route were selling at a premium, bragged up as "on the Burke-Gilman" or "handy to Burke-Gilman." Nevertheless, no subsequent conversion of an abandoned rail grade to an urban trail has occurred in the Seattle area without opposition by people who have not learned. They are joined — nay, they are stirred up — by other people who seek to acquire portions of rail routes for personal gain. When Burlington Northern abandoned 4.88 miles of the Burke-Gilman line, the stretch from Kenmore to Woodinville, the old battle between public rights and private profit resumed. However, in 1987 King County moved to begin condemnation proceedings and in 1989-90 or so will complete the "missing link" between Logboom Park and Blyth Park.

As of 1988, the stretch from Logboom north through Kenmore must be done (or not done) on the shoulder of Bothell Way. The rail grade is partly obliterated, partly fenced, and partly posted with mean-it NO TRESPASSING signs. Not that there is much scenery to be regretted; Kenmore is an industrial area, an anomaly in so pretty a valley; in the 1930s the place had such a reputation a young lady could lose hers simply by driving through.

At length the rail grade leaves the grime, at the head of Lake Washington, diverges from the highway shoulder, and enters pastoral greenery of the Sammamish River. From Wayne Golf Course onward the route is or soon will be public. A sidetrip to a bridge gives vistas up and down the duck freeway. At 2½ miles from Logboom Park the trail crosses the river on a splendid old

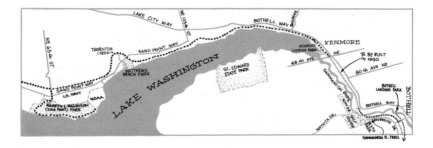

Burke-Gilman Trail near Lake Washington

railroad bridge to Blyth Park. (As of 1988 this bridge has gates which make it awkward to cross; the traveler may well wish to proceed the short way to the new bridge built for the Sammamish River Trail.) Blyth Park is the terminus of the Tolt Pipeline Trail (which see). Here, too, is the end of the Burke-Gilman and the start of the Sammamish River Trail (which see).

One-way distance from Chittenden Locks to Blyth Park 19 miles
High point 150 feet, minor elevation gain
Bus: Metro 17 and 43 at Chittenden Locks; 15, 17, 18, and 43 in Ballard; 26 and 28 at Fremont; a dozen lines in the University District; 30 in Laurelhurst; 8 and 41 on Sand Point Way; 25 on 37 Avenue NE; 307 on Bothell Way; many lines in Bothell

Sand Point (Warren G. Magnuson) Park (map — page 80)

By the time the people of Seattle realized the local supply of waterfront was finite, somebody was sitting on just about every inch. How could the public obtain more room for children to go wading? Since only God and the military have the power to create a shore, and She finished Her engineering millennia ago, it was left to the U.S. Navy to save the scene — by going away. The 196-acre park presently recalls all too vividly its past as an invasion of marsh and lake, as a desert of pavement reeking of aviation fuel. Future generations will stroll across the plain in cool shadows of stately trees (now being planted), along a shore restored to nature, and honor this as a jewel of the city. It's not too bad now.

From Sand Point Way turn east on NE 65 Street and follow signs to the parking area at the south end of the park. Elevation, 25 feet.

There's no shore trail and probably never should be. The walking is on old roads closed to motorized vehicles and on paths mowed or foot-beaten through tall grass. Countless sidepaths wend off through Scotch broom, hellberry, or willow thicket to nooks on the shore for looking out to sailboats, the north and south of Lake Washington, the Issaquah Alps, and the Cascades. The only developed areas are the boat-launch (bring your canoe or sailing surfboard) and the swimming beach. At a long 1 mile from the south fence is the NOAA boundary, where the Great White Fleet of scientists sallies forth into salt seas of the world. That the public not nourish excessive hostilities toward the Rover Boys for muscling in on what could have been a much larger public park, NOAA has provided 2000 feet of waterfront walking into the complex, featuring such little niceties as basalt chairs and tables, pedestrian bridges inscribed with texts from *Moby Dick,* and a "sand garden" made of pipes.

The New Forest is growing taller by the year and the Navy junk (chunks of old concrete, twisted masses of rusty iron) is being removed from the shore it was used to make and every year the park is getting better and better. Even when first opened it was nothing for a birder to sneeze at. The shore brush and the inland fields each had its distinctive bunch. On his initial tour, while angry "general aviation" pilots were still buzzing the abandoned runways dropping petitions demanding that the City of Seattle be impeached, the surveyor watched a vicious redwing blackbird chase a heron clear to the far side of the lake, then harass a hawk out of the country, after which the surveyor himself was sent packing.

Round trip 2 miles, allow 1½ hours
High point 25 feet, no elevation gain
Bus: Metro 8 and 41

Beacon Ridge (maps — pages 82 and 83)

A 200-foot-wide lawn rolling up hill and down dale for miles, in broad views west to saltwater and Olympics, east to Lake Washington and Cascades. And if you don't bother them the Seattle City Light power lines won't bother you. The hike can begin and end at any number of places; the full tour, starting at the north end, will be described here.

Park at or near Maple Wood Playground Park, Corson Avenue S and South Snoqualmie, in itself a nice little broad-view stroll around the greensward. Elevation, 200 feet.

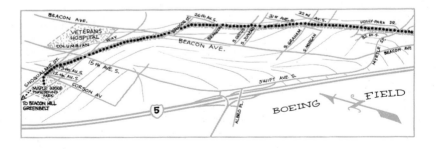

Walk a long block north to the powerline lawn; here is a panorama over I-5 and the Duwamish industrial plain to Elliott Bay and downtown Seattle and Queen Anne Hill and Magnolia Bluff and Olympics.

Ascend the lawn 1 mile to the crossing of busy Beacon Avenue (good parking), just south of the Veterans Administration Hospital and Jefferson Park Golf Course. Here the lawn bends right to follow on or near the crest of Beacon Ridge. Streets (mostly quiet) are crossed and backyards merge into public lawn, but the walk-anywhere no-trail-needed strip is so spacious and calm (no motorcycles permitted) that despite the all-aroundness of Puget Sound City a person feels the green peace.

Ascending grassy knolls, dipping to hollows, the way offers looks south over Lake Washington to Renton and Rainier, up to jets sliding down to land, and east over Mercer Island to the Issaquah Alps. Beyond Martin Luther King Way the ridge assumes a rural air, often wildwooded on either side, pleasantly invaded by garden plots and orchards and horses pasturing and roosters crowing. And dogs barking. After crossing 51 Avenue S, the green lane drops a bit to fruit trees in a vale and rises to a hilltop weather station, 5 miles from the start and the recommended lunch spot and turnaround. The view extends back the full length of the route to the Veterans Hospital and beyond to downtown towers and Capitol Hill, as well as over the Duwamish Valley and Boeing Field to West Seattle and the Olympics.

Round trip 10 miles, allow 7 hours
High point 350 feet, elevation gain 800 feet
Bus: Metro 3, 31, and 48 to Beacon Avenue; 42 to Martin Luther King Way

The route continues, but in dropping from Weather Station Knoll the powerline leaves the wide lawn and the realm of city police and enters a grubby motorcycle hell which continues to Skyway, relieved only by the oasis of Skyway County Park. However, Seattle and King County and Renton easily could put their heads together to devise a route down from the ridge to the Cedar River, connecting there to the trail which ultimately will lead to Snoqualmie Pass, or near.

LAKE WASHINGTON TO EAST SAMMAMISH PLATEAU

When the Canadian ice melted away, some 13,500 years ago, it left two long lake troughs and — to their west, east, and in between — three long highlands of glacial debris. It was, from a hydrological standpoint, an "unorganized" landscape. The rivers which had flowed from this point and that of the glacier front were gone, their valleys now containing only the seeps and dribbles of rain-fed streams. Where ice blocks had melted late, leaving pits in the moraine surface, there were *kettle* lakes which commenced the evolution through the phases of marsh, bog, and meadow to forest.

The landscape was still "infant" when European settlers arrived. In a century, however, ditches, culverts, sewers, landfills, and pavement had brought the westernmost of the highlands, occupied by Seattle and appendage communities, to maturity. The process was well along on the middle highland, the site of Bellevue-Kirkland-Bothell, when a spiritual conversion of society brought a new attitude toward wetlands. The lesson sank in that if a tract is half dry, half wet, 90 percent of the wildlife will be found in the wet half. The people always had been fond of wild creatures but had been led to believe that when a chunk of their living room was preempted, they'd simply move over. Now they learned it wasn't so, that destruction of habitat means destruction of wildlife. Thus it was that before the middle highland was totally dried up for houses and shopping centers, public policy began to emphasize the protection of wetlands. The opportunities for wetland protection were very great in the easternmost highland, which entered the 1980s in very nearly a state of nature, resembling the scene a traveler between Seattle and Everett would have observed early in the century, and between Bellevue and Bothell in mid-century. When the developers projected instant cities, they were met by the defenders of wildlife habitat. Unfortunately, the government is dominated by the philosophy that the developer has more rights than the wildlife.

Walkers (who tend to be attracted to water almost as strongly as wild creatures are) are well-served by the Bellevue Parks Department, which has specialized in the linear swamps, marshes, bogs, and kettle lakes left by the meltwater. Further, the Bellevue City Council has adopted a Natural Determinants Ordinance which gives Nature as loud a voice in land planning as that of developers. New annexations will enlarge the city into the Issaquah Alps, up from wetlands to steep lands, where Nature has more opinions on other matters than water. Bellevue Parks proposes to listen carefully and to build a trail system to hook everything together — Lake Washington to Lake Sammamish to Issaquah Alps — and to trail systems of cities on all sides and of King County.

Kirkland Parks concentrates on Lake Washington; the "City on the Lakeshore" vows eventually to have a walkway beside or near the water the full distance from Juanita Bay to Moss Bay to Yarrow Bay.

Other government units important on the middle highland are the cities of Redmond and Bothell in minor ways; Washington State Parks, with two major units; and King County Parks, with several parks/trails.

Chickadee

Separating the two overlake highlands is the valley of Lake Sammamish-Sammamish River. The story here is one major state park, one major county park, one super-major county trail in existence and in process of cloning.

The easternmost of the three glacial highlands is largest of all, extending 25-odd miles from I-90 on the south to the Snohomish River on the north. The southern section, Grand Ridge, belongs geologically to the Issaquah Alps. North from there the highland goes variously by the names of East Sammamish Plateau, Pine Lake Plateau, Bear Creek Plateau, East Union Hill, Union Hill, Novelty Hill, Ring Hill, and etcetera. In the past the pedestrian and equestrian had hundreds of miles of walking-riding routes, largely following old logging railroad grades. Most of these either have been closed off by private fences or soon will be obliterated by developments. What will be left by the turn of the century cannot be predicted. The past is dead or dying. The shape of the future can be but dimly seen.

Two cities presently reach up onto the plateau. Issaquah is developing a trail plan. Redmond has two superb parks on the highland and envisions a trail system looping from the Sammamish River to Bear Creek to the Tolt River Trail. Inter-agency plans are underway to develop a comprehensive trail system, as well as a Grand Ridge Regional Wildland Park.

Other cities may be incorporated before long. The General Development Plan adopted by King County in 1985 was the best compromise the planners could get The Powers to swallow, but left many questions unresolved. If the King County Council doesn't do so, the developers and/or the people will, the one seeking greater freedom than King County will permit, the other seeking greater freedom from developers. "Novelty Hill City" would center on 1500 Weyerhaeuser acres and 1100 Port Blakeley Tree Farm acres. These firms, having followed the bottom line away from growing trees to growing cities, propose homes for some 25,000 people, plus the accompanying golf courses and business parks. The companies describe themselves as "sensitive" and promise to take good care of the 230 acres of major wetlands identified by county planners on the Weyerhaeuser property alone. The pedestrian and the wildlife would feel better if these folks did not cite the Klahanie development, the core of "Pine Lake City," as "sensitive." If government will permit Klahanie to do as it is doing to Yellow Lake, what good can it do the wet acres of Weyerhaeuser and Port Blakeley?

Jane Ace, of *Easy Aces,* used to counsel her family and friends to learn to "take the bitter with the better." Walkers will find much of both on the two overlake highlands and in the broad valley between. The trails are open the year around, the highest elevations topping out at around 600 feet (save for Grand Ridge). The trailheads are close to home — next door if you live there, but very largely accessible by Metro bus from any part of Puget Sound City.

USGS maps: Mercer Island, Bothell, Maltby, Kirkland, Redmond, Issaquah, Fall City
Walkable all year

Mercer Island: Luther Burbank County Park (map — page 87)

The City of Seattle once debated whether to buy Mercer Island — the whole thing. It could have done so, easily, with the petty cash clinking unused in the

Luther Burbank County Park

civic pocket. Scoffed the great civic brains, "Who would ever have any use for that much green?"

Rather than becoming a park for Puget Sound City for the ages, the island was divided and subdivided into thousands of private parks. Indeed, public parks are controversial on the island, the community vitals gnawed by a fear of an invasion by off-islanders. Respecting the feelings of the City of Mercer Island, we will not mention in this space its few bits of trails, which are best considered strictly community resources. In fact, none is worth the time of an off-islander. However, a King County park on the north shore of the island keeps alive the memory of what might have been.

Beside the lake, under the big sky, on the 77 acres of a former school for delinquents, are meadows, marshes, groves of trees, and 3000 feet of waterside walking.

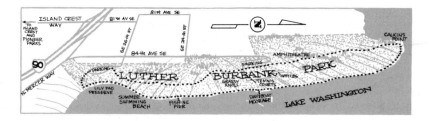

From the Mercer Island business district go off I-90 on Exit 7, "Island Crest Way," cross under the freeway onto 84 Avenue SE and from it at SE 24 Street enter the park.

To methodically "do" the park, walk a loop. From the parking lot by the headquarters building and tennis courts head north. Pass the amphitheater and a froggy cattail marsh to Calkins Point and views north over the water to Meydenbauer Bay and towers of the University District. Walk the meadow shore south, by clumps of willow and cottonwood, to views of the East Channel Bridge and the peaks of Cougar Mountain enclosing Coal Creek. Pass below the old school building, by the old brick power plant, walk out on docks where, in season, boats moor for picnicking. Follow the waterfront trail in willow-madrona-Indian plum woods to the fishing pier, lawns by the swimming beach, and the marsh at the park border. Loop back inland through meadows, including an ascent of the Grassy Knoll.

Loop trip 1½ miles, allow 1 hour
High point 50 feet, elevation gain 50 feet
Bus: Metro 202, 210, 226, and 235

Mercer Slough–Kelsey Creek–Wilburton Hill (map — page 90)

The original settlers didn't like bogs and did their darndest to drain them to grow vegetables and hay. Eventually some decided to go with the natural flow and took up the cultivation of blueberries, which like bogs. Then came the Bellevue Shopping Square and the city-builders, who staged an annual Blueberry Festival to hawk the properties they were developing on paved-over bogs. At last an incipient civic maturity provided the Bellevue Parks Department the support needed to preserve surviving wetlands. The new ethic was too late to save the entirety of the 8-mile loop of bogs, marshes, lakes, and creeks through the heart of the city. However, two lengthy stretches are pretty much intact.

The first extends from Lake Washington up Mercer Slough to Kelsey Creek, which curves around the base of Wilburton Hill, one of Bellevue's higher rises and its only sizable wildwood. Each of the several parks can be and usually is walked separately, though convenient linkages permit combination trips. In any event, they should be viewed as parts of a whole — as Bellevue Parks has viewed them. Indeed, a plan exists and, given funding, soon will be implemented to supply the "missing link" between Kelsey Creek Park and the Lake Hills Greenbelt and (with several other small linkages) provide a continuous foot trail from Lake Washington to Lake Sammamish. Watch this space.

Sweyolocken Boat-Launch to Enetai Beach Park

Drive Bellevue Way a bit north of I-90. Where 113th goes west, an unmarked (probably) road drops off southerly to the bank of Mercer Slough, elevation 17 feet.

The boat-launch is of no interest to the boatless pedestrian. (Canoes and kayaks sometimes are for rent on weekends at a house on 113th, across Bellevue Way from the entry road to the boat launch; watch for temporary signs.) However, two neat little walks take off from the parking area.

For Enetai Beach, go south from the parking lot on a paved bike path. In several hundred feet is a T. The left is to Bellefields Park (see below).

Go right, crossing under I-90, emerging to sky between marsh and lawns. In season, the marsh is brilliant with yellow flag, the cattails raucous with blackbirds, the lawns crowded with Canada goslings. The way touches the lake shore, in views over the waters to Newport Yacht Basin and Cougar Mountain, and ends at SE Lake Road. This narrow and quiet residential lane leads in ¼ mile to Enetai Bathing Beach Park, a fine place to sit and watch ducks and sailboats.

Round trip 1¼ miles, allow 1 hour
High point 17 feet, no elevation gain

Sweyolocken Boat-Launch to Bellefields Nature Park

At the T (see above) turn left and ascend a graceful bridge arching over Mercer Slough. Look south to the gray geometry of freeway. Look down to murky waters of the slough. Look north (with binoculars) along the tantalizing alleyway hemmed in by impenetrable willow jungle.

Beyond the bridge a floating path through reeds beside and under I-90 arrives in ½ mile on the east side of the valley. Surrealistic, that's the word for this half-mile: the wide expanse of cattails and willow thickets a-rustle with flitting birds, the lakewater a-ripple with swimming birds, wary creatures lurking in the bushes — and inches away, the massive concrete and roaring traffic of I-90.

At the east side of the valley is 118 Avenue SE (or Lake Washington Boulevard, as it was). Less than 1 mile south along this little old onetime highway is Coal Creek. (Bellevue Parks intends a trail connection to Coal Creek Park and also to the new Newcastle Beach Park.) The bikeway turns north, paralleling 118th at the edge of the Mercer Slough Open Space (see below). In a long ½ mile the path turns up to 118th and (1988) ends — just a couple hundred feet from the entry to trails of Bellefields Nature Park (see below), which thus can be combined with all of the above for a very rich day.

Bellevue Parks intends, when funding is obtained, to complete the trail route to Kelsey Creek Park, so keep your eyes open.

Round trip to Bellefields trailhead 2 miles, allow 1½ hours
High point 50 feet, elevation gain 30 feet

Mercer Slough Open Space (map — page 90)

The lowering of Lake Washington by 10 feet in 1916 converted a bay to a wetland. Truck-gardening and blueberry-ranching invaded the bogs. Then business and industry, which love flat land, began running out of the dry variety and began invading the wet. But by now Bellevue Parks was vigorously on the scene. Since the 1970s, some 180 acres have been protected from blacktopping; more will be if the city gets a fair day in court against the speculators.

The city owns most of the boggy bottom east of Mercer Slough. Walkways may ultimately be provided from the existing bikeway along 118th (see above) to areas for viewing the 150-plus birds and mammals that live here, virtually in downtown Bellevue.

The future of the wetlands west of the slough is problematical. Bellevue Parks owns two large chunks but developers hold the rest and have deployed legal armies to attack the city and the birds. The goals of Bellevue Parks are: (1) the enhancement and protection of wildlife habitat; (2) perpetuation on the west side of diversified agriculture (strawberries, blueberries, whatever-berries, daffodils, garden truck); (3) a trail system to improve public access; (4) an interpretive center to enrich enjoyment of the scene.

At present (1988), Overlake Farm No. 2 is located off the entry road to Sweyolocken Boat Launch; for information on buying berries — by picking your own — call Bellevue Parks.

North of 112th the Overlake Blueberry Farm (no U-pick) operates on city lands under lease. One suggested plan would place a nature center here, the starting point for a system of paths carefully located not to bother the plants and animals. The walkways might circle several "made" ponds, cross and recross the slough, and total perhaps 7-8 miles.

As of 1988, the only walking is on the east-side bikeway and in Bellefields Nature Park (and perhaps while picking blueberries).

Bellefields Nature Park (map — page 90)
Something there is about a marsh that makes man want to fill it or drain it and turn it into "useful" land — a farm, freeway, or subdivision. Or maybe a golf course or baseball field. Siegfried K. Semrau, former Bellevue Park Director, was among the earliest folk hereabouts to appreciate the intrinsic value of marshes. Thanks to his leadership, here is a beautifully useless soggy tanglewood.

Go off I-405 on Exit 12, turn west to 118 Avenue SE, then south 1 mile to the park sign and a small parking area. Spot the sign, "To the Trails," and go.

Artfully arranged to make the 50 acres seem a dozen times larger, the 3 miles of trails weave through forest, over little creeks, beside Mercer Slough and its (often) hundreds of ducks and coots. Most of the trails are literally

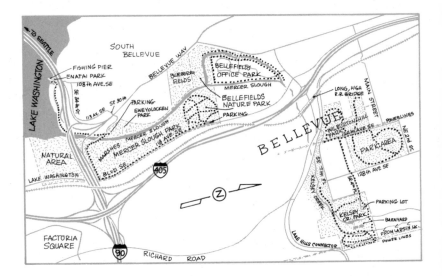

Bellefields Office Park

floating on a deep peat deposit. Brush from trail-clearing was placed as a base, over which was spread a layer of sandy loam from the hillside, then a layer of wood chips, also from the trail-clearing. The result is a unique springy surface. Names of the paths, signed at intersections, are evocative and entertaining as well as descriptive: Mud Lake Boulevard, Nightshade Avenue, Willow Grove, Skunk Cabbage Lane, Cottonwood Avenue, Cattail Way, Fireweed Lane, Gooseberry Avenue, Bee Trail, and so forth.

No map or guide is needed to savor this "living museum of natural history." Start on any trail, take any turns, keep going until it's time to go home. A good introduction is a perimeter loop, taking lefts at all junctions and thus circling the edge of the park. Then, on a second go-around, take all the right turns. Finally criss-cross to make sure you haven't missed anything.

Perimeter loop and embellishments 2 miles, allow 1½ hours
High point 50 feet, elevation gain 30 feet

Bellefields Office Park (map — page 90)

Bellefields Nature Park was supposed to be larger — 200 acres larger. However, the citizens of that day were too busy keeping up payments on

Cadillacs and planning moves to Houston and Yuma to vote the purchase price. So, developers moved in, to dabble in the enormous peat bog (2 miles long and 90 feet deep). They dredged a Second Slough parallel to Mercer Slough, creating a 160-acre island. They set the buildings back from the sloughs and surrounded them with lawns and trees. Along the sloughs are paths with spots to fish, launch canoes, picnic, and watch ducks, coots, gulls, crows, banties, and weirds.

Enter the Office Park either from 112 Avenue SE at SE 15 Street or SE 8 Street. Circle the island shores on cinder paths and lawns, eked out with connections across blacktop roads and lots. There also are paths in the strip along 112 Avenue.

This is couth and kempt slough. It is not Bellefields Nature Park. But it's better than no slough at all.

Island loop 2 miles, allow 1½ hours
High point 50 feet, no elevation gain
Bus: Metro 226 to Bellevue Way, walk ¼ mile to island entrance

Kelsey Creek Park (map — page 90)

That the agricultural past of the Bellevue area be not utterly forgotten, and that children may know animals other than dogs and cats, this former farm has been revived, complete with barns and pastures, cows, pigs, horses, burros, goats and sheep. Other attractions of the 80-acre park are the Fraser House, a cabin of squared-off logs built nearby in 1888 and moved here to be preserved, and an Oriental Garden to commemorate Bellevue's sister city, Yao, in Japan. There also are undeveloped natural areas, both valley marshes and hillside forests.

Go off I-405 on Exit 12, turn east on SE 8 Street, cross Lake Hills Connector at a stoplight onto SE 7 Place, and proceed via 128 Place SE and SE 4 Place into the park.

The maximum walk is the Kelsey Figure Eight — the Farm Loop plus the Hillside Loop. Start in the entrance parking lot and spend much time in the Oriental Garden. Then turn right to the path along the west edge of the lawns, with views to barns atop the central ridge. Bend left over West Fork Kelsey Creek to the Fraser House and cross the Barn parking lot to the trail along fenced-off preserves of cows and sheep and horses. Keep bending left, now upstream along East Fork Kelsey Creek, pastures on the left, wild wetlands on the right.

At about 1 mile from the start the Hillside Loop takes off from the Farm Loop. Turn right over East Fork into forest, to a T. For the recommended clockwise direction, take the left. On trail that invariably has solid boardwalks over ook and creeks and staircases up mucky slopes, ascend in a glory of mostly deciduous forest. The way turns right and sidehills; several sidetrails climb left a short way to the powerline and neighborhoods. After crossing several nice gullies from which Kelsey draws watery substance, the way drops back to the bottom and recrosses the tributaries to the T, closing the loop in about 1 long mile.

Finish the Farm Loop by climbing over the ridge of Douglas fir forest and dropping back to the north parking lot.

Kelsey Figure Eight 2½ miles, allow 2 hours
High point 160 feet, elevation gain 300 feet

In 1986 the city, having learned that the cheapest and best way to control stormwater is to retain natural wetlands, bought 24 acres south of the park, the confluence of the main and west forks of Kelsey Creek and of Richards Creek. The seller donated 16 acres of adjoining upland too steep to develop. Ultimately Bellevue Parks will run a trail along the bottomland to connect Mercer Slough Open Space and will provide viewing-platform sidetrails into the marshes. Something good might be done here for pedestrians. Meanwhile, the ducks and hawks love it.

Wilburton Hill Park (map — page 90)
How a piece of country survived amid the building of an All-American City is too wondrous a story for these pages. That 132 acres (or is it 90 acres?) were acquired for a park was a triumph of the New (1980s) Bellevue. But then came the question, what to do with the land? The Little League vowed it must have it all as "bawfields." The neighbors declared they would not tolerate the destruction of their quiet life. Bellevue Parks deliberated at great length and eventually the City Council chose a middle course that gave everybody something, but failed to preserve the largest forest wildland in the city's park system.

Go off I-405 on Exit 12, turn east on SE 8 Street, turn left at the stoplight onto Lake Hills Connector, which bends north to become 116 Avenue SE. Turn right on SE 1 Street, over the railroad tracks. Turn right on Main Street and continue to Wilburton School, elevation 200 feet.

As of 1988 there are some 3 miles of paths in the park. The ultimate trail system will be systematized in some fashion, as yet unknown. Until then the explorer should make up his own route. The "main" trail, an old woods road, sets out east, divides and redivides, is joined by entries from neighborhoods along streets west, north, and east. The forest has glorious groves of large maple, stands of Douglas fir that weren't choice enough for the old sawmill town of Wilburton (once larger than Bellevue) but now are on the way to becoming old-growth, patches of madrona, and all the usual companions of canopy, understory, and groundcover. Amid the natives are the escapes — apple trees, hawthorns, forget-me-not. Watch for raccoon, deer, coyote.

The apex is the hilltop field, elevation 230 feet, where the spirit is liberated into the sky, out to horizons. Here on a sunny day is the spot to have a picnic, to lie in the grass and look to the Issaquah Alps and the flitting swallows and the good-weather clouds. Unfortunately, the bawplayers have been awarded this hilltop.

In addition to these woodland paths, a powerline swath south from Wilburton School is worth walking for three reasons: (1) it passes SE 4 Place, the entry street to Kelsey Creek Park, a few blocks distant, permitting the two parks to be done on a single walk; (2) the powerline path descends past the footbaw field of Hyak Junior High to bottomland marshes of Kelsey Creek and SE 7th, elevation 25 feet. A large road shoulder close to Lake Hills Connector provides a good trailhead. A pedestrian crossing of the Connector leads to the Kelsey Creek Trestle, which lies on the railroad trail to Renton; (3) where the swath passes Hyak School, a closed-off woods road goes ⅓ mile west along the wildwood scarp to SE 5 Street, passing paths down the scarp and up through the woods to Wilburton School.

Sample loop trip 2 miles, allow 1½ hours
High point 230 feet, elevation gain 50 feet

A portion of the park will become the 20-acre Bellevue Botanical Garden. The beginning was in 1947, when Harriet and Cal Shorts commenced converting 7.5 acres of wildwoods to a "sample of paradise." When they gave their creation to the city, they stipulated only that it remain open space. The Bellevue Botanical Garden Society saw the start of something even grander and Bellevue Parks has agreed. For information on guided tours of the garden-as-is and the garden-to-be, write President Iris Jewett, P.O. Box 6091, Bellevue 98007.

Lake Hills Greenbelt (map — page 97)

The eastern segment of the 8-mile-long wetland of yore extends from I-90 at Eastgate north through the Lake Hills Greenbelt. Two upland trail systems at the south end, one in a business park and the other in a park park, complement the bog-walking. When the Bellevue Parks plan is carried out, all the pieces will fit neatly into a single outing. Further, when this system is connected by trail to Kelsey Creek Park, there will be a veritable "Lake to Lake Trail," Washington to Sammamish.

Robinswood Park (map — page 97)

Bellevue Parks acquired a "hobby" farm and has maintained it very much as the owners did, with the exception that animals no longer graze the pasture vale ringed by forest nor dip snouts in the pretty little lake. The farm buildings, however, have been retained for use as community meeting places, receptions for weddings, coming-outs, and the like. Trees, grass, lake, and buildings would fit beautifully in a calendar; with some snow, on a Christmas card.

Drive 148 Avenue SE to the park entrance at SE 24 Street.

For an introductory loop that saves the centerpiece for last, walk south from the parking lot on a path near 148th. Enter a fir forest and hit the blacktop remains of an old road now closed to cars. Turn left (east) to houses at the park's east boundary.

(Note: This old road continues as a public walkway to 156 Avenue SE and the Old Bellevue Airfield Trail discussed below. Robinswood Park is the best starting point for that trail.)

Find a path left into park forest. Emerge from firs on the greensward beside the air-supported tennis domes above the lake. Admire the prospect from this eminence, then descend the meadow to weeping willows and cattails and circle the shore. A couple times. Complete the loop up to the parking lot.

Loop trip 1½ miles, allow 1 hour
High point 425 feet, elevation gain 200 feet
Bus: Metro 252

Old Bellevue Airfield (map — page 97)

Folks who live close by or work in the business park find the path a pleasant bit of exercise. The developers who provided the trail as a public relations gesture and as an amenity which justifies higher rents have done a nice job of

Robinswood Park

preserving a narrow strip of forest along the route or, when that has not been feasible, installing lawns and shrubs. The tread is a mat of wood chips, easy on the feet. Wheels, horses, and unleashed pets are banned. The worst harassment is the thud-thud and huff-puff of the joggers.

All around the circuit are feeder paths from parking lots and office buildings. For the outsider, however, the recommended access is Robinswood Park (see above). The public walkway from the south end of Robinswood hits 156 Avenue SE exactly across from the west entry to the Airfield Trail. Elevation, 375 feet.

The path, wide enough for two or three people to walk side by side, starts off easterly, then turns north beside a fence on the edge of the undeveloped (1988) portion of the airfield. Along the way, beginning here, are constructions designed to give hyperactive pedestrians something to do besides walking, such as chinning. In ½ mile of (mainly) woods, the trail bends easterly around the end of the garbage dump that extended the landing strip into the vale draining to Phantom Lake. A fenced-off marshy bowl now serves as a retention pond, with a filtration system to halt noxious chemicals from seeping into the lake. Or so it is hoped.

Phantom Lake is glimpsed through the trees to the north. A few feet from the trail is SE 24 Street, with a small parking area for walkers and good shoulder parking elsewhere. After paralleling 24th for ¼ mile, the route bends southerly, behind the homes of Spirit Ridge, and emerges from fir and Indian plum and salal to become a lawn path beside 161 Avenue SE, through the business park.

At ¾ mile from 24th, trail yields to sidewalk extending ⅓ mile west along Eastgate Way, then north ¾ mile to sidewalk's end at the trail from Robinswood.

Loop trip 2½ miles, allow 1½ hours
High point 375 feet, elevation gain 100 feet
Bus: Metro 252

Lake Hills Greenbelt Park (map — page 97)

The original inhabitants doubtless rendezvoused here annually to pick the native blueberries and cranberries. It is said the bogs and marshes of that day bordered a single large lake, draining northward to Kelsey Creek. Then a homesteader dug a ditch east from the wetland to drain the waters over the scarp to Lake Sammamish. The former lake divided and shrank to two small lakes, Phantom and Larsen, yielding dry land for growing hay and truck. Ove and Mary Larsen homesteaded at "Blueberry Lake" about 1890, combining farming with his job in the Newcastle mines. In 1918 he sold half his land to the four Aries brothers, who ran the area's largest farm, producing carrots, celery, peas, lettuce, and cauliflower until 1960, when K Mart rolled out the blacktop. However, in the 1940s Louis Weinzirl had bought a slice of the Larsen homestead and replaced the wild native blueberries with the domestic blueberries which continue to thrive. (History courtesy of Lucile McDonald.)

Of the 8-mile wetland once continuous from Lake Washington to Eastgate, the middle 2½ miles between Kelsey Creek Park and Larsen Lake went the way of business and residence. However, Bellevue Parks was aided and abetted in its preservation goals by the city's Surface Water Department, which demonstrated that the cheapest way to control stormwater was to let Nature do it. The Lake Hills Greenbelt serves utilitarian as well as esthetic and recreational purposes.

The plan for the Greenbelt Park (one of the city's two largest) will develop only 2 percent of the 123 acres of land and 17 acres of lake, keeping 78 acres as woodland and wetland, 22 acres in blueberry bushes, and 20 acres as community vegetable garden plots leased to individuals growing for family tables. It is a "sensitive" park — sensitive to the needs of wild creatures, who have large preserves left strictly to them with no human entry — and sensitive to the needs of neighbors for peace and quiet — and sensitive to the needs of folks who want to come listen to birds.

At the south end is 75-acre Phantom Lake, elevation 250 feet. A sidewalk along SE 156 Avenue connects south ½ mile to the trail linking Old Bellevue Airfield and Robinswood Park. The lake is designated a "quiet zone" — no motorboats, no loud radios, no whooping and hollering. There are two public accesses, one at the south end of the Greenbelt Park. Pond lilies bloom yellow. Muskrats ramble through the willow swamps. Great blue herons fish. Bald eagles perch in snags. A viewing platform permits a little stroll out over the waters to watch little birds chasing big birds away from nests, and littler birds chasing...

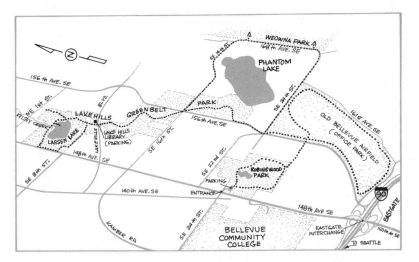

The trail sets out north from Phantom Lake through marsh grasses, the path 8 feet wide, with picnic tables and resting benches, bridges over canals, signs interpreting the history and the wildlife — the osprey and red-tail hawk and kingfisher, the river otter and coyote. Passing between a working farm on the left (see the rich, black, peaty soil, the good green crops) and a "wildlife enhancement area" on the right (let 'em alone), in ½ mile the route crosses the intersection of SE 156th and SE 16th to a 40-car parking lot. A path from here leads to the Community Garden, where folks can sign up for a patch of earth and grow their own peas and tomatoes and corn and thus learn (remember) the taste of fresh vegetables.

Winding through willow woods and by farms, in ½ mile the path crosses Lake Hills Boulevard to Lake Hills Library. Walkers usually can find parking space at the Little League field or the library or the adjoining shopping center.

Past the library the way comes to a T. The left goes ½ mile through woods and blueberry farms to 148 Avenue SE and a small parking area. Sidewalk connects north ¼ mile to the north end of the Larsen Lake trail.

The lake trail goes right from the T, between untamed marsh and tamed blueberries, fenced off lest ye be tempted, to lakeside woods. The way rounds the shore in hardhack and willow, the blackbirds as tyrannical in nesting season as the motorcycles used to be when school let out. Frogs splash, ducks paddle, fish swim. Pond lilies spread green pads and bloom bright yellow. A fishing pier provides a viewpoint in the lake. At ¾ mile from the T is 148th and the sidewalk which permits a loop walk, if wanted.

From near the lake a sidepath goes due north ¼ mile to the north end of the Greenbelt Park on 151 Place SE, at K Mart Center. The woods here are distinguished by the uncommon (hereabouts) aspen and beech.

Round trip from Phantom Lake to Lake Hills Library 2 miles, allow 1½ hours
High point 275 feet, elevation gain 25 feet
Bus: Metro 252
Loop trip around Larsen Lake 1½ miles, allow 1 hour

Lake Hills Greenbelt Trail

Phantom Lake Loop (map — page 97)

In 1988 a 10-foot wide asphalt walkway was completed, linking the Lake Hills Greenbelt and Weowna Park. The route is entirely beside or near streams: from 156 Avenue SE, east along SE 16 Street through the Greenbelt Park farm area to 168 Avenue SE; south along the edge of Weowna Park to SE 24 Street; east past the Old Bellevue Airfield to 156 Avenue SE; and north past Phantom Lake to complete the loop.

This is an important new link in the "Lake to Lake Trail." In future a high-standard trail will be built down through Weowna Park to Sammamish Parkway, paralleling the lake. One may hope that someday Bellevue can acquire a shore property so that a "Lake to Lake" walker who began at Enetai Park, gazing over Lake Washington, can conclude by gazing over Lake Sammamish.

Loop trip 3 miles, allow 2 hours
High point 375 feet, elevation gain 100 feet
Bus: Metro 252

Weowna Park (map — page 99)

In the heart of the Overlake Borough of Puget Sound City, where for a third of a century the land-developers have been hyperactive, a strip of forest 1 mile long and ¼ mile wide has survived. More preposterous, it is *virgin* forest. The hiker accustomed to lowland second-growth becomes giddy, confronted by Douglas firs up to 6 feet in diameter and equally majestic cedars and hemlocks and that lushness and solemnity that say "old growth."

And the ravines! The creeks! Situated on the "breaks" from the Lake Hills highland to Lake Sammamish, the park is deeply incised by streams. The outstanding one is not natural; Phantom Creek flows from Phantom Lake, just ¼ mile away, and enters the park in a 5-foot-deep trench hand-dug in glacial till nigh onto a century ago to convert lake to pasture. Before that, Phantom Lake drained to Larsen Lake — that is, the two were part of a single large lake which drained out Kelsey Creek to Lake Washington. The raw newness of the creek is evidenced by its superb waterfalls over till and blue glacial clay and its deep canyon sliced in drift.

That the virgin forest has been preserved seems due to the difficulty of logging the precipice in early days, then the nostalgia for deep woods felt by the owner, a retired logger himself, and then a subdivision scheme (don't try to figure out an Indian source for the name — it's "We own a park" — catch?), and finally a Forward Thrust purchase. There is no development and never will be much; plans are to keep it a wilderness park, little done except someday to systematize the trails.

The trails are accessible from the bottom, West Lake Sammamish Parkway SE, elevation 100 feet, but parking is a problem — the west shoulder is bikeway-walkway and the east shoulder is very skinny. Bottom accesses will be noted but the wise plan is to hike from the top.

Drive to 168 Avenue SE, which runs most of the park length on the upper side. The Phantom Lake Loop Trail runs beside 168th from SE 16th to SE 24th; the walkway goes west on both these streets. Park carefully on shoulders to not block traffic. Elevation, 275 feet.

Local folks have beaten out many paths over the years but not with any system. For a full survey one must either fight brush to hook up trails or return frequently to 168th. The most imporant paths are here described in sequence from the south.

North a short way from where 168th curves north a small King County Parks sign marks where an obvious trail enters the woods and descends easily and

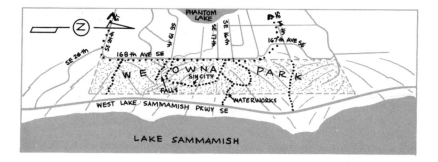

pleasantly. Note evergreen huckleberry, unusual hereabouts, and a fruity reason for visiting Weowna in fall. At a T go left and continue down to Sammamish Parkway; the trail widens to a blacktop stub and is chained; a highway sign just here says "Speed Zone Ahead."

The park's chief spectacularity is Phantom Creek, its pretty falls located among some of the largest of the Douglas firs. By SE 19th spot a trio of white concrete posts marking the culvert and take the path on the right (south) side, behind the paper-deliverers' shelter. Hang onto the children! The way skirts the perilous brinks of "Till Falls," frothing to a cirque-like basin, and then "Clay Grotto Falls," where the creek goes underground and plunges into a clay-walled cave. Sidepaths permit safe explorations of the bottoms of both falls. The main trail ends but a root ladder drops into the gorge jungle; a doughty soul could slither on down to Sammamish Parkway and likely find secret nooks that would excite Tarzan, and even Boy.

North of SE 17th another King County Parks sign marks a good path, not obvious at the start, which winds across a splendid flat of mixed forest to a Y. The right fork sidehills through Sinners' City (not a Boy Scout camp, according to evidence of beer bottles and pinup girls scattered around shacks and treehouses) and connects to the falls area of Phantom Creek. The left fork samples superb groves of big alders and maples, big firs, big madronas, and eventually comes out on 168th at SE 16th, obscured by neighborhood lawn-clippings and hedge-trimmings. Loveliest of all, the Trillium Trail takes off — very obscurely — from this fork and descends a luscious big-tree ravine, passes a fenced watershed and covered reservoir, an old waterworks, and hits Sammamish Parkway 500 feet south of the gated road noted below.

For the final path, turn right from 168th onto SE 14th, right onto 167th, and right on SE 12th to the deadend. Skid down to a trail-road in the gully and descend by a series of concrete retaining dams and stormwater drains to Sammamish Parkway, where the trail-road is prominently gated. The feature of this walk is a 7-foot Douglas fir snag.

Total of all round trips about 4 miles, allow 3 hours
High point 275 feet, elevation gain 800 feet
Bus: Metro 252 to SE 16th and 148th, walk 1 mile to park

Bridle Trails State Park (map — page 102)

In 1942 a cowboy could ride from Renton to Bothell on trails (abandoned logging roads, mainly) and country lanes, crossing only several paved highways. However, the opening of the Lake Washington Floating Bridge signaled the end of the open range. The riders talked the Legislature into transferring 481.5 acres of school lands to the state parks system. It wasn't topographically interesting property. The forest, largely Douglas fir several decades old, was in its most monotonous phase.

But behold how wilderness can rebuild itself. The second-growth firs are three-quarters of a century old; they, and companion hemlock and cedar and understory and groundcover, are evolving from simple-souled childhood to the complexity of maturity. Foreshadowing the future is the past — a scattering of old-growth firs that were too fire-scarred to interest the railroad loggers.

Trail in Bridle Trails State Park

Honeycombing the wildland are 23 miles of major trails plus 25 miles of minor paths — 48 miles! As the ranger warns newcomers, "You can get lost in there." There are no trail signs! But you couldn't get dangerously lost. Just long enough for the thrill.

Go off I-405 on Exit 17, turn east to 116 Avenue NE, and south to the park entrance between NE 40 and NE 60 Streets. The popularity of the trails is suggested by the enormous size of the parking lot, elevation 400 feet.

Hikers should keep in mind that on all trails where horses are permitted, not just in this park, the animals have the right of way. The hiker should step off the path, act nonchalant, talk to the beast so it'll recognize the stranger as a human, and avoid sudden motions. Because of the park name, one may suppose hikers are not welcome and/or might be trampled by the cavalry. Neither is true. Despite the popularity with horsefolk the park is too large to get crowded; on an ordinary day a hiker won't meet many horses, particularly if he stays off the main trails that in winter are anyway churned to muck. Moreover, improvements of the 1980s drained and turnpiked some mudholes, easing the way for both hooves and feet.

There is, nevertheless, a lot of mud, mucho mud. Further, the figure of 122,000 horse-days of use a year means an average of 334 horses a day, or 7 per mile, and not a diaper among them. Pedestrians, be warned.

To describe the complete 48 miles would require many pages — and be superfluous. There is little in the way of views out and the plateau has minor topographical variety; one place is much like another, one trail like another.

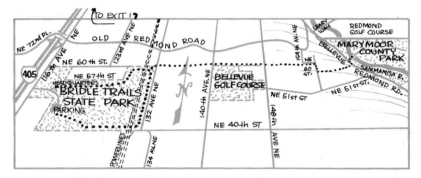

Getting confused is a distinct possibility but to stay lost would require dedication; listening for the roar of I-405 gives a western baseline; the powerline swath down the center of the park provides north-south orientation. But since there are no signs, and myriad feeder trails enter from horse ranches, riding academies, and stables all around, even describing a basic introduction could get out of hand. One can only try.

For an introductory perimeter loop, start on the prominent wide trail taking off to the left from the far south end of the parking lot. At major junctions take right turns, avoid minor paths, and shortly reach the south boundary. Proceed easterly, left (shunning paths that enter the park), cross the powerline, reenter woods, and reach the east boundary, 132 Avenue NE. Turn left to the north boundary, NE 60, and turn left, west, jogging left to pass a large indentation of ranches. Return by the headquarter corrals to the parking lot.

That's the basic introduction — but not the best hike. To escape the major trails, to lose the sights and nearly the sounds of civilization, leave the perimeter, dive into the interior on the smaller paths. Get lost.

Perimeter loop 4 miles, allow 2½ hours
High point 566 feet, elevation gain 300 feet
Bus: Metro 251 to NE 70 and 116th, walk ¾ mile to park

Kirkland Watershed Park (map — page 103)

How much good stuff can be crammed into 60 acres? The forest grown since turn-of-the-century logging — large Douglas fir, huge maples dripping licorice fern, groves of madrona, fine big cedars, alder, and hemlock, the occasional gigantic cottonwood, mysterious plantations of two-needle (lodgepole?) pine. Thickets of yellowberries, white lawns of candyflower. Canyons carved in glacial drift, creeks trickling through horsetail bottoms. Mysterious artifacts of a vanished civilization. And sampling it all, a roundabout, up-and-down-and-up loop trail of some 2 miles.

Go off I-405 on Exit 17, turn west on SE 70 Place, which bends south as NE 68 Street. Turn south on 108 Avenue NE, then east on NE 45th to the main park entrance. No signs except "No horses, no motorcycles." Elevation, 400 feet.

To do the loop in the recommended clockwise direction, set off up the main trail (old service road, abandoned). Pass a major trail descending to the right; this is the return leg. The path skirts the edge of a precipice plunging into a

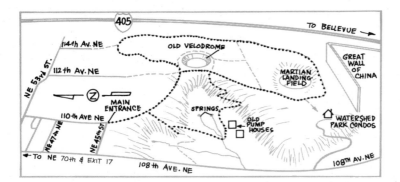

green canyon on the right and ascends to the plateau top at 425 feet. An entry trail from 112th joins on the left just before the first of the artifacts, hypothesized by David Quimby, who introduced the surveyor to the watershed, to be an Old Velodrome.

For the loop, keep north through fine woods. But hark! What is that roar? One had forgotten there are freeways. The trail bends around to head south, passing an entry from 114th, and emerges from forest at the huge bowl Quimby identifies as the Martian Landing Pad. What is that emptiness above, where formerly was a green roof? It is the sky! With swallows in it! Keep straight ahead to the Great Wall of China at the far side of the Pad. Pass an entry trail used by the people who live behind the Great Wall. Turn west along the Pad to its west end. Pass an entry from Watershed Park Condos. Look out to towers of downtown Bellevue, to heights of the Issaquah Alps. Reenter forest, the canyon gaping on the left, and proceed north to a Y a few steps short of the Old Velodrome.

Now for the nicest part of the walk, though the trail is thin and steep and slippery. Take the left fork and switchback down the precipice, deeper and deeper into the green. Pause for rest on hillside benches. Look through the treetops, *down* to the birds, out to glimpses of Lake Washington. But what has happened to one's hearing? The roaring has stopped! When the ears dropped off the brink the freeway dematerialized, was shipped to Mars. Birdsongs submerge the generalized hum-rumble of the distant City.

At the bottom of the canyon the springs seep out of aquifers, through horsetails, joining to form a creek. About time, say the panting dogs in the party. The path crosses the creek, climbs to the narrow crest of a ridge between this canyon and another. Atop the crest is a T. The left is an entry from 108 Avenue, the right climbs to complete the loop.

People care about this park, care deeply. Once it was a horrifying motorcycle and four-wheeler playground, but though there are six trail entries, all are under watch by residents who are quick to call for reinforcements. Further, they are diligent garbage-collectors. On the survey day not a speck of trash was seen and not a single wheel track. Moreover, in contrast to the state park on the other side of I-405, the nose encountered no aroma louder than skunk cabbage.

Loop trip 2 miles, allow 1½ hours
High point 425 feet, elevation gain 150 feet

Kirkland marina

Kirkland Waterfront (maps — page 106)

Kirkland planners vow that someday there will be a continuous shore or near-shore trail along Lake Washington from Juanita Bay to Yarrow Bay, some 5 miles, partly in open marsh, partly on beach, partly through lanes of marinas and condos and eateries and shoppes.

Why wait? The route can be walked now, in bits suitable for afternoon and evening strolls. The imaginative way is to do the whole thing in a single go, loitering as lazily as may be wished, counting on the Metro bus to whip the bones back to the start.

Complete round trip 13 miles, allow 8 hours
(Ride the bus one way and cut the walking in half)

Juanita Beach (King County) Park (map — page 106)

To do the entire walk starting from the north, leave the car or get off the bus at Juanita Beach (King County) Park, located on NE Juanita Drive, elevation 20 feet.

Begin in the park, walking the ¼-mile promenade that encloses the swimming beach. Views past Juanita and Nelson Points across the lake to Sand Point and the tip of the Space Needle, down the lake to Hunts Point and the Evergreen Point Bridge. Beware of the ducks and geese and crows — they'll grab your lunch.

Looping-around trip ¾ mile, allow 1 hour

Juanita Bay Park (map — page 106)

This "largest jewel in Kirkland's tiara of waterfront parks" is also the city's largest park, 63 acres, with 2100 feet of shoreline. It became possible when the Juanita Golf Course was abandoned, conveniently next to an abandoned stretch of the Lake Washington Boulevard. But Kirkland Parks had to have the vigor to convert possibility to actuality and the citizens had to vote the money to keep the golf course free of mansions.

Sidewalks along Juanita Drive hitch the second segment to the first in a scant ¼ mile. To do this park separately, where 98 Avenue NE rises from the swamps of Forbes Creek, spot a small parking area below the street on the west. Elevation, 50 feet.

The city does not plan bawfields, boat-launch, or putting greens. Rather, it intends "an alternative to our structured everyday lives." The highest priority is wildlife habitat. The existing parking lot will be slightly enlarged. The Southern Meadow (upland) will be mowed, irrigated, manicured, and provided with play area, picnic shelter, benches, and a paved trail winding through groves of weeping willow and birch, Douglas fir and maple. The Wetland Meadow will be left for Nature to manage, with help from the bossy blackbirds. Two deadend boardwalks will be built out through the buttercups and yellow flag and cattails to viewing areas of marsh and open lake.

The other abandonment, of highway, converted the causeway built in 1935 to a foot and bicycle path crossing ½ mile of bayshore and Forbes Creek wetlands. Muskrat and raccoon and opossum and beaver live here, and more than 70 species of birds; in winter, as many as 1600 birds have been counted at a time. Salmon spawn in Forbes Creek. What a happy sight, to see green grass growing from cracks in sterile concrete! Old dock pilings topped with little gardens point out through acres of lily pads, brilliant in season with large white flowers. The only changes envisioned here are a possible fishing pier, an interpretive center, and a replacement of the existing path along 98th with "finer landscaping" and better separation from machines.

Thorough walkabout 1¾ miles, allow 2 hours
High point 50 feet, minor elevation gain
Bus: Metro 241

Kiwanis Park–Waverly Park–David Brink Park (map — page 106)

The third stretch of the route is not by the water, though it has two dips to the shore, and thus is ordinarily only walked by a person doing the straight-through. However, so few automobiles disturb the quiet residential streets that one may walk down the middle without attracting attention, except from the dogs, who make sure you stay in the middle.

From the southwest edge of the golf course climb a path to public streets. Walk 10 Street W; at a Y, follow it left, uphill, then right. When it bends left as 14 Avenue W find an obscure path down the bluff to Kiwanis Park, with huge cottonwoods on 2.5 acres of wild shore. Return to the street, go left on 8th, right on 16th, right on 7th, left on 14th, right on 6th, and finally right on Waverly Way, reached near its northern deadend. Descend left on the entry road through forest to the beach of Waverly ("Skinnydipper") Park and walk out on the fishing pier for views south to Moss Bay. Return to Waverly and proceed south. The bluff side is virtually free of houses, opening long views north past

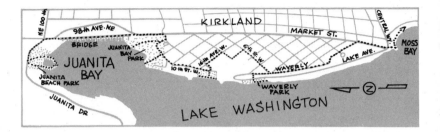

Champaign Point and across to Sand Point and the tips of Seattle towers. In 1984 Kirkland bought the 9-acre site of Waverly School. Named David Brink Park after the longtime director of Kirkland Parks, it and blufftop sidewalk will connect Waverly and Marina Parks. At Market Street turn downhill to the water.

One-way trip 2 miles, allow 1 hour
High point 175 feet, elevation gain 400 feet

Kirkland Shoreline Trail (map — page 106)

When Kirkland says "shoreline trail," this is what it means. That it exists and will grow is due partly to the heritage of olden times but mainly to the determination of modern times that the citizens shall not be cut off from the water. Since the early 1970s the city has required of developers wishing to build on or over the water that they donate a public easement through their property. The requirement also covers requests for remodeling and renovation, so that though seven over-the-water condos were built before the rule was adopted, walling off the water, sooner or later they will need to be rehabilitated. Then, zap.

The start is Marina Park, built in 1970 exactly where Market Street used to run out onto a ferry dock; until the end of War II a person could walk on the boat, debark 4 miles later at Madison Park, and catch the bus to downtown Seattle. That cannot be done anymore, another example of entropy. However, there is a public dock for people arriving in Kirkland by boat; poor folks are permitted vicarious enjoyment. The 2.6 acres of walkway, beach, and lawn give fine views of lake and people and "so many ducks that swimming would be hazardous to the health."

When Kirkland decided to be "a lakeside town rather than a town near a lake" (nothing personal there, Bellevue), it was the first city in the state to

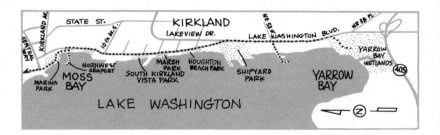

Moss Bay on Kirkland's shoreline trail

complete — in 1974 — its own shoreline master program, pursuant to the state Shoreline Management Act of 1971. It is the only city in the state to seek to create a public trail all the way along the lake. So far from fighting in the courts, developers generally have seen the light and gone along happily, donating (so far) some 1000 feet of public paths over private property.

From Marina Park the walking route (presently) returns via Kirkland Avenue to Lake Street and proceeds past shops and bistros to the Port of Moss Bay Marina, present home of Northwest Seaport.

The way southward is partly on sidewalks (past those pre-Enlightenment, over-the-water condos), partly on shore walkways (through the post-Enlightenment condos), pleasured by a series of parklets. The first is .02-acre Street End Park, providing a view of Harbor Lights Condominium, protruding 250 feet into the lake (modern laws would forbid this) and boasting the city's only over-the-water swimming pool. South Kirkland Park is the next opening in the wall of buildings. Then comes Marsh Park, or "Muscle Beach," where adolescents take off their clothes to perform mating rituals, and finally Houghton

Beach, where families huddle under the benign eye of a lifeguard who doubles as morals guard. Along the way to here, at the old boundary of Kirkland-Houghton, Lake Street has become Lake Washington Boulevard.

Sidewalks continue to Yarrow Bay Marina, a nice sidetrip to observe how rich people play. The city has obtained two shore easements to the south but cannot hook them together without more easements — that is, more building.

One-way trip from Marina Park to Yarrow Bay Marina 2 miles,
allow 2 hours
Bus: Metro 235, 251, and 254

Shipyard (map — page 106)

In 1946 the Lake Washington Shipyard, which built ferries, War I wooden freighters, postwar steel freighters, and, in War II, destroyer escorts and seaplane tenders, closed. The Skinner Corporation leased parts of the land to other industrial uses and to a professional football team from Seattle. Then it put forth a plan for "Shipyard Park," which on 18 shoreline acres would have a 100-room hotel, a 461-slip marina, 40,000 square feet of space for eating, boozing, and shopping, 467,000 square feet of office space, a 24-unit condo, 125 apartments and 1746 parking stalls. Promising, in addition, a path along the entire ¼ mile of shore, a rebuilt stream freed from its culvert and stocked with salmon, and two small beach parklets, Skinner declared this would be "the pendant on the necklace of Kirkland waterfront parks." In 1987 a compromise reduced the marina to 220 or 240 slips and opponents abandoned their court action. Completion is planned for 1992.

Yarrow Bay Wetlands (map — page 106)

Since the 1950s one grandiose scheme after another has been proposed to dry up the third-largest marsh on Lake Washington. Since the 1950s one schemer after another has slunk away with his battered lawyers and his crumpled architects' pretty pictures, defeated by the citizens of Yarrow Bay. In 1986 a developer got around them, obtaining permission from Kirkland to build The Plaza at Yarrow Bay in exchange for giving the city 66 acres of cattails, blackbirds, muskrats, and woodpeckers. Hardhack and willow-tangle and hellberries forbid human entry. The place serves people by storing floodwaters and cleaning polluted runoff. Mainly, however, it serves as habitat for salmon, bass, pheasant, hawks, bullfrogs, and water rats. It never will be a major park; at most there may be a path to a viewpoint.

O.O. Denny Park–Big Finn Hill Park (map — page 109)

Stroll a sandy beach in views across Lake Washington. Leave the sun for cool shadows of Big Finn Canyon. And suddenly yelp in surprise, ambushed by a genuine, flabbergasting, holy-cow and oh-my-golly of a Douglas fir claimed to be the largest in (urban?) King County.

From Juanita Drive NE turn off on Holmes Point Drive to O.O. Denny (Seattle City) Park, located on Holmes Point, elevation 20 feet.

The 46-acre park is well-known for its ¼ mile of beach, Cougar Mountain rising on the horizon to the south and Sand Point jutting from the west. Fewer folks are familiar with the two trail systems, one either side of Big Finn Creek.

Find the start of one just south of the culvert under the highway. A broad path ascends beside the gorge through impressive forest of cedar and fir and hemlock, yew and hazelnut and huckleberry, coolwort and fairy bells. Skid-paths plummet to the creek jungle. The path ends at a gravel road, 175 feet, that drops to the creek and someday may be an access to Big Finn Hill (King County) Park.

The gorge section of Big Finn Park presently has no trails worth recommending, just 80 acres of creek and wildwood walls, a critter preserve. Getting the land set aside from the usual process of maximizing the tax base took local activists 10 years of crusading. Ultimately 1-mile trails might be built along both sides of the gorge, if the critters don't mount a crusade against it. (Also, 120 acres on the plateau east of Juanita Drive have been added; this woodland has meandering paths beaten out by local feet but not surveyed for this guide.)

The major trail system of the gorge area begins at a sign, "No Motor Vehicles," at the overflow parking lot northeast of the creek. The path soon forks, and each fork forks again, and each eventually ends in somebody's back yard. However, along the way...

At the first split, a short bit from the parking lot, the left ascends a tributary ravine in mixed forest of big old conifers and hardwoods. Then the eye is caught by large Douglas firs — and larger — the bark blackened by charcoal. The walker suddenly sees the history of the park area: burned a century-odd ago by a forest fire that killed all but the thick-barked old-growth firs; the second-growth attaining size rivaling the old-growth; the Denny family acquiring the property as a summer retreat, then giving it to the city of Seattle. The path repeatedly divides, each piece worth wandering up ravine walls through spacious green chambers of the forest. One climbs to the top of a 300-foot ridge, where a final split leads (left) to a skywide vista over the gorge and (right) to a madrona grove where kids long have camped. These endpoints are about ¾ mile from the parking lot.

Now, back to that first split: Take the right fork up the main valley, near the creek, through plants lushly growing from black ook. A sidepath climbs left; follow it a few yards and gasp and wow-ee — these are the biggest old firs yet,

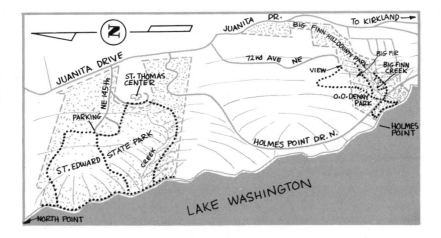

and the young cedars aren't much smaller. Return from the sidetrip, take a few more steps. For maximum effect keep your eyes on the ground. There, spot the plaque:

  "King County's Largest Douglas Fir
    Height 255 feet
    Circumference 26.3 feet
    Bark thickness 12 inches
    Age 575 years
    Shatanka Campfire Girls, Kirkland, 1978"
  Now lift your eyes.

Round trip all trails 4 miles, allow 3 hours
High point 300 feet, elevation gain all trails 1000 feet
Bus: Metro 240 to NE 122 Place and Juanita Drive NE, walk 1 long mile to
    O.O. Denny Park

King County's largest lowland Douglas fir in O.O. Denny Park

Trail in St. Edwards State Park

St. Edwards State Park (map — page 109)

So far as sufficient and proper "parking" is concerned, Puget Sound City has been saved from shame less by planning than by fortuitous circumstance, or in simpler language, dumb luck. For example, in 1977 the people obtained — half a century after any realist would have said the last chances were gone — a large wildland park on the shore of Lake Washington. The fortuities were: a property owner (the Archdiocese of Seattle) with soul; and an alert partnership of state and federal legislators and officials.

This was not raw wasteland, such as was obtained from the U.S. Navy the same year, at Sand Point. This was Instant Wildland Park, the forests already installed. Development is focused on the upland plateau, in and around the former seminary buildings. Most of the 316 acres — all the steep bluff and the several superb ravines and the 3000 feet of waterfront — will remain as they were under stewardship of The Church — green and quiet.

Drive Juanita Drive NE north from Kirkland or south from Kenmore to the park entrance at NE 145th. (The park sign is inconspicuous behind the one for St. Thomas Center, which is outshouted by the one for Milam Center.) Turn west on the entry road to a Y; keep right, following signs to the parking area behind the main St. Edward building, elevation 350 feet.

Where to walk? Where seminary students did for years and the deer and coyote still do, beating out a trail system of a dozen-odd miles. For openers, to sample just about all the good things, do a figure-8 loop.

At the front of the seminary building take the Beach Trail ⅔ mile, losing 338 feet, to the lake. Always at an easy grade, this onetime woods road winds down the bluff, in and out of valleys, through a forest of maple, alder, dogwood, hazelnut, and cedar but especially notable for the combination of two dominant species, Douglas fir and madrona. Views into shadowed vales give the feeling of touring the great halls of a forest mansion. Sidetrails invite left and right; mentally note them for later.

At the lakeshore picnic lawn watch mallard hens lead flotillas of ducklings, gaze over log rafts to boats on the water, look up the lake to Kenmore, down to Sand Point.

For the first loop of the figure 8, follow the shore trail down the waterside terrace (underwater until the lake was lowered), through alders and cottonwoods leaning far out from the bank, ¼ mile to the south boundary. Now, having satisfied your curiosity about *that,* retreat all the way back to the trickle-creek just south of the picnic lawn, and just south of this ooze take the prominent path up the bluff. The way ascends slopes of a ravine and tops out on the narrow crest of a ridge crowned with a cathedral of a fir forest. At ⅔ mile from the shore the way leaves trees for grass at the St. Thomas water tower; follow roads and lawns north ½ mile to the start.

For the second loop, again descend the Beach Trail — or one of those mentally noted sidepaths. Turn north on the shore through a succession of monster cottonwoods, two with caves that invite kids to crawl in. In ½ mile the park ends. Retreat a few hundred steps to the only major up-trail. (There are several lesser up-paths.) The way climbs steeply through glorious fir forest, then sidehills a jungle gorge where devils club grows tall as trees. At the Y the left fork drops to the creek and climbs to suburbia; take the right a final bit up to the plateau and at ⅔ mile from the lake return to the parking lot.

Figure-8 loop trip 4½ miles, allow 3 hours
High point 350 feet, elevation gain 700 feet
Bus: Metro 240 to NE 153rd, walk to entrance

Lake Sammamish State Park (map — page 114)

Not for a hot summer Sunday, when this is the most Coney Island-crowded of state parks, but for any quieter day, are the walks over the fields, through the marshes, along the lakeshore and the creek banks, always in views up the lake and to the Issaquah Alps — Grand, Cougar, Squak, and Tiger. The least known of the wonders is a wildwood gorge with a secret waterfall. Three tours may be done separately or combined.

The Lakeshore Way

Leave I-90 on Exit 15, drive a short bit north to SE 56 Street, and turn left to the park entrance. To maximize the walk, park at the first opportunity. Elevation, 25 feet.

Cross lawns through groves of cottonwood and weeping willow to the lake and follow the sandy shore east to the mouth of Issaquah Creek. Turn right upstream to the charming footbridge and return downstream nearly to the mouth. Manicured park yields to reeds and tall grass and willow tangles and masses of lilypads, and to soggy footing of a meager mucky path that may require getting the ankles wet. Soon the path improves and pavement is reached at the boat-launch area, some 1¾ miles by this devious route from the start. For a 3½-mile round trip, turn back.

Round trip 3½ miles, allow 2 hours
High point 25 feet, no elevation gain
Bus: Metro 210

The Birding Way

The Chief Birder of the lake, Marty Murphy, tells us how to see and hear the park residents and visitors who do not shout and scream and never kick baws around or hit them with clubs.

Before entering the main gate, stop by the first soccer field along SE 56th. Go around the second gate, veer left on a service road by a superb weeping willow, a stand of alders, and a small grove of young firs where the deer hang out. Watch for great blue heron perched high in cottonwoods along Issaquah Creek or feeding in the field beyond.

From the parking lot closest to the main park entrance go left in spring toward the jogging field and be overwhelmed by northern flickers and red-wing blackbirds. Veer to the water and up to late autumn see bufflehead, pied-bill grebe, western grebe, belted kingfisher, Canada geese, American widgeon, and yellow-breasted chat. Sometimes a common loon rests on the shore. Go left on a wet path to Tibbetts Creek and note the nesting habitat for small birds and mallards. Returning along the shore see gulls, geese, coots, and mallards waiting for their bread.

Enjoy the cattails at the mouth of Issaquah Creek and head upstream, past the bridge, to open fields. Look left with binoculars to see great blue heron. Veer over the fields on the watch for eagles, hawks, herons, and a pair of coyotes watching you. Also keep an eye out for barn owls. Near the end of the field turn right to a bank of Issaquah Creek. Note the rock island — great hunting territory for heron. Killdeer and kingfisher call.

Round trip 2 miles, allow all day

Laughing Jacob's Creek (map — page 114)

Walk from the main park to the boat-launch, as described above, or drive there via East Lake Sammamish Parkway from Exit 17 on I-90.

Cross the railroad tracks into the boat-launch parking lot; King County Parks has proposed ultimately obtaining the right-of-way and providing a trail up Lake Sammamish to Marymoor Park and the Sammamish River Trail. Issaquah Parks dreams of a trail south to the city center and connections there to the Issaquah Alps.

From the parking lot go back over the tracks and the parkway, jog right, and enter the Hans Jensen Youth Group Area. Proceed through the campground field up the valley of Laughing Jacob's Creek to the edge of the woods. There, in a cool-shadowed cedar grove by babbling water, the trail splits.

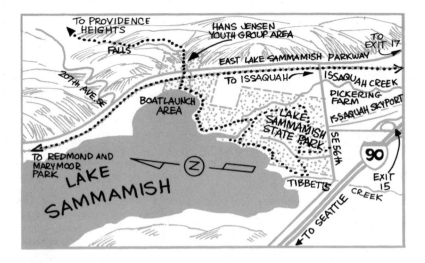

For one tour, cross the little bridge and ascend a steep ¼ mile up the gorge wall on a rude path. On the rim are big firs and views some 200 vertical feet down to the fine frenzy of greenery along the creek.

For the other, don't cross the bridge, continue on the trail up the gorge into a pocket wilderness. In about ⅓ mile, ¾ mile from the highway, gentlefolk may wish to conclude the tour. Walkers willing to brave the tangle can continue some ¼ mile and be bewitched. There it is, the water splashing down moss-black sandstone slabs in a jackstraw of moss-green logs, Laughing Jacob's Falls.

Much of this walk was outside the park until 1987, when the state Department of Natural Resources transferred 120 acres to State Parks. The DNR and State Parks are now (1988) negotiating a land exchange with a developer which would give the public a trail corridor up the creek to Providence Heights.

Round trip to falls 2 miles, allow 1½ hours
High point 350 feet, elevation gain 400 feet

Lake Sammamish Trail (maps — pages 114 and 116)

Summer cottages of the remote past, when the lake was way out in the boondocks, grew to the ramblers and splitlevels of commuting suburbia which, except at north and south ends, block off the public from this smaller but by no means inconsiderable (9 miles long) sibling of Lake Washington. However, as happened elsewhere around Whulj country, the railroad very early on pre-empted some prime view property, still remains, and breaks through what otherwise would be hundreds upon hundreds of fences.

In 1980 Burlington Northern announced intentions of ultimately abandoning the rail line. King County Parks began drawing plans for a Lake Sammamish Trail that would connect the Sammamish River Trail and Marymoor Park to Lake Sammamish State Park, Issaquah — and thus to the Issaquah-to-

Snoqualmie Falls Trail—which will link to the Snoqualmie River Trail—which via the Tolt Pipeline Trail will hitch to the Sammamish River Trail. A loop! A superloop! Hooked up at Bothell with the Burke-Gilman Trail. A system! A county system! A bounty for the millions, for the ages!

However, several wealthy property owners along the route are agin it. The legalities remain to be settled in court.

In years past—indeed, for not many years short of a century (raising the legal question whether any fences ever can be legally erected along the grade, rails or not)—hoboes and local residents have been walking the rail line. There never was any complaint until the prospects arose of the long-public trail becoming forever-public. However, as of 1988 the feelings are running so high that King County surveyors have had the dogs set on them, joggers have been chased and cursed and threatened with "birdshot britches." Therefore, we do not discuss this as an open trail—at present—but as a future—and if not that, as a past.

Let us say, then, that until recently what a walker did was leave I-90 on Exit 17, signed "East Sammamish Road," and drive East Lake Sammamish Parkway 2 miles north. He then turned left to the parking area of the Lake Sammamish State Park boat-launch area, elevation 25 feet.

He walked back out the entry road to the railroad tracks, still in use once or twice a week (to the deadend in Issaquah), and headed north. The route paralleled (and continues to do so) East Lake Sammamish Parkway but at sufficient distance to feel safely removed, and for substantial sections out of sight and sound of traffic. The water was (is) always near and sometimes beside the tracks. However, all beaches being private, the walker stayed on the railbed. The foreground entertained him — the lakeside architecture and docks and boats, the stretches of wild-tangled swamp greenery. The background was a constant joy — sun-sparkling waves, sailboats, ducks, and far forest shores. Rising above all was (and is) the vertical panorama from the Squak Plain to the Issaquah Alps — to the ravines and peaks of Cougar, here

Issaquah Creek in Lake Sammamish State Park

seen to its best advantage, and Squak and Tiger, and on either side of Squak, the deep glacial troughs of Issaquah and Tibbetts Creeks.

North from the state park the walker found other places to park the car without blocking traffic and to get from the public highway to the quasi-public rails. Gaps between houses increased and more wild spots gave close looks at shore and water. At 8 miles from the park the walker mused over stubs of old pilings reaching far out in the water — steamer dock? Sawmill? Booming grounds? Here at the north end of the lake began (begin) the mile-wide marshes-pastures of Marymoor Park. Shoulders here suggested parking to explore paths from highway over tracks into the willows and onward to the soccer fields. In another 1½ miles of woods and fields the tracks led the walker into the heart of downtown Redmond, where he picked up the Sammamish River Trail and just-like-that whizzed through Bothell and Logboom Park on the shore of Lake Washington to Gasworks Park on the shore of Lake Union.

One-way trip from boat-launch to lakehead was, when possible without danger of being yelled at, 8 miles, 4 hours
High point 50 feet, elevation gain 25 feet

Marymoor Park (map — page 116)

Until establishment of the Cougar Mountain Regional Wildland Park, Marymoor Park was King County's largest, occupying 485 acres of the flats at the north end of Lake Sammamish and along its outlet, the Sammamish River. In this spacious plain are soccer and baseball fields, children's play area, archery butts, model airplane airport, tennis courts, bicycle track, picnic tables, Pea Patch. In an open-air shelter is an exhibit of the archeological dig that established the fact of human residence on this spot 7000 years ago. An historical museum occupies the 28-room Clise (Marymoor) Mansion, headquarters of what began in 1904 as the Clise family hunting preserve, called Willowmoor, then was a dairy farm until purchased for a park in 1963. And there are lines of majestic poplars up to 4 feet in diameter, and groves of Douglas fir. A Dutch-like windmill. A river. A lake.

Just south of the center of Redmond, cross the bridge from West Lake Sammamish Parkway over the river to the park, elevation 36 feet.

What's to be done in the way of walking? By no means disdain simply striking off in the grass and roaming the fields. This book spends much of its time in forests. It's bracing to wander wide-open spaces under the big sky of pastures and lake.

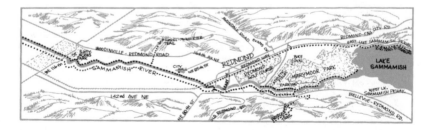

Spectator along Bridlecrest Trail

The basic walk, of course, is downstream along the machine-free riverbank, first in fields and by the Pea Patch, then in willow thickets, finally in people-free marshes, a great big critter refuge. Mingle with ducks and coots, blackbirds and hawks. In pre-park days the walk would have ended in the frustration of impassable marshes; now, a wooden walkway leads through muck and reeds to a concrete viewing pier at the meeting of marsh and open lake, by the beginning of the Sammamish River, with views down the 9-mile-long lake to Tiger Mountain rising a tall 3000 feet above the south end.

Described separately, but best done as a walk from Marymoor Park, is the Bridlecrest Trail (which see).

Round trip to lake 2 miles, allow 1½ hours
High point 35 feet, no elevation gain
Bus: Metro 251, 253, and 254 to West Lake Sammamish Parkway, walk ½ mile to park

Bridlecrest Trail (map — page 116)

A gorgeous forest seemingly virgin, of huge firs, including a snagtop some 7 feet in diameter, and big hemlocks and maples. That's the best part of a trail that connects Marymoor Park to Bridle Trails State Park. Most of the route is primarily of interest to horseriders and local walkers, but no hiker visiting Marymoor should miss the first stretch.

From Marymoor Park (which see) walk out the entrance road. Cross the river bridge, walk the riverbank trail south, cross Lake Sammamish Parkway to a "Bridlecrest" sign and enter the forest.

Ascend the steep hill in the marvelous trees. Down in the mossy bottom of the creek to the right, spot an ancient bridge, an old concrete water tank, nurselogs. The trail climbs above the splendid ravine to a ridge between two gullies, through a fine alder-maple jungle, to lawns of a Redmond city park at 156 Avenue NE. This is as far as most hikers will care to go. But the way west has attractions, particularly to a fan of horses, an admirer of horse ranches. There also are cows and views to the Cascades.

From the neighborhood park the trail jogs north a block, then turns west on the line of NE 60 Street, which except for a couple blocks at the start is not cut through, so the trail is a lane between fences, removed from vehicles except for crossings of 148 and 140 Avenues. Passing pastures, a posh apartment complex, greensward of a golf course, at 132nd Avenue the trail reaches the northeast corner of Bridle Trails State Park.

Round trip 4 miles, allow 2½ hours
High point 500 feet, elevation gain 450 feet
Bus: Metro 251 to NE 70 and 116th, walk ¾ mile to Bridle Trails Park, thence to the trail; Metro 251, 253, and 254 to West Lake Sammamish Parkway, walk ¾ mile to trail

Sammamish River Trail (maps — pages 116 and 120)

Pastures and cornfields and "instant lawn" farms sprawling table-flat east and west to forested valley walls. The murky river floating ducks and coots for 14 meandering miles. Tweety birds flitting in reeds, clouds of gulls circling, hawks on patrol above. The path along the bank, far out in the quiet plain, distant from noisy roads. To a hiker accustomed to skulking in dank woods, an airy, wide-sky, liberated trail sure to have sun if there's any to be had.

On first survey in 1977, before the trail formally existed, the solitary walker met only bored cows and friendly horses. On a fine Saturday in the summer of 1981 the entire 9½ miles between the Park at Bothell Landing and Marymoor Park were one big smile: bicyclists by the family (bike rentals in Bothell and Redmond), rollerskaters by the platoon (rentals on fine weekends at the Leary Way crossing in Redmond), horses (with riders), runners, joggers, walkers, not to forget paddlers in canoes and rubber rafts. There were tiny children carried on mothers' backs, in kiddyseats on bikes, in strollers being pushed by fathers on rollerskates. There were seniors enjoying the scenery from a flat, paved, no-problem path. Where were all these folks before the trail was created through the efforts of Save the Sammamish Valley Trail Association, King County Parks, Forward Thrust, and IAC? Wherever, they weren't having this much fun. Anybody who supposes motorized recreation is the future, quiet travel is the past, should spend a day here — and then get active promoting more urban-area trails. By 1988 the one trail wasn't enough and a second route on the other side of the river was being developed.

Great things have happened in this valley in the 1980s. The King County Farmlands Preservation Program was at last funded by the voters and overcame legal challenges. Through 1985 the county had bought development rights to 70 percent of the valley's agricultural lands, nearly 1000 acres in total, saving these from urbanization and industrialization. (Lest we rejoice too much, far more acres than that are being held by speculators.)

Further, King County Parks has consolidated its ownership and easements along the west bank of the river, the route of the second and parallel Sammamish River Trail. One will serve feet, the other bicycles and rollerskates. (Read the trailhead signs that will be installed to be sure you are where you belong.) The west bank is open to walking now, even before the trail formally exists; park the car at any of the cross streets shown on the map and go.

Finally, the trees planted along the trail are reaching for the sky, providing more shade by the year and fine music on a windy day. Benches are an amenity not present in the barbed-wire-fence era of the 1970s. Patrol by King County police has largely eliminated illegal dirtbiking; the cops can't be outrun by chortling scofflaws because the cops are riding dirtbikes themselves. (Therefore do not, here or on the Tolt Pipeline Trail, reflexively assault dirtbikers — check first to see if they are Theirs or Ours.)

The walk can begin at either end or any number of convenient put-ins along the way. Here it will be described from the north end, where the Sammamish River Trail ultimately will be linked to the Burke-Gilman Trail.

Blyth Park is the grand junction of these two trails and of the Tolt Pipeline Trail as well. Bothell's biggest park, at 36 acres, it sits at an elevation of 25 feet on the bank of the Sammamish River below the wooded slopes of Norway Hill. From Main Street in old Bothell drive the 102 Avenue bridge over the river. Turn right on Riverside Drive to the park, which abuts the Wayne Golf Course.

(Note: As of 1988 the "formal" start of the Sammamish River Trail is marked by a prominent sign on Bothell Way at 96 Avenue NE. The blacktopped path drops to the river, crosses on a new foot-bicycle bridge with views downstream to the abandoned railroad bridge, ultimately to be the Burke-Gilman entry to Blyth Park. On the far bank a path goes right to the entry road to Blyth Park, which is close by through the trees.)

The trail turns upstream, through cottonwood-alder-willow forest, beside cattails and reeds raucous with blackbirds. At ½ mile from Bothell Way/Blyth Park is the Park at Bothell Landing.

When Bothell turned its back on its beginnings as a stop for the steamers coming up from Lake Washington and — in high enough water — proceeding to Lake Sammamish, it became just another hick village selling gas and groceries and the occasional hamburger. Briefly, after 1912, it could boast of lying on the Pacific Highway from Seattle to Everett. However, this soon became "the old Everett Highway" and the hamlet mouldered. When it once again turned its face to the river it got Soul. The shops on the mall of Bothell Landing offer ice cream cones, books, and T-shirts — and they rent bicycles for the ride to Marymoor Park. The Park at Bothell Landing is a dandy spot to watch ducks and canoes, to picnic, to swim. Of historic interest are the buildings: the 1885 Beckstrom Log House; the 1896 Lytle House, now the Senior Center; and the 1893 William Hannan Home, now the Bothell Historical Museum (Sundays, 1-4 P.M.)

Landing Park, elevation 20 feet, lies just off Bothell Way. At ¼ mile from its graceful wooden bridge arching over the river is 102 Avenue NE, a popular starting point. At ¾ mile from the bridge (1¼ miles from Blyth) the trail crosses the river to another popular parking-starting place just off Highway 522. For a short bit the way is a sidewalk along the old Bothell-Woodinville Road, which now deadends at the river. A bridge over North Creek leads to a forest of concrete pillars whose foliage is concrete ramps — the interchanges of I-405 and Highway 522 and whatnot.

North Creek has been talked up as a trail corridor north to Snohomish County. The channel has been relocated and remodeled by developers, who have provided a creekside walkway about 1 mile through business parks.

At 2¾ miles from Blyth Park the trail crosses Bear Creek; trail corridors are being developed on both banks, leading initially through business parks and the like but eventually, perhaps, to the planned city trail system of Redmond.

Past Bear Creek bridge the trail goes under NE 175 Street in Woodinville (parking) and the scene changes. To this point there have been river and greenery but also trailer courts, apartment houses, assorted urbia, and concrete — pleasant walking but "busy." Now begins ruralia as the broad trail and companion river strike out into the center of the peaceful plain. At 4¼ miles is the junction with the Tolt Pipeline Trail (which see), and at 4¾ miles the underpass crossing of NE 145 Street (parking, and a sidetrip to Ste. Michelle Winery, ¼ mile away, to buy cheese and crackers for lunch. The winery has 90 manicured acres for strolling. A second winery on the other side of 145th plans a "French village" complete with 200 houses, a shopping center, and a thousand imported Frenchmen).

Shortly beyond the underpass crossing of NE 124 Street (parking), at 7¼ miles is NE 116 Street and the county's Sixty Acres Park — stay out unless your're wearing team togs and kicking a soccer baw. At 8 miles is the junction with the Farrel-McWhirter Trail (which see).

At 8⅓ miles the scene again changes at Redmond City Hall, located beside the river at the deadend of NE 85 Street (parking). Watch for the Levine sculpture, *Sitting Woman,* who is doing it without a chair and badly needs attentions of the sort given the folks *Waiting for the Interurban* in the Fremont District.

Quitting farms, the trail follows the river through the city, passing under the railroad to Issaquah (see Lake Sammamish Trail) and then lofty masses of highway concrete. At 8¾ miles it crosses Leary Way (parking) next to "downtown" Redmond. Across the river lies the golf course which the city mothers have determined must stop being green and start generating traffic. At 10 miles from Blyth Park is the entrance to Marymore Park (which see).

(Historical notes: The primeval Sammamish River was 30 miles long. Lowering of Lake Washington made its waters lower and slower. The U.S. Army

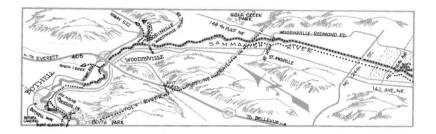

Sammamish River Trail

Corps of Engineers shortened up the meanders with their jungled shores and slough swamps to 14 miles and mowed the banks lest muskrats ramble and birdies nest. When King County Parks proposed to restore some of the meanders, the Corps threatened to call in the Coast Artillery. Someday, however, Parks will overcome.)

(Travelers' notes: As the foot goes, it is 23 miles from Gasworks Park on Lake Union to Marymoor. As the kayak, canoe, and rubber raft float, it is 15 miles from Redmond to Logboom Park.)

One way from Blyth Park to Marymoor Park 10 miles, allow minutes or all day
High point 35 feet, minor elevation gain
Bus: Metro 307 to Bothell; 251, 253, and 254 to Redmond

Grand Ridge–East Sammamish Plateau (map — page 123)

"Between two worlds, the one dying, the other agonizing through the birthing" — this is how it is, here, in 1988. Early in the decade the local horsefolk published a map showing trails totaling hundreds of miles. Late in the decade most either had been closed off by houses and fences or were on the verge. That's the dying world. What of the world that is being born? King County Parks long has had hopes for a mainline, regional trail extending 18 miles from the Issaquah-Snoqualmie Falls Trail north to the Tolt Pipeline Trail, probably along the Northwest Natural Gas Pipeline and/or the Bonneville Powerline. Now, public officials and citizen groups are developing a grand plan for a Grand Ridge Regional Wildland Park that would link the regional trails to the Issaquah Alps. The three walks described here recall the past and foreshadow the future.

Grand Ridge Trail (map — page 123)

Cedars and firs and hemlocks so big one wonders they weren't logged in olden days — until one goggles at olden-day stumps. An exuberance of vine maple and salmonberry and devils club. Creeks and swamps. Tracks of — maybe meetings with — deer and coyote and bear. A deep experience of the insides of a second-growth wildland at lowland's edge, suburbia's edge.

Leave I-90 on Exit 20, turn north to Preston Way, and drive east to 280 Drive SE. Turn steeply uphill 0.6 mile. Where the road turns sharp east and is signed SE 63, "Private Road, Dead End," park on the shoulder, elevation 880 feet.

The trail may not be visible at the start but definitely is there—close beside the fence, which is barbed and may be electrified—and definitely is on public land, though not so signed. In a short bit the way opens out onto an ancient woods road. Cross a pleasant creek and ascend its lush valley to a Y—the two ends of what used to be called the Hour Trail because it was a 1-hour loop from the long-gone Black Nugget Stables.

From the Y go left, ascend a vale to a ridge crest, a glory of old alder forest, and another Y. Go either way, it doesn't matter, both are wild and nice and they rejoin in ½ (right) and ¾ (left) mile, at about 1½ miles from the road.

Gently descending slopes of Grand Ridge northward, the path splits and resplits. Keep the compass handy and keep taking lefts and you'll find trails to the Bonneville powerline (see Issaquah Alps, Issaquah to High Point) and/or the Black Nugget Road (see East Fork Issaquah Creek-Grand Ridge-North Fork Issaquah Creek).

To approximate the horse's hour, keep taking rights. Thus you will stay on public land in superb forest, swinging in and out from a marvelous creek that drains to North Fork Issaquah Creek. The path curves around a steep and

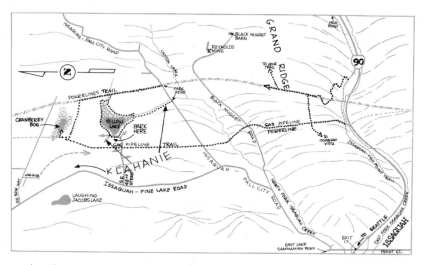

rocky slope above the gulch of another thoroughly admirable North Fork tributary. A final scant 1 mile completes the trail — this leg, with windows through big firs to Snoqualmie Valley and the Cascades, is the most outer-scenic.

The Grand Ridge Trail is the central circuit of the proposed Grand Ridge Regional Wildland Park. The intention is to eventually have additional trailheads around the periphery, as well as connections to the regional trail system.

Round trip 4 miles, allow 3 hours
High point 1100 feet, elevation gain 600 feet

East Fork Issaquah Creek–Grand Ridge–North Fork Issaquah Creek (map — page 123)

From the Issaquah-High Point Trail (which see) at 1½ miles west of High Point, ¾ mile east of the site of the old railroad trestle, turn steeply up the gas line swath, climbing from 325 feet to the gentling out of Grand Ridge at 500 feet. Gaze south to the Tradition Plateau, Tiger and Squak.

In ⅓ mile intersect the telephone cable (buried): the woods road left leads to Issaquah Vista; the right connects in a scant ½ mile to the Bonneville powerline swath, which runs south to the Issaquah-High Point Trail and north to SE Black Nugget Road—on the way passing a sidetrail to the Grand Ridge Trail (which see).

From the high point of 550 feet the gas line slopes gently, then plummets to the valley of North Fork Issaquah Creek, crossing the Black Nugget Road at 375 feet. (To drive to this point, go ¾ mile from Issaquah-Fall City Road.)

For the best part of this whole section, cross the road, climb a 100-foot ridge, and drop to the broad bottom of the North Fork. The gas line has dammed the vigorous creek of "mountain tea" into a dark-watered pond-marsh-swamp, a place of cattails and pond lilies, fish and frogs and blackbirds.

Round trip from Issaquah-High Point Trail 3 miles, allow 2 hours
High point 550 feet, elevation gain 400 feet

Yellow Lake–Cranberry Bog (map — page 123)

The previous edition of this book rhapsodized over the finest lake on the East Sammamish Plateau, the only sizable sphagnum peat bog surviving so near Seattle, and the area's grandest wildlife refuge and its best birding. This edition comes not to praise but to mourn.

Go off I-90 on Exit 17 to East Lake Sammamish Parkway and turn right up the Issaquah-Fall City Road. (Before construction of the Sunset Highway over High Point to the Raging River, this was the Snoqualmie Pass Highway.) At a Y in ¾ mile keep left on Issaquah-Pine Lake Road. At 0.9 mile from this junction, turn right on SE 43 Street, the entrance to Klahanie, a "sensitive" development, by which is meant that any sensitive person who knew the area of old can't go through now without wanting to spread his lunch on the land. In 0.5 mile from the entrance spot Yellow Lake to the right. Park on the street, elevation 400 feet.

The developers have provided a trail along the Northwest Natural Gas Pipeline and will build another along the Bonneville Powerline; neither is of any interest except to local residents walking the dog or jogging, though someday a regional trail may make use of these segments. The 1½-mile loop path around Yellow Lake will be nicely landscaped and will have viewpoints and (probably) places to launch boats. Possibly the lake may be legally made a "Quiet Zone" (see Phantom Lake), so that it will be permissible to beat radios to death and stuff socks in the mouths of shrieking children. But who knows? The sure things are these: the buffer zone recommended by environmentalists was cut to a third by King County planners and this was cut to a third by the King County Council; no honest provision was made to maintain the purity of the springs which feed the lake and thus are the headwaters of the North Fork Issaquah Creek (a salmon-spawning stream) which is the lake's outlet; the promised trail-greenbelt along the North Fork to the Issaquah-Fall City Road will not fend off the sour juices from streets and houses. When Klahanie is "built out" the lake will continue the slow dying that began with the first bulldozer in 1986. Ironically, sometime in the 1990s the folks who live in Klahanie will have come to love Yellow Lake and will rise up to save it. Millions in public funds will be spent — millions that in effect went into the developers' pockets.

For those who weren't here before, Yellow Lake will be a delight. There will still be birds and for a time the native trout — until thrown-away goldfish drive them out. The native pond lily will bloom yellow in spring — until somebody introduces the exotic white-flowered pond lily and it becomes White Lake. The surveyor won't go back because it is too painful to recall the hours spent wandering, semi-lost, where the cougar and bear and coyote lived, and the muskrat and mountain beaver and deer, and the eagle, osprey, red-tailed hawk, great blue heron, snow geese, Canada geese, and many species of ducks, and where grew the forests that mingled gone-wild crabapple trees with stands of aspen and birch. How much will survive to century's end?

The Cranberry Bog will continue to be worth visiting simply because there isn't another in the vicinity, not anymore. The Klahanie Natural Gas Trail goes north from Yellow Lake and down the slope to the bog. Park on the street and descend to the shore. Come in late May or early June to see the kalmia in rosy bloom, some days later for the white flowers of Labrador tea, and then the pink glow of hardhack. Come in fall to pick a mouthful of wild cranberries growing in sphagnum moss. Stay out of the bog — and keep the kids out. Can the bog survive Klahanie? Probably not.

Round trips 2 miles, allow 2 hours
High point 400 feet, minor elevation gain

Farrel-McWhirter Park and Trail (map — page 125)

In 1971, when Elise Farrel-McWhirter bequeathed to Redmond the 68 acres of pasture and forest that had been her summer retreat since 1938, she gave the city what became in 1980 "the jewel of its park system." That title now must be yielded up to the Redmond Watershed — at least so long as that preserve retains park-like status. However, the older jewel has 2 miles of in-park trails; they connect to the 3-mile trail to the Sammamish River.

The recommended itinerary is to start at (near, that is) the Sammamish, saving the park for the luncheon climax. Drive Woodinville-Redmond Road 1.5 miles north of NE Redmond Way (via 164th), 1½ miles south of NE 124 Street (via 140 Place NE) to the pushbutton traffic signal signed "Trail Crossing." Park on the shoulder, elevation 175 feet.

The "Puget Power City of Redmond Trail" descends the powerline swath west ¼ mile to the Sammamish River Trail at 25 feet. The city may bridge the river to extend the trail westward.

Eastward, however, is the direction of the park. Ascend alder forest to the powerline swath and plateau top, 275 feet, with a view back over the Sammamish valley. In the first 1 mile the swath zigs left, zags right, crosses two streets (bus stop at NE 110) and a private drive — very suburban. The next 1¼ miles to Avondale Road have long woodland vistas and a country feel. Houses are few, cows many, fields and woods line the way. Twice, to dodge a swamp bottom and a farm fence, the trail swings from powerline through woodland cool. Two well-beaten sidetrails lead right into nicer and wilder forest than anything on the main route. The swath drops from a high point of 300 feet to 82 feet at "Trail Crossing" (and bus stop) of Avondale Road. The final ½ mile to the

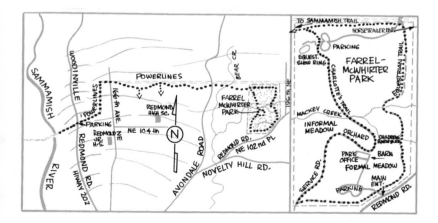

park boundary crosses the fish avenue of Bear Creek and winds through birdy woods of willow, alder, ocean spray, and honeysuckle.

A perimeter (approximately) trail covers park highlights in a 1½-mile loop. From the Equestrian Show Ring veer left to the powerline and climb to the 175-foot top of Novelty Hill. Turn right along 196 Avenue NE to the park's horse-trailer entrance. Continue through middling Douglas fir shading a floor of bracken and coolwort, dip to Mackey Creek, climb to the park's main entrance on Redmond Road, and proceed to a service road — the old farm road. Turn right beside picnic grounds on the Formal Meadow to the Orchard, the Red Barn (display of old farm implements) and Children's Barnyard (animals to pet), and Grain Silo (restrooms and observation deck). Skirt the Informal Meadow, recross Mackey Creek, and return to the Show Ring.

Development of the park continues. A ½-mile nature trail has been marked. Mackey Creek is intended as the corridor of the main arterial trail through the Bear Creek basin. A trail is planned from the park to the Redmond Watershed.

To drive to the park, take Avondale Road northeast from Redmond 1½ miles, turn right ½ mile on Novelty Hill Road, and turn left ½ mile on Redmond Road.

Round trip 7 miles, allow 4 hours
High point 300 feet, elevation gain 500 feet
Bus: Metro 251 to trail crossing of Avondale Road; 254 to trail crossing of
NE 110th

Redmond Watershed (map — page 126)

The Redmond city mothers and fathers call it "a jewel" to be treasured as an "urban wildland park." The 806 acres were bought between 1926 and 1944 as a buffer to Seidel Creek; its waters never met purity standards and except for service roads (abandoned) the tract has seen little human disturbance since the railroad loggers left in the 1920s. The master plan adopted in 1986 calls for no development through the end of the century, preserving the land for "low intensity" use. A 1-mile trail is proposed west to Farrel-McWhirter Park. The Tolt Pipeline Trail lies a mere ¾ mile to the north. Seidel Creek is tributary to Bear Creek, projected as the central axis of the Redmond trail system. When

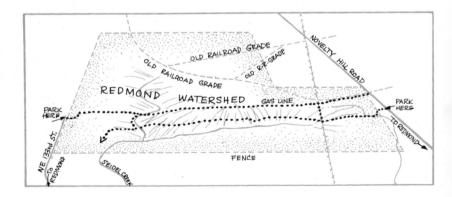

Novelty Hill City is built adjoining the watershed, the trail corridors dedicated by Weyerhaeuser and Port Blakely Tree Farms will lead in. That is the future.

As of 1988, the walker must hear a discouraging word — "dirtbikes." The watershed and the adjoining 2600 acres held for massive development are the regional center for razzing about in machines and firing pistols and rifles. The place absolutely must not be attempted by a rational person on weekends or after school lets out, in the afternoon or for the summer.

The northern access is the less attractive. From Redmond Way in "downtown" Redmond drive northeasterly on Avondale Way-Avondale Road. Turn east on Bear Creek Road-132nd, in 0.3 mile turn right on 133rd, and in 0.6 mile more come to the Northwest Natural Gas Pipeline swath. Park here, elevation 425 feet.

The swath at this point is private property on both sides of the road. However, a path open to the public sets out north from the west edge and if it is a lucky path, crosses the outlet of Welcome Lake and intersects the Tolt Pipeline Trail ¾ mile from 133rd. Perhaps keep it in mind.

A trail also heads south and shortly swerves to the swath inside the watershed. The swath dips to a wide, deep vale with a nice creek, climbs out, and at ½ mile from 133rd passes a trail entering on the right. Definitely keep this trail in mind (see below).

The swath runs a compass line 1¾ miles from 133rd to Novelty Hill Road — up and down, down and up, and naught but grass and wheel tracks. It could be a nice exercise on a winter Tuesday morning when one wanted a brisk walk under the sky, out of the wet brush. With the single exception noted above, no trails invite the feet into the forests on either side. Granted, the surveyor was distinctly defatigable, as he tends to be on pipeline swaths which reek of dirtbike scat. He had high hopes for the "old railroad grades" on the GS map, but the only one he could get to from public land was choked with greenery. If the watershed had a Chief Ranger of the sort who overlooks trail construction in the Issaquah Alps, the grades readily could be brushed out for some 2 miles or more in the northeast sector of the watershed, the plateau portion which doubtless is rich in secret wetlands.

The recommended — and highly endorsed — introduction is from the southern access. (But again, never try it when the children are not securely locked up.) Drive Avondale Road from downtown Redmond. At a Y bear easterly on Novelty Hill Road, which in 2.3 miles crosses the gas swath, elevation 525 feet. However, rather than parking and starting from here, return west a scant 0.2 mile, to the end of the guardrail, and a woods road, usually gated shut, signed "No Unauthorized Dumping Allowed" and "No Trespassing"; the well-used bypass trail is plain to see.

Walk the road to a beaver-like pond dammed by the road. Pass a Redmond Public Works dump off to the left and proceed straight ahead, the old road becoming trail. In a scant ½ mile cross the Puget Power swath.

The abandoned service road, which has seen no legal wheels in decades, sidehills above Seidel Creek, the waters too quiet to be heard and too heavily defended to be visited. The way is flat at the start, then has minor ups and downs, and finally some major-minor downs and ups. The trail burrows through mixed forest of silvery alder, lacy hemlock, sprawling maple, and cottonwoods that in spring fluff the air. Cedars form graceful shrubs. Red huckleberries top old stumps dating from the railroad logging. Trickle-creeks slake the thirsts of panting dogs. Vine maple arches over. The forest becomes a mix of large maple and biggish fir, then bigger fir.

At 1½ miles of twisty-turning the path drops to a cathedral-type forest vale and crosses a sparkling creek whose waters send the dogs into delirium; this is a tributary of Seidel Creek and a hike destination if ever the surveyor saw one.

A few steps beyond is a T with another old service road. The right climbs to the gas swath, which a person could use for a loop. But why? The way you came is the best way back, after the picnic lunch.

The left was not surveyed because the map shows it leaving the watershed in ⅓ mile. The dirtbike tracks are distinctly not "low intensity" and heavy traffic comes from the private lands.

Round trip to Picnic Creek 3 miles, allow 2 hours
High point 525 feet, elevation gain 250 feet

Round trip on pipeline 3½ miles, allow 2 hours
High point 540 feet, elevation gain 350 feet

Tolt Pipeline Trail (maps — page 129)

When the Seattle Water Department built the pipeline in 1963 from its new Tolt River Reservoir 30 miles to the city, it acquired for the purpose a strip of land some 100 feet wide. As an admirable demonstration of multiple use of such utility corridors, cooperation with King County Parks led to establishment of the first King County Forward Thrust trail. The route is 12 miles, up hill and down dale, from city's edge through suburbia to wildland, from Bothell to the Snoqualmie River valley.

The trail may be hiked straight through if return transportation can be arranged. Most hikers, of course, start at one end or somewhere in the middle and walk this way or that as far as inclination leads. Parking availability is a consideration. Some accesses have room for one or two cars, others for a half-dozen, others for none. On busy days the lot at the chosen start may be full up, forcing a switch to an alternate.

Blyth Park to Norway Hill, ½ mile, elevation gain 450 feet

Officially the trail is not open up the wooded slopes of Norway Hill from Blyth Park. Some problems with the neighbors, perhaps. It is walked unofficially all the time and will be more and more as the junction of three great trails — Burke-Gilman, Sammamish River, and Tolt Pipeline — makes Bothell famous.

From Main Street in old Bothell drive the 102 Avenue NE bridge over the Sammamish River and turn right on Riverside Drive to the park, which abuts the Wayne Golf Course.

Whether or not hiking the Tolt Pipeline, one easily can spend an hour or two poking along the riverbank and wandering paths on the hillside. One of these informally intersects the pipeline swath, where the official trail eventually will go.

Norway Hill to I-405, 1 mile, elevation gain 50 feet

To drive to the present official trail start, cross the Sammamish River from Bothell and turn left. In 0.5 mile turn right on a road signed "Norway Hill." In 0.5 mile pass a road to the right, signed "Norway Hill"; this leads to 104th and the

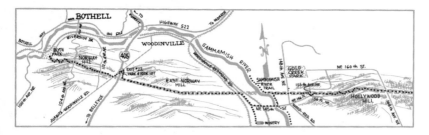

present official trail start, but at a point with poor parking. So continue 0.3 mile on 112th to the pipeline and parking for three-four cars.

Now, to back up and describe the route in sequence: From Blyth Park the (future) trail switchbacks ½ mile to the 480-foot top of Norway Hill and the official (present) trail start at 104th. Superb views down to the Sammamish, out Bothell Way and the valley to Kenmore, Lake Washington, and Olympics. From 104th the trail descends by houses, through woods a long ½ mile to 112th and parking. In ¼ mile more is the concrete jungle of I-405.

To cross the freeway, from the trail turn left up a farm road to a freeway access. Follow footpaths plainly marked on the pavement. Pass a Pool It Parking Lot (to get here to dump your car, take Exit 22 from I-405 and cross the freeway on NE 160th to the lot on the west side). Beyond the freeway the route turns right to rejoin the pipeline, all this crossing business taking about ⅓ mile.

I-405 to Sammamish River, scant 2 miles, elevation gain 125 feet

Backyards. A good rest stop in tall firs of East Norway Hill County Park. Climb to cross busy 124th (some parking). A nursery marsh-field left, houses right.

Ascend to 400-foot top of East Norway Hill. Fields. Acreage estates. Horses. Broad view east to Cascades. Descend to Sammamish valley. At bottom, cross railroad tracks to limited parking by Woodinville-Redmond Road.

The short stretch of trail to the Sammamish River is not officially open. And there's no bridge. So, to continue onward a detour is necessary.

Sammamish River to Bear Creek Valley, 4 miles, elevation gain 650 feet

Until a bridge is built, detour south to 145th. For compensation, at that point take a sidetrip into park-like grounds of Chateau Ste. Michelle Winery. Walk the trails. See the duck ponds.

Cross the river and turn north on the riverbank path (see Sammamish River Trail). Alternatively, if driving, go north on 148th to the swath and good parking.

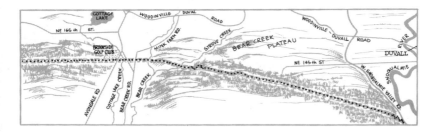

Tolt Pipeline Trail

From the riverbank to 148th the trail is in Sammamish County Park; nice fields, marsh grasses, river, waterfowl. Total distance of this detour is 1 mile.

Ascend steeply from 148th to a 350-foot crest. Horse ranches. Nice woods. Views back down to the Sammamish and over to East Norway Hill.

Where the pipeline makes an air crossing of the deep gulch of 155 Avenue, find a path to the right down in woods. On the far side of the gulch climb steeply to a subtop hill at 350 feet. Big stable here. Horse estates.

Drop to a tangled ravine, then begin a steady uphill in big-fir forest. Pass a pleasant vale to left — pastures, barn, horses, sheep. Climb to the 545-foot summit of Hollywood Hill and a road, 168 Avenue NE; limited parking. Grand views west to downtown Seattle, Puget Sound, Olympics. Continue through pastures, cows, horses, old barns. Then into forest. At the east edge of the high plateau, views of Pilchuck, Sultan, Index, Phelps.

Descend in wildland to remote quiet. Continue on the flat, by pastures, marshes, to the green valley bottom of Bear Creek and Brookside Golf Course. Here at Avondale Road is good parking.

Note that all along this Hollywood Hill stretch are paths taking off this way and that. What marvels lie hidden in these woods?

In 1977 the question might well have been asked. In 1988 the answer, for the most part, is "new houses — bushels of new houses — googols of new houses — miles of new fences."

Bear Creek Valley to Snoqualmie Valley, 4 miles, elevation gain 350 feet

Cross the splendid flat bottom of Bear Creek Valley, which actually has three creeks and tributaries, plus marshes, pastures, woods. In succession cross Avondale Road (parking), Cottage Lake Creek, Bear Creek Road (parking), Mink Farm Road (parking), Bear Creek, and Struve Creek. Passing houses secluded in woods, start upward in wildwoods, climbing to the summit of Bear Creek Plateau at 525 feet.

Stay high nearly 2 miles, largely in woods, much still wild, though the developers have in mind building several New Redmonds up here by the end of the century. Until that happens, trails will continue to take off every which way over the plateau, many not posted "Private Keep Out" and thus open to exploration.

The pipeline gives views out to the Cascades, down to Snoqualmie pastures. At last it descends on a switchbacking service road to the West Snoqualmie Valley Road at 50 feet, close to the Snoqualmie River. Very cramped parking here.

To continue, turn south ½ mile, then east on Novelty Hill Road (NE 124th) 1 mile across the river and valley to join the Snoqualmie River Trail at Novelty.

To pick up the Tolt Pipeline and follow it east into the Cascades, see *Footsore 2.*

One-way trip 11½ miles, allow 8 hours
High points 480, 400, 545, and 525 feet, elevation gain 1600 feet
Bus: many Metro lines to Bothell, walk ½ mile to Blyth Park

ISSAQUAH ALPS

When Puget Sound City began sprawling eastward beyond Lake Washington the developments concentrated on the lower and flatter lands, leaving the higher and steeper for later. Notably spared from overnight citification was the finger of highlands reaching 20 miles out from the Cascade front to the shores of Lake Washington. So dramatic was the contrast between homes and highways and shopping centers proliferating below and wilderness lingering above that a social opportunity was easily recognized — the chance to have spacious wildlands and long forest trails within the heart of the megalopolis predicted by century's end to be pushing its frontiers against the upthrust of the Cascade Mountains.

Not only are these trails accessible by private automobile in a half-hour or less from any home in King County (and northern Pierce and southern Snohomish Counties and — not counting ferry time — eastern Kitsap County) but many of the trailheads, existing or potential, lie on public transit lines, giving rise to the description, "Wilderness on the Metro 210" — a crucial consideration in years ahead when gridlocks and/or $5-a-gallon gasoline will phase out the dominance of the private automobile.

Westernmost of the Issaquah Alps is Cougar Mountain, leaping from the waters of Lake Washington to a highest peak of 1595 feet — an astounding elevation so near Seattle, as tall as three and a half Queen Anne Hills one atop the other. Here, in 1985, was established King County's largest park, the Cougar Mountain Regional Wildland Park. When complete, the regional park, the adjoining Coal Creek County Park, and the trail corridors leading in from all sides will comprise an "in city" green retreat totaling at least 5000 acres.

Next east in line is Squak Mountain State Park, occupying 600-odd acres of the summit ridge, topping out at an elevation of 2000 feet. Given to the people by the Bullitt family and guaranteed by terms of the gift to remain "forever wild," the park can — and must — be tripled in size by acquiring the cliffs on the east and west sides of the mountain, at once expanding the wildness and preserving wildlife travel corridors connecting Cougar to Squak to Tiger — which connects to the Cascades.

Tiger Mountain, next east, is a range of peaks extending from West Tiger to Middle Tiger to South Tiger and culminating in East Tiger, 3004 feet. The altitude is enough that snows can pile deep from October to May, to stay for weeks or melt off overnight. So subjected are the heights to frost, hot sun, and strong winds from every point of the compass that the plant communities — the silver fir and the Alaska huckleberry and the lupine and paintbrush and penstemon — give verisimilitude to "Alps." In 1980 the state Department of Natural Resources established the Tiger Mountain State Forest. Details of management remain to be worked out but quiet-trail recreation and wildlife habitat will be prominent.

Completing the Issaquah Alps are Grand Ridge, glanced at in this chapter and the one preceding; Taylor Mountain, the vital connecting link in the wildlife travel route from Tiger to the Cedar River watershed and the Cascades; and beyond the Raging River — a stream with no pretensions to origins in the high

Cougar Mountain trail

Cascades, belonging wholly to the Alps — Rattlesnake Mountain, treated in *Footsore 2.*

To see how much progress has been made in the last decade preserving green and quiet spaces in the Alps, the reader is referred to the first edition of this book, wherein the newly invented term "Issaquah Alps" first was given more than ephemeral status. There now are *no trails* on Cougar, Squak, or Tiger legally open to vehicles. *No shooting* of any kind (gun, bow-and-arrow, slingshot) is permitted on Cougar and Squak; on Tiger only shotguns are allowed and these only during hunting season. There are scofflaws in the Alps, just as there are in Bellevue Shopping Square. But the vigilance of law-abiding — and law-enforcing — citizens is helping officials tame the crazies.

In this edition, unlike predecessors, all the described trails are either on public land or on private lands open to hikers through the traditional pass-through ("tolerated trespassing") policy.

However, to date not an inch of trail in the Alps has been built by — or is maintained by — public funds. Everything has been done and *is* done by unpaid volunteers — the Volunteers of Washington, The Mountaineers, the Issaquah Alps Trails Club, Scouts and Campfire Girls and other youth groups, senior groups, school groups, church groups, and bushwhacking hermits. Many of the trails are so regularly brushed out by participants in the Adopt-a-Trail Program or are so well-tromped by throngs that they have the look of national park promenades. Others, though, obvious to the eye in winter, are annually swallowed by the spring growth of salmonberries-nettles-sword-ferns-bracken. The trails described in these pages all are "findable" but some are "keepable" only by the experienced wildland navigator equipped with the proper maps.

Fuller treatment of all the trails, with detailed maps, is in the books published by the Issaquah Alps Trails Club: *Guide to Trails of Tiger Mountain,* by William K. Longwell, Jr.; *Trails of Cougar Mountain Regional Wildland Park,* by Ralph Owen and the author of this here book; and *Trails of Squak Mountain,* by Jack Hornung, and *Trails of Grand Ridge and East Sammamish Plateau.*

USGS maps: Mercer Island, Issaquah, Maple Valley, Hobart, Fall City, Snoqualmie
Maps and guidebooks of the Issaquah Alps Trails Club are available at map shops, hike shops, and bookstores.
Walkable all year

COUGAR MOUNTAIN REGIONAL WILDLAND PARK

In 1980 the then-new Issaquah Alps Trails Club publicly proposed that the inner sanctuary of Cougar Mountain (as the Newcastle Hills had come to be called) be preserved as a "great big green and quiet place." In 1983 the King County Council and Executive formally adopted the plan. Acquisitions began in 1984 and continue in 1987, with major steps remaining before the optimum boundaries are achieved. However, in 1985 it already was King County's largest park and seemed sure to ultimately become one of the largest urban-core parks in the nation devoted solely to non-mechanized trail recreation and to wildlife habitat.

A companion goal is a Newcastle Historic District, ideally as part of a more comprehensive Coal Country National Historic District. The excitement up north is properly honored by a Klondike National Historic Park, with one of its segments on Seattle's Skid Road. But the distant gold was no more than a flash in the pan. The local coal, exported from docks at the edge of the Skid Road, fueled the Puget Sound economy from the 1860s into the 20th century. Mining continued at Newcastle until 1963 — and is still underway a few miles to the south at Black Diamond. The story is treated at length, with maps and photos, in *Coals of Newcastle,* by Dick and Lucile McDonald.

The Regional Wildland Park exemplifies the geographical phenomenon of the whole being greater than the sum of its parts. Taken individually, the Newcastle Historic District, the Western Creeks (Coal, May, and China), the Curious Valley (the Long Marsh), the Far Country, De Leo Wall, the High Basins, the Summit Ridge, The Precipice, and The Wilderness are splendid, each in its own way. Assembled together and made one, they form a unity the greater for the diversity.

The park boundaries are "opportunistic," meaning they are flexible, ready to take advantage of opportunities that may arise between the present day and the time — not too far off — when Cougar Mountain is "built out." The core park may total something between 3000 and 4000 acres. This, however, will be only a portion of the Cougar Mountain greenlands. Contiguous to the park and essentially part of it is Coal Creek Park; close by, with a trail connection sought, is May Creek Park.

As land-developers seek approval of their plats, they consult with government and the citizenry to determine the wants for greenbelt dedication. Corridors have been obtained by such dedications along Far Country Creek from the south, De Leo Wall and China Creek from the west, and Hilltop Creek and Anti-Aircraft Creek from the north. All will carry trails that lead from the neighborhoods and from Metro bus stops to the park. Other such corridors are being sought on the north from the Metro 210 bus stop at Eastgate, I-90's Exit 13, and the Metro 210 Park & Ride lot at Goode's Corner, and on the east from West Fork Tibbetts Creek and Newcastle Queen Creek. The proposed Precipice Trail would wrap around the north and east sides of Cougar, hooking up a number of trails.

King County Parks will not have the trailheads signed and "officially open" until 1989 or later and for that reason they are described here in some detail. Keep in mind that until County Parks arrives in force, most of the signs and trail maintenance will be by volunteers. If you don't like their work, you can't fire them — but you can join them.

Trailheads

King County Parks eventually will install official trailhead signs and provide for parking. Until then a bit of careful navigation will be required. However, all the trailheads described here are readily findable and fully open to the public. (*Note:* these are the *major* trailheads; lesser ones are described in *50+ Hikes.*)

Coal Creek Townsite Trailhead

Newcastle was a floating sort of town. The initial main settlement was off the Coal Creek-Newcastle Road on 72 Street; still inhabited, it was known as "Old Newcastle" or "Old Town." The final center of activity, farther up Coal Creek, was officially designated on the maps as "Coal Creek" and locally known as "New Town." In these pages we refer to it as Coal Creek Townsite.

Go off I-90 at Exit 11 or Exit 13 to Newport Way. Turn east or west, as the case may be, to SE 164th. Turn south on this arterial, which changes names at every turn, at last becoming Lakemont Boulevard. At 3 miles from Newport Way the road makes a horseshoe bend around a crossing of Coal Creek.

Alternatively, go off I-405 on Exit 10 to Coal Creek Parkway. In 2.7 miles turn left on Coal Creek-Newcastle Road, which in 2 miles comes to the horseshoe bend, where it changes name to Lakemont Boulevard.

Parking (1988) is on a gravel deadend stub that goes off the county road at the horseshoe bend to a gate blocking access to public vehicles. Elevation, 600 feet.

Nike Park Trailhead

Drive SE 164th-Lakemont Boulevard 2.3 miles south from Newport Way or 0.8 mile north from Coal Creek Townsite. Turn east and up on SE Cougar Mountain Way. In 0.6 mile, where it turns sharp northeast to become 168th, go off south on 166 Way SE. In 0.7 mile is Nike Park, planned to be the point where public vehicles stop. Now become a King County park serving as a trailhead for the Regional Park, this is where the Army had its Nikes in underground silos. Elevation, 1200 feet.

Radar Park Trailhead

From the turnoff to 166th (see above) continue on 168th, which turns sharp right to become SE 60th. At 0.6 mile from 166th, turn steeply uphill right on Cougar Mountain Drive. At 0.8 mile from SE 60th is the outer gate, closed much of the day and much of the year. Elevation, 1350 feet. When the outer gate is open, drive 0.3 mile more to the inner gate at the entry to Radar Park, containing the summit of Anti-Aircraft Peak. This is where the Army had its command radar for the Nikes. The trailhead is at the outside of the inner gate. Elevation, 1400 feet.

Lakemont Gorge (Exit 13) Trailhead

Go off I-90 on Exit 13 and park by the concrete barricade on the stub-end pointing south into the gorge. Or, get off the Metro 210 bus at the stop just across I-90 and walk back through the underpass. Pass the barricade and drop off the bank to the trailhead sign. Elevation, 200 feet.

West Tibbetts Creek Trailhead

Go off I-90 on Exit 15 and drive south on Highway 900 to the Newport Way stoplight. Continue on Highway 900 for 0.9 mile south from the stoplight. The obscure trailhead is on the north bank of Clay Pit Creek (unsigned) just where it crosses under the highway. Park on nearby shoulders — carefully. Elevation, 200 feet.

Wilderness Creek Trailhead

From the Newport Way stoplight (see above) drive Highway 900 south 2.6 miles to an official and well-signed trailhead parking area. Elevation, 365 feet.

Other Trailheads

The Far Country Creek Trailhead will follow a corridor — already dedicated to King County Parks — along Far Country Creek from May Valley near the May Valley School. This will be the main southern entry to the Regional Park, which it will enter in the Far Country basin, there connecting to the Duxduwabc Trail and the Far Country Lookout trail.

The park will have two entries from the southwest (south of Coal Creek). The corridors for both have been dedicated. Both will emanate from Lake Boren (King County) Park and will proceed easterly, one along China Creek, the other along the south face (De Leo Wall) of Marshall's Hill.

These lesser trailheads can be used as of 1988 but will not be fully developed until perhaps 1990 or later.

Bus: Metro 210 to Exit 13 (Ultimately, Metro 210 trailheads will be located on Newport Way in Eastgate and at the junction of Newport Way and Highway 900.)

Seattle & Walla Walla Railroad–Coal Creek Park (map — page 137)

The peaks of Cougar Mountain — the Newcastle Hills — wrap in a horseshoe around the basin of Coal Creek. Seattle's first railroad never got to the Inland Empire nor even the Cascades, but in 1878 it did attain a profitable deadend at Coal Creek's Newcastle mines, then King County's major industry. In 1933, with the "company" mine already three years defunct, the railroad gave up the ghost — the 55 years of ghosts who nowadays walk the woods in company of coyote and deer and bear. A campaign is in progress, led by the Seattle & Walla Walla RR Committee, to place the 22-mile route from the site of the King Street coal docks on Elliott Bay through Renton to Newcastle on the National Historic Register. The final stretch of grade to the deadend has

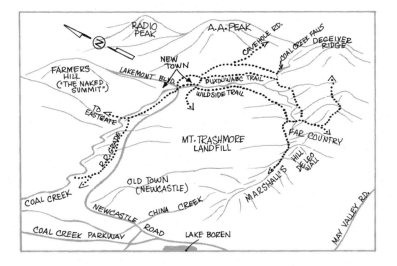

become a favorite among walkers seeking the flavor of history and the sounds of creeks and birds, preserved as it is in Coal Creek (King County) Park.

Park at Coal Creek Townsite trailhead, elevation 600 feet.

Cross the county road to a field, pass a remnant of concrete foundation from the hotel, and at the field edge find Elizabeth's Trail, descending the ravine dug for a tram which brought supplies up to the hotel and company store. Beyond the footbridge over Coal Creek (dry in summer, the water seeping into the mines) turn downvalley onto the rail grade, a wide and level path except for the short detours around the heaps of waste rock dumped from the "gypo" mines which operated after the company mine and railroad quit.

The perceptive and sensitive walker will spot bits and pieces of the past and conjure up that half-century bustle of railroading and mining: chunks of coal, brick, rusty iron; concrete foundations of a power plant and of the locomotive turntable; climbing roses blooming high in trees, the pinkish gaiety of apple-blossom time. Signs note the location of the railroad ticket office-waiting room, the coal bunkers, the Newcastle School (1914-1969), the takeoff of the spur line of the Washington Lumber & Spar logging railroad, which from 1920 to 1925 extended 13 miles of lines through the high basins.

The history is near-submerged in the "new wilderness" rebuilt by nature in the past half-century; the tall, steep walls and lush forest of the gorge block out sights of civilization and soak up the noise, making room for the babble of creek and chirping of birds. In season, spawning salmon are fed upon by bald eagles, great blue heron, kingfishers, bears, coyotes, raccoons, and weasels; Coal Creek serves as a major link in the wildlife travel corridor between Lake Washington and the Cascades.

At 1 mile the grade is obliterated by the Cinder Mine, where waste rock dumped from the company mines was cooked by the spontaneous combustion of coal into pink and yellow clinkers. Until 1984 these were mined for processing into cinder blocks and running tracks.

Beyond the pit the grade resumes and enters The Farm, as it was until 1977. The short-trip stroller turns around here, 1½ flat and easy miles from the trailhead. However, roaming the fields where the cows so recently grazed adds a pastoral element to the historical picture. A farm lane winds down the slope, past a made pond (cattails, frogs, and ducks) to a petite Grand Canyon where the creek cuts a wall of tawny sandstone and tumbles over tawny blocks. Peer into tawny-bottomed pools for trout.

Round trip 3 miles, allow 2 hours
High point 600 feet, elevation gain (on return) 50 feet

Coal Creek Park continues downstream from The Farm 1½ miles to a crossing of Coal Creek Parkway, location of a very good (unsigned) trailhead for folks who don't mind wading the creek, over and over again. This stretch of gorge-protected wildland forest will be more popular when the boot-built path is improved — substantially. The park extends farther downstream, to I-405, but the walking there is more of community than regional interest.

As for the Seattle & Walla Walla Railroad, at The Farm it leaves Coal Creek and takes aim on Renton. The route to there and onward to Seattle is fully described in *Trails of Cougar Mountain Regional Wildland Park.*

Coal Creek Townsite Loop (map — page 137)

Totally ignorant of the past, a person can stroll this little loop with great pleasure, enjoying the creek, the forest mixture of native maple and cotton-wood and exotic poplar, the intermingling of blossoms of wildflowers with those of garden escapes gone wild. The deeper appreciation, of course, is to look beneath the half-century of greening to the decades of industrial grime and noise, of human work and play, happiness and tragedy. "But where," asks the visitor, informed that Coal Creek town was the second and last site of Newcastle life and labor, "Did it all *go*?" Some of it rotted into the ground and was grown over by the green. Most of it was hauled away piece by piece, salvaged and scavenged and recycled, as was America's way of life in the Great Depression.

Interpretive signs aid the imagination in reconstructing the scene of olden days. The books published by the Trails Club help more. The fullest introduction is the annual (first Sunday in June) Return to Newcastle, when a History Tent displays photos, maps, and artifacts; former residents tell of mine days, school days, railroad days; guides lead tours of the historical district.

Park at Coal Creek Townsite trailhead, elevation 600 feet.

For a prelude, take the short path into the ravine of Red Town Creek on the upslope side of the parking area. In the creek bed is exposed coal of the No. 4 Seam; this was how the wealth of Coal Creek was discovered in 1863.

Then, walk past the gate. Hill Street climbs steeply left, the return leg of the loop. Go straight ahead into the woods on the Wildside Trail. The path follows the grade of a road once used to haul logs to a sawmill and, after that, by the gypo miners who took over the area after the Pacific Coast Coal Company quit in 1930. The Bagley Seam lies beneath the trail as it crosses Coal Creek to the site of the Wash House, whose foundations lie buried under a heap of waste rock dumped by the gypos. The miners coming off shift went directly to the Wash House and then home, where they were cleaner than their wives — who were, however, eventually granted a weekly Ladies Day. The way intersects a modern truck road, now abandoned. Turn left on it to the 22-foot concrete arch of the Ford Slope, which from 1910 to 1926 was the center of company mining, embodying the newest and highest technology. It went down the Muldoon Seam at a 42-degree angle for 1740 feet (850 vertical feet, to 250 feet below sea level). Eleven electric locomotives worked underground on a number of levels in the Muldoon and adjoining seams. The coal was lifted to the surface by a steam hoist, the mine cars hauled down Coal Creek by the electrics for dumping in the top of the bunkers, which loaded from the bottom into rail cars for transport to Seattle.

Continue on the road from the Ford Slope, passing a sidetrail, right, to the concrete foundations of the steam hoist and onward to a concrete dam in Coal Creek. The reservoir supplied water to the mining operation and doubled as a sawmill pond. It tripled as the ol' swimmin' hole, where on alternate days in summer the girls swam and the boys hid out in the woods, and the boys swam and the girls hid out, neither sex owning any swimming garb other than that provided by Mother Nature.

The road climbs to a T, 750 feet, with the Duxduwabc Trail, the approximate route used by the Duwamish and Snoqualmie peoples for overland travel between Coal Creek and May Creek, and later by farmers and miners. Turn left through Red Town, the major neighborhood of Coal Creek Town, with 80 houses on four streets running parallel to the existing trail. The name came from the color the houses were painted by the company, which owned them. Other neighborhoods were White Town, Rainbow Town, Finn Town, and Greek Village. The trail crosses the 1000-foot-wide band in which the coal seams of the Newcastle Anticline intersect the surface: from south to north, the Jones, Dolly Varden, Ragtime, Shoo Fly, Muldoon, May Creek, Bagley, No. 3, and No. 4; off by itself to the north, dating from a later geological age, is the Primrose Seam.

Pass a sidepath, right, to an old strip mine in the Bagley Seam; a sidepath, left, down a ravine formed by the collapse of an entry tunnel into the Bagley Seam; the Cave Hole Road, right; and the site, on the right, of the palatial Superintendent's House. Turn left and descend Hill Street past the sites of the Hospital, the Doctor's House, and the Saloon.

Loop trip 1 mile, allow 1 hour
High point 750 feet, elevation gain 150 feet

De Leo Wall via the Wildside Trail (map — page 137)

Plummeting 600 feet from the 1125-foot summit of Marshall's Hill, the naked cliffs of De Leo Wall (named for a homesteader family) are as tall as several hundred feet. The views over May Valley to Renton and Tacoma and Mt. Rainier make a satisfying spot to sit and eat corned beef sandwiches and apple pie. The trail beside marsh and swamp, through forest young and old, is the choicest in the vicinity.

Park at Coal Creek Townsite trailhead, elevation 600 feet.

Walk past the gate and straight ahead into the woods on the Wildside Trail. Crossing Coal Creek and passing the Wash House site, in a short bit it intersects a modern (now abandoned) truck road. On the far side it climbs from the valley floor onto the valley wall and pretty much stays there, upsy-downsy.

This is the Curious Valley, trenched by a considerable stream flowing from the glacier front and vastly "over-size" for the amount of modern water. For a mile and more the valley bottom, up to ⅛ mile wide, is occupied by the Long Marsh (Swamp), an impenetrable tulgeywood. The north end of the wetland drains through the mine yards around the Ford Slope into Coal Creek; the south end, over the andesite outcrop of Far Country Falls and down to May Creek.

Along the east valley wall runs the Duxduwabc Trail, leading from Red Town to the Ball Park to the Far Country and on down Far Country Creek to May Valley. This is the hypothesized route of the Duwamish-Snoqualmie peoples — and the certain route of the firewood loggers who worked here until establishment of the Regional Park. But the west valley wall hasn't seen wheels in years; it's the wild side.

At ¼ mile from the trailhead is a major junction, 700 feet. The right fork ascends to China Summit and follows China Creek out to Old Newcastle. Go left, dropping to the valley floor, to a junction at 1 mile. The left fork is a cross-valley connector to the Duxduwabc Trail at the Ball Park. Go right, up a bit and along the sidehill to the horse-mucked Marshall's Hill Trail. Jog left on it 90 steps and turn right on the Wildside, which quickly Ts with a woods road. Go right, close by the edge of a large bog to the left; no cranberries, kalmia, or sundew have been found in the bog but Labrador tea is prominent.

Coal Creek

The longest, wildest stretch ensues, the path at one point splitting into two alternates which soon rejoin, passing a cattail marsh and Cottonwood Creek, and ending at a junction, 1¾ miles, 700 feet.

To the left is a connector trail across the Curious Valley to the Duxduwabc Trail at the entry to the secluded basin of the Far Country, the route to the Far Country Lookout and The Wilderness, as well as out to May Valley.

Go right from the junction on Dave's Trail, rounding a spur from Marshall's Hill, crossing the cool trickle of Dave's Creek, and ascending into fine dark forest of mixed conifers. At 2¾ miles, 950 feet, the path emerges on a sky-open buttress, an outcrop of andesite plucked steep by that old glacier. Gaze over pastures where cows graze and dogs bark, to Renton and Southcenter, I-5 and Sea-Tac Airport, Lake Washington and the southern Olympics, Rainier and the Tacoma Smelter stack and the steam plume of a pulpmill and the sometimes steam of what's left of Mt. St. Helens. The grassy bald is edged by madrona, serviceberry, *Ceanothus sanguineus,* and not far off are a few Oregon white oak. In spring the top of the wall is brightened by paintbrush and blue-eyed Mary and strawberry, Easter lily and chocolate lily, a garden growing to one side of the sky.

Round trip 5½ miles, allow 4 hours
High point 950 feet, elevation gain 350 feet plus many ups and downs

Coal Creek Falls (map — page 137)

Hikers had pioneered trails throughout Cougar Mountain from Old New-castle through China Creek and the Curious Valley to the Far Country and The Wilderness, were thronging here, thronging there, thronging everywhere — and yet this secret nook escaped detection. To be sure, after heavy rains when all the creeks were up, a mighty suspicion lurked in the ears of pedestrians hearing the sound of thunder in the brush. But the brush was of a sort to make an ape quail. Then a neat sequence of ancient logging roads was found, the nook was revealed to human eyes, and instantly became one of the best-loved short hikes.

Park at Coal Creek Townsite trailhead, elevation 600 feet.

Walk by the gate and turn left up Hill Street, which on the flat of Red Town, 750 feet, bends right and becomes the Duxduwabc Trail. Just past the site of the Superintendent's House turn left, uphill, on the Cave Hole Road. Aban-doned now to be a trail, until establishment of the Regional Park this route was driven by trucks of firewood loggers; earlier in the century, it was the horse-and-wagon access to the Klondike Reservoir and various coal prospects. The Pacific Coast Coal Company, builder of the road, took care not to undermine it by digging too close to the surface, but the gypos mined to the grass roots, causing the subsequent slumps of the ground surface known as "cave holes." Thus the name, given by hikers, because until the federal Office of Surface Mining began filling them, the road gave access to scores of fascinating pits. The road-trail ascends to the Clay Pit Road at 1200 feet, 1½ miles from Coal Creek Townsite trailhead.

The ascent from Red Town begins with a zig left across an open-pit mine in the No. 3 Seam and a zag right to recross the No. 3, then the Bagley Seam; at the corner a sidetrail goes off left to Red Town Creek dam and the Military Road. At ⅔ mile, 950 feet, go off the Cave Hole Road right, on the signed trail to Coal Creek Falls. The way crosses the Bagley and Muldoon Seams, contours (up and down) south along slopes high above the Curious Valley, and at last turns sharp left into the deep cleft of Coal Creek, 950 feet.

In winter the falls do often roar, boiling up gales of spray to fill the gorge. But in that season they often fall dead silent, a crystal palace of icicles. In summer they also are quiet, a drip-drip-drip down the 30-foot slab — yet enough on the hottest of days to cool the shadows under the big hemlocks and maples of the mist forest. A litter of granite erratics dropped by the glacier contrasts with potholes swirled out in the tawny bedrock sandstone. Of interest to geology students: though Coal Creek here is flowing over sedimentary structures, a stone's throw to the south the bedrock is volcanic, an andesite breccia. Something to muse upon while picnicking.

Round trip 2½ miles, allow 2 hours
High point 950 feet, elevation gain 350 feet plus ups and downs

Anti-Aircraft Peak–Clay Pit Peak Loop (map — page 144)

Here is the sky country of Cougar Mountain, in the high basins where Coal Creek pulls itself together from the seepages of Klondike Swamp, Coyote

Swamp, and the Wilderness Fork, and where — across the low divide of Cougar Pass — West Fork Tibbetts Creek has its source in Lame Bear Swamp. This is wind country, where living gales roar through the trees, and cloud country, where the storm-driven mists extinguish exterior reality. Finally, it's snow country, often white for weeks at a time and subject to blizzarding from October through April. Above the basins, ringing them to exclude too-vivid reminders of Puget Sound City, are three of Cougar's summits. A loop that samples the basins also leads to the longest and widest views.

Park at Nike Park trailhead, elevation 1200 feet.

Poke about Nike Park. There's little to see because the Nike missiles were underground and the silos have been welded shut. With Cold War curiosity satisfied, let the hike begin.

The start is on the Clay Pit Road, where trucks haul fire clay out to the Newcastle Brick Plant. The lease predates the Regional Park and has some years to run. However, the trucks roll only a few weeks of the year, when the clay is dry enough, and only on weekdays; when the trucks *are* rolling, walkers will not wish to spend much time on the road and definitely will want to keep an eye out.

Pass the Radio Peak trail, left, and the Cave Hole Road, right. At a long ¼ mile go off left on a narrow lane, the Klondike Trail. Primevally the headwaters basin of Coal Creek held a lake a mile long and a thousand feet wide. With a dam across the lower end to increase storage capacity to 10,000,000 gallons, it was the principal water supply for the mines at Coal Creek Town, to wash coal and make steam. Perhaps partly due to leakage into the mines, but largely because of evaporation when the old-growth forest was logged in the 1920s, the lake became the Klondike Swamp, an enormously complex (partly, it's cattail marsh) and rich wetland, certain to remain a secure wildlife refuge even when the trails are thronged.

At ¼ mile from the Clay Pit Road pass the trail, right, to Cougar Pass; for a shorter loop hike, take this trail (see below). In a scant 1 mile from the road turn right on the Lost Beagle Trail, which ascends forest above the swamp to the Cyclone Fence enclosing Radar Park, barring hikers from easy backdoor access to the summit of Anti-Aircraft Peak. The trail follows the fence, passing the Anti-Aircraft (A-A) Ridge Trail, right; mark it, because this is the route of the loop, after a sidetrip for views.

The trail emerges from woods at Radar Park trailhead, 1400 feet, ¾ mile from the Klondike Trail. A few steps to the left is the entry to Radar Park, location of the radar and command facilities for the missiles in Nike Park. Nothing remains now but the broad lawns, the broad views to Lake Washington and Seattle, and the summit knoll, 1450 feet. Come here on an icy winter day to see the winds pile snowdrifts in a North Dakota-like manner. The biggest views — the airplane-wing views — are not inside the Cyclone Fence but across the entry road, on the grassy knoll of the Million Dollar View. When the brush has been cut back, as in future it will be regularly, the vista extends from Olympics to Cascades, Seattle to Bellevue, Lake Sammamish (a swan-dive below) to Mt. Baker and the San Juan Islands.

Full up on views, retreat into the woods and set out down the A-A Ridge Trail, through alder-maple forests, fir-hemlock-cedar forests. In a short bit cross a railroad grade (taken left, it loops back to Radar Park) and continue down, marveling at the enormous stumps of old-growth Douglas fir, enjoying the standing trees, 60 and 100 years young. At 1 mile from the Lost Beagle Trail is

Cougar Pass, 1250 feet, the divide between Coal Creek and West Fork Tibbetts Creek. At the junction here the right fork leads in a scant ¼ mile to the Klondike Trail; a loop from there to here, skipping Anti-Aircraft Peak, is much shorter.

Turn left along the edge of Lame Bear Swamp, as formidably inaccessible to humans (though not bears) as a wetland gets. At ⅓ mile from Cougar Pass the Tibbetts Marsh Trail is intersected. The left descends to cross West Fork Tibbetts Creek and climb Anti-Aircraft Peak (another loop, you see). Turn right, uphill, ¼ mile and emerge from woods to the wide-open spaces of the Clay Pit, 1375 feet.

The Clay Pit Road goes right 1 mile to the trailhead. But first, ascend the stripped slopes of the pit (note black streaks — the Primrose Seam) to the top, a few yards from the wooded summit of Clay Pit Peak, 1525 feet. The views are out over the Sammamish basin and East Sammamish Plateau to the Cascades, from Pilchuck and Baker to Glacier and Index and Teneriffe and Si.

When the mining ceases, as it may any year or not for some years, it is proposed that the notch cut in the impervious clay to drain the pit floor be dammed. Nature would then take care of creating a large lake-marsh, so shaped during the final days of mining to provide wildlife islets and peninsulas and coves. Within a decade or two the great blue herons would begin nesting.

Loop trip 5½ miles, allow 4 hours
High point 1525 feet, elevation gain 550 feet

Wilderness Peak via the Clay Pit (map — page 144)

The name, "The Wilderness," was not given lightly. It truly is a wildland, partly railroad-logged in the 1920s and cat-logged in the 1940s, but in each case by a quick once-through, man's intrusion limited to a few days, nature then let alone to rebuild. Part never was logged at all and the virgin forest of Douglas fir on the slopes of Wilderness Peak is as noble an assemblage of ancient snagtops and wolves as is to be found so near Seattle. Wilderness

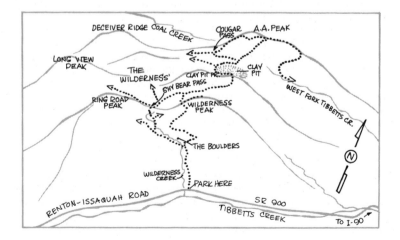

Peak is the culmination of The Wilderness, and of Cougar Mountain, its elevation of 1595 feet the highest peak. The route described here is the fastest way to the summit — and it is not all that fast — and that's what makes wilderness.

Park at Nike Park trailhead, elevation 1200 feet.

Walk the Clay Pit Road, then cat tracks, to the uppermost gouge of the Clay Pit, 1¼ miles, 1500 feet. Proceed southeasterly around the summit plateau of Clay Pit Peak and in a short bit drop off the end of a cat track to another, a trench, and turn right. When this trench deadends, go left a few feet and drop to another. The trenches are the means by which fire clay miners "prospect," and here they continue all the way to the end of sedimentary rocks in Blackwater Saddle, low point in the ridge between Clay Pit and Wilderness Peaks and the divide between Coal Creek headwaters and May Creek drainage. Blackwater Pond, colored by decomposing alder leaves, marks the end of the railroad logging and the subsequent growth of alder-maple, a forest now in climax luxuriance, cool-cloistered in summer, starkly bare-limbed and sky-bright in winter.

From the pond, 1450 feet, the animal-man path turns steeply up the slopes of Wilderness Peak, the underlying rocks now volcanic, the forest a mix of conifers and fern-draped maples. The way flattens out in the devils club and elderberry of the soggy-bottomed Penultimate Plateau and intersects a major trail. To the right it is the Wilderness Creek Mainline, descending to Shy Bear Pass and thence down Wilderness Creek to The Boulders. To the left it is the Wilderness Cliffs Mainline, which gets to The Boulders via Wild View Cliff and Big View Cliff. Turn left a few steps, then left on the path climbing to the Ultimate Plateau and the summit of Wilderness Peak, 1595 feet, 1⅓ miles from the top of the Clay Pit.

There is no view. The Douglas firs growing here were perhaps half a century old when the gypos came through, high-grading, and weren't big enough to bother with. But now they're getting on to the century mark. — And a few steps away is where the gypos quit and the old-growth virgin forest begins. When clouds slide through, dimming the trees to Platonic essences, or snowflakes float through white-sagging branches, who needs to see Southcenter?

Round trip 5 miles, allow 4 hours
High point 1595 feet, elevation gain 400 feet

Ingenuities On and About Anti-Aircraft Peak (map — page 147)

The objection to a trailhead on top of a mountain is that the hikes have to be upside-down, descending at the start, ascending at the finish. It doesn't feel natural. What's to be done, then, about the embarrassment of the Radar Park trailhead, barely a hoot and a holler from the summit of A-A Peak?

The throngs find no problem. They love being able to drive to Radar Park, where during World War II a battery of guns protected Issaquah against Japanese attack, and during the Cold War the command radar for the Nikes of Nike Park stood on guard against bombers the Russians didn't have. The picnicking is pleasant, the views are grand, and the excitement is high when the winds blow clouds from the south or snow from the north. An afternoon easily can be spent eating the tuna fish sandwiches and potato salad, strolling the greensward.

For lengthier exercise, a nice little loop can be done from the northeast corner of the Cyclone Fence. See the sign, "To the Trails," just outside the park gate to the east. Find the path at the fence corner, follow it through the woods to a split, take the right (the Lost Beagle Trail) along the fence to the summit plateau, go off and down left on the A-A Ridge Trail, and at the railroad grade turn left to square one, for a loop of about ¾ mile, a sauntering hour.

But to come to grips with the crux, why *not* start by descending? From the Radar Park trailhead, elevation 1400 feet, a person can do the Anti-Aircraft Peak-Clay Pit Peak loop, as described earlier in these pages, and the Lakemont Gorge-Peggy's Trail and West Fork Tibbetts Creek, as described later.

Is it looping you would be? Get a copy of *Trails of Cougar Mountain Regional Wildland Park* and hook up Radio Peak, A-A Peak, Clay Pit Peak, Wilderness Peak. Or confront the ultimate challenge, the Cougar Ring.

Finally, however decadent it may seem to hardy aerobics, there's something to be said for *not* walking uphill. The two-car shuttle, leaving one at the Exit 13 trailhead or the West Fork Tibbetts Creek trailhead, then driving to Radar Park, permits easy enjoyment of the natural splendors without breaking a sweat. Indeed, once a person gets hooked on the two-car dodge, great notions arise of one-way hikes from Radar Park to Coal Creek Townsite, to May Valley, to Lake Washington, to the pot of gold at the bottom end of the rainbow.

Round trips a little bit to a long stretch, allow minutes or hours

Lewis Creek Gorge–Peggy's Trail (map — page 147)

Cougar Mountain offers no happier walk than this ascent through a "virtual rain forest," then a veritable virgin forest, past spectacular waterfalls tumbling down The Precipice, and culminating in the mountain's grandest panoramas of far horizons. Moreover, this is at present the solitary "bus-easy" gateway to the Cougar Mountain Regional Wildland Park, off the Metro 210 and onto the trail. Development will bring some change in the route but the permanence of the trail is guaranteed by the developer and the government.

Park at Exit 13 trailhead, elevation 200 feet. — Or get off the Metro 210 at its regular stop just the other side of I-90.

Walk past the concrete-block barrier, drop off a bank, and cross a soggy meadow to the trailhead sign. A short stretch of boot-beaten trail leads across the hillside to the lower end of a cat road gouged in 1975 to prepare for building Lakemont Boulevard up the gorge; defeated then by a Peasant's Revolt, the project has been revived and soon will require relocation of the trail and destruction of the forest.

The strolling is easy on road-become-trail, up through lovely mixed forest that in a hot summer afternoon is 20 degrees cooler than outside. No logger has been here since the 19th century; in the rich soil and wet bottom the cedars and hemlocks have grown huge, the great maples are hanging gardens of licorice fern, and the understory is a richness of four other ferns, devils club, salmonberry, plus a mysterious patch of periwinkle, last survivor of an 1890s homestead. A walker feels magically transported to an Olympic rain forest. Sidepaths lead off to choice picnic spots.

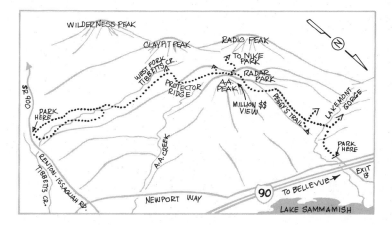

In ½ mile, at 325 feet, turn off the pilot road onto Peggy's Trail, which crosses Lewis-Peltola Creek, runs up against the gorge wall, and gets serious. The tread is narrow and slippery when wet; descending is even more of a trial than ascending, due to the frequency of falling down. But — oh — how fine it is! The forest of the gorge wall is virgin, grown up since a forest fire of the 19th century, and never molested by man except for this skinny little trail. Close to the left is the perilous ravine of Owen Creek, a marvel to gaze down into. The looking also is impressive out through the tops of the virgin trees to the greater chasm of Lewis Creek Gorge. Along about now the hiker newly introduced to the area is likely to join the masses who believe that this is the single most spectacular section of Cougar Mountain, park-worthy in its own right, independently of the Regional Park.

At 600 feet, ½ mile from the pilot road, Peggy's Trail abruptly flattens out on the bench that wraps all around this sector of Cougar, to the joy of the land-developers. A few steps from the brink is Falls Junction. The right fork follows an old railroad grade ¾ mile to the Bears' Orchard, a farm and sometime moonshine factory from 1912 to 1940, now harvested mainly by — who else? (Railroad grade and orchard will be bulldozed into building lots in 1989 or so.)

Turn left, down into and up out of the notch cut in the lip of the bench by Owen Creek. In a few steps is another junction. The summit trail turns right. Left, however, is a sidetrip urged on those adventurers willing to risk injury (should they fall off a log or over a cliff) to view the most awesome geography of the mountain. A precarious path plummets down a wooded rib between twin chasms with sandstone walls, to views this way of Ralph's Falls, that way of Peggy's Falls. Beware!

Peggy's (summit) Trail, having turned right, proceeds gently up beside the creek, passes the Precipice Trail, left, and at 880 feet, 1¾ miles from Exit 13, bursts out on SE 60th. On the far side of the road the way resumes, reverting to steepness to ascend the Upper Precipice. Having crossed the historic Military Road at 1300 feet, a long ¼ mile from SE 60th, it levels out once more at a stone's throw from where Cougar Mountain Drive passes the outer gate of Radar Park. Turn left on the road ¼ mile to Radar Park trailhead. Go off left to the Million Dollar View. Then go right, up the park meadows to the summit of Anti-Aircraft Peak, 1470 feet.

Round trip 5½ miles, allow 4 hours
High point 1470 feet, elevation gain 1300 feet
Bus: Metro 210

West Fork Tibbetts Creek–Bear Ridge–Protector Ridge (map — page 147)

The east slope of Cougar Mountain rises virtually from sea level through The Precipice to the highest peaks. Hidden beneath the treetops of the forest grown up since the railroad logging of the 1920s are deep ravines and sharp-crested ridges, a land-developer's dismay but the delight of hikers. Age-old game traces traveled by the deer and the bear, the coyote and the cougar, on their commute between Cougar and Squak (and east to Tiger and the Cascades), doubling over the centuries as shortcut routes for people on their way to or from Lake Sammamish and Coal Creek, have been taken over by modern pedestrians.

Park on a shoulder of Highway 900 near the West Tibbetts trailhead, elevation 200 feet.

The path begins obscurely on the north bank of Clay Pit Creek and follows an ancient road-trail along the south side of Bear Ridge, the prominent spur between Clay Pit Creek and West Fork Tibbetts Creek. In several hundred feet the trail splits.

The left fork is the Bear Ridge trail, ascending the green shadows deep in the gulch of Clay Pit Creek; bear trails branch off right to the ridge crest and overviews of the awesome gorge of West Tibbetts Creek. In ¾ mile, 600 feet, the way briefly touches West Tibbetts trail, diverges left, and steeply ascends The Precipice atop a thin crest. It then trends westerly to the Fantastic Erratic (largest chunk of glacier-dropped rock known in the Issaquah Alps), to more views of West Tibbetts Gorge, and ends at an intersection with The Precipice Trail, 900 feet, 1 mile from the road.

The right fork is the West Tibbetts trail, rounding the foot of Bear Ridge to West Tibbetts Creek, a year-round joy, cooling a grand gorge. The way follows the creek closely, crossing back and forth, nearly to the touch-and-go junction with Bear Ridge trail at ¾ mile, 600 feet. Leaving the junction, it crosses the creek once more and heads for higher ground near the north rim of the gorge. At 1¼ mile, 1025 feet, the way crosses The Precipice Trail, and at a scant 1½ miles, splits.

The left fork, the West Tibbetts trail, proceeds straight ahead ¼ mile to intersect the Tibbetts Marsh trail, 1235 feet; the left leads to Clay Pit Peak, the right to Anti-Aircraft Peak.

The right fork, the Protector Ridge trail, traverses the low ridge which separates the high basins, containing Lame Bear Swamp and associated wetlands, from the steep east slopes, providing a natural barrier between the Cougar Mountain Regional Wildland Park and the low-density residential development which ultimately may reach this high. It is therefore the park's "protector." In ½ mile the path comes to Radar Park trailhead, 1400 feet, a few steps from the Million Dollar View on one hand and the summit of Anti-Aircraft Peak on the other.

A popular way to do the loopings made possible by these trails is from the top, with a two-car switch, everything downhill.

Round trip 4 miles, allow 3 hours
High point 1400 feet, elevation gain 1200 feet

Wilderness Peak via The Boulders (map — page 144)

The east ridge of Cougar's highest peak is a wonder to behold: from an elevation of 1595 feet it plummets down a virgin forest of cantankerous old Douglas firs, mostly snagtops and wolves, through cliffs of andesite plucked to precipices by the Pleistocene glacier. Slicing a gorge along the south side of the ridge is another marvel, Wilderness Creek, an all-year stream that in winter tumbles and in summer dribbles over rock outcrops beneath house-size chunks of volcanic rock tumbled from the cliffs plucked by the ice.

Much of Cougar Mountain bears manifold marks of man — mining for a century, logging early and logging late, roads built and abandoned, homesteads reclaimed by forest, forests felled for once and all by advancing suburbia. But in The Wilderness man passed through once, swiftly, in a matter of days, a long time ago, and never returned. In the wake of the loggers who spent barely hours in any one spot, there have walked, since then, only bear and cougar and deer and coyote — and, rather recently, hikers.

Park at Wilderness Creek trailhead, elevation 365 feet.

Ascend the straight-up cat track-trail, a gypo gouge of the 1940s. The "high-graders" cut only a few trees and the remaining forest has so thrived in the lush valley as to seem a virgin splendor of large maples and cedars. Close left sounds waterfalling Wilderness Creek; sidepaths lead to nooks for sitting and musing.

In ⅓ mile, 800 feet, is Boulders Junction. The right fork is the Wilderness Cliffs Mainline, ascending steeply to Big View Cliff, Wild View Cliff, and on through virgin forest to Wilderness Peak. However, the route is a bit spooky for the inexperienced wildlander.

The best introductory route is the left fork, the Wilderness Creek Mainline, which contours a short bit to The Boulders, huge blocks of andesite covered with ferns and moss. Picnic here amid the green gloom of handsome big trees, beside the splashing creek, all the cooler on a hot summer afternoon.

The Mainline splits, one piece on either side of the creek, forming a nice little loop; at 975 feet they rejoin. For more distant goals, the best path is on the left (true right).

At 1020 feet, ⅔ mile from the road, the trail splits. The left fork proceeds up the valley wall to Ring Road Peak, with connections to Long View Peak, Doughty Falls, Malignant Deceiver Ridge, and Far Country Lookout.

For the Creek Mainline, diverge right on a side-track to the creek bottom. From here the Fall Line Trail crosses the valley bottom on a log and clambers up cliffs to join the Wilderness Cliffs Mainline.

For the Creek Mainline, go left along the creek. Cross it to the fabulous Cougar Mountain Cave, a nook beneath a chunk of andesite with sleeping room for three bobcats or one bear. Pass the Upper Boulders and recross the

Ferns growing beside Wilderness Creek

creek to a fine, large boggy flat—the Big Bottom. The path hits the lower end of a cat road and ascends to the beautiful fern-hung maples and beautiful big hemlocks of Beautiful Bottom, ¾ mile, 1100 feet. The Beautiful Bottom Trail clambers straight up right to join the Cliffs Mainline.

For the Creek Mainline, continue up the creek to its all-year source in springs seeping from the rock, pass any number of connector trails, and top out at Shy Bear Pass, 1320 feet, 1¼ miles.

At the four-way junction here on the divide between Wilderness Creek and Cabbage Creek, the Long View Peak trail goes left, the Shy Bear Trail straight ahead down Cabbage Creek. The Creek Mainline turns right and ascends to the Penultimate Plateau, 1575 feet. At a junction here, the Blackwater Trail goes left to Clay Pit Peak, the Creek Mainline proceeds straight ahead — changing name to the Cliffs Mainline, a grand looping return for the experienced wildlander.

The summit path goes off left a short bit to the Ultimate Plateau, 1595 feet. Bring a rock from below to add to the summit cairn.

Round trip 3½ miles, allow 3 hours
High point 1595 feet, elevation gain 1230 feet

SQUAK MOUNTAIN STATE PARK

Between 1595-foot Cougar on the west and 3000-foot Tiger on the east is 2000-foot Squak, in some opinion the noblest beast of them all. That it has fewer trails than neighbor mountains is owing not to inferior quality but a smaller floor plan. It's a "pinched" mountain — squeezed between two channels of the Canadian ice. But because of that it's the steepest of the Alps and thus, pound for pound, most challenging. For some years Squak had an evil reputation among hikers because of the illegal wheels. However, in 1987 State Parks received funds that permit it to intensify enforcement. Peace! It's wonderful!

Squak forests were not extensive enough to finance a logging railroad of the sort boasted by Cougar and Tiger. What Squak got was narrow-gauge trucks, a breed of vehicle not much wider than today's ATVs, able to cling to cliffs on skinny little gouges. The gypos high-graded more forests than they clearcut and left large sections strictly alone; the mountain has more virgin timber than any patch of real estate so close to downtown Seattle.

The greatest event in the history of Squak was the purchase of Section 4 by the Bullitt family as a country retreat. In the 1970s the family gave the land — more than 600 acres — to Washington State Parks, stipulating that it be kept "forever wild" — no roads, no tree-cutting, no wheeled machines, not even any horses. (Note: some of the trails described herein are referred to as roads ("North Ridge Road") because that's what they used to be. They aren't anymore.)

Note: As of 1989 a splendid new trail system is being constructed on Squak Mountain by citizen volunteers. There will be trailheads in downtown Issaquah, on Highway 900, and on the southwest side of the mountain. In late 1989 the Issaquah Alps Trails Club published a guidebook to the enhanced trail system.

Trailheads

Washington State Parks has been embarrassed by its ownership of land which lacks official public access. It has in mind two prospective entries.

City of Issaquah Trailhead

The most-wanted trailhead is one that connects to City of Issaquah trails and walkways so that city residents and visitors — including those arriving by Metro 210 bus from all parts of Puget Sound City — can walk from downtown Issaquah along Issaquah Creek and up its tributary, Cabin Creek, to the park boundary. As of 1988 Issaquah Parks and State Parks are considering ways and means. Given success, this will become the most-used trailhead, and could be open as early as 1989.

Highway 900 Trailhead

Purchased by State Parks when the outlook in Issaquah was dim, this land has not been funded by the State Legislature for development. However, it provides an official public route from Highway 900 to the park.

Go off I-90 on Exit 15 and drive south on Highway 900 to the Newport Way stoplight. Continue straight ahead 1.7 miles to the (gated) entry road to the Interpace Clay Pit, where the eventual parking lot will be. Until then, park on the commodious highway shoulder. Elevation, 450 feet.

From the parking lot (to be) the trail (to be, yet already there, de facto, or close enough) ascends to the northwest park corner and intersects the North Ridge Road (now a trail).

Burlington Northern Trailhead

Until State Parks (and the City of Issaquah and the State Legislature) get together, hikers will continue to prefer a trailhead that starts from Highway 900 and ascends the west face of Squak through Burlington Northern lands, which are open to the public through the walk-through ("tolerated trespassing") policy.

From the Newport Way stoplight drive Highway 900 for 2.1 miles south. A few feet south of Milepost 19 and just north of Sunset Quarry, spot a narrow woods road, almost blocked by garbage. Do not drive in. Park nearby on the very narrow highway shoulder. Elevation, 425 feet. (Better, park 0.4 mile north at the "State Parks Trailhead" and walk the powerline service road south to intersect the "garbage road." The latter, gated against public vehicles, is referred to herein as the West Face Road.)

Central Peak–Northeast Face Loop (map — page 152)

This grand loop is a classic of the Alps, on everybody's list of favorites. The whole route is in splendid forest, some ot it alder-maple grown up since the 1920s, some of it big old firs and hemlocks the gypo loggers were in too much of a hurry to molest, and some of it virgin. Though no single smashing view elicits sighs and gasps, at a number of points are windows — cumulatively, to every point of the compass. However, some hikers prefer to do the route when all the windows are closed by clouds, all the views are inward to the forest.

Start at the Burlington Northern trailhead, elevation 425 feet.

Ascend the West Face Road past the wheel-barring gate (feet, feel free), gaining elevation at a meaningful rate but with plenty of things to keep the mind off the hard labor. (Note: this road *is* a road, used by the very occasional

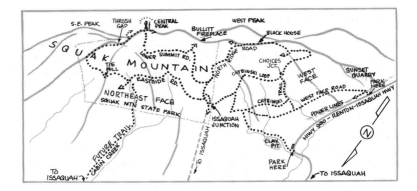

Squak Mountain "over-communication" towers

service vehicles of a radio facility. These are the only wheel tracks you will see
— except for those of the occasional hardened criminal.) The firs and hemlocks and maples and alders are big and old, a classic beauty of a mixed forest.
Creeklets waterfall down green gulches. The mountainside drops steeply off,
opening interior panoramas through a sky of green leaves. Fairy bells and
columbine line the way, and swordfern and lady fern and licorice fern and
maidenhair fern.

At 1¼ miles, 1090 feet, the road switchbacks right, and soon left, and in a
scant 1½ miles passes close by the North Ridge Road, on the left; a few steps
up the latter is Issaquah Junction, 1275 feet, where the East Side Road goes
off left — remember it, it's the return leg of the loop.

Continue up the West Face Road onto the North Ridge Road. For the
simplest route to the summit, at 1400 feet, ¼ mile from the junction, go off left
on Lower Summit Road, which curves south, in and out of forest vales, around
spurs, a joy. At 1700 feet, 2¼ miles, a sideroad climbs right a short distance to
the Bullitt Fireplace, all that remains of their summer home. Continue straight
ahead to Central Peak, 2½ miles, 2000 feet, decorated with a thicket of radio
towers.

Views would be meager were it not for slots cut in the forest to let microwaves
in and out. One gives views of May Valley, Cougar Mountain, Renton, Lake
Washington, Puget Sound, Vashon Island, and the Tacoma Smelter. Another
shows Lakes Sammamish and Washington, Bellevue, the Space Needle, and

Seattle and the Olympic Mountains (Mount Constance, left) from Radar Park

Mt. Baker. To the south is a screened view of the Cedar Hills Garbage Dump, Enumclaw, and Rainier.

Don't quit just because you've bagged the peak — the best of the loop lies ahead. Descend the service road a short bit to 1925 feet and turn left on the Summit Trail, a lovely wildland path down a ravine of lush mixed forest. At a scant 3 miles, in the notch between Central Peak and Southeast Peak, is Thrush Gap Junction, 1500 feet. Turn left, north, on a trail that in the 1920s was a narrow road that barely held the primitive Mack trucks and chain-drive Reos. At little A Creek are stringers of an old bridge, fern gardens in the air. The road contours, blasted from andesite cliffs, a wonderful stroll in ginger, solomon's seal, and oak fern, with screened views out to Issaquah and Tiger Mountain.

At a scant 3½ miles the road-trail abruptly ends on the crest of a spur ridge, 1600 feet. Traces of grade go out on the spur a few feet to a strange clearing. Sawdust! The whole slope is sawdust, partly covered with a gorgeous sprawl of twinflower. Here, high above the valley, a portable sawmill operated — a "tie mill," carted around on a truck, that squared small trees into railroad ties. Another surprise: a view — not of the expected Issaquah but over Cougar Mountain to towers of downtown Seattle.

Plunge down the sawdust into woods, quickly hitting the East Side Road-Trail at 1300 feet. Turn left and contour around tips of spur ridges, deep into an alder-maple ravine, by windows out on the valley. At 4¾ miles the East Side Road completes the loop at Issaquah Junction.

Loop trip 6 miles, allow 5 hours
High point 2000 feet, elevation gain 1600 feet

West Peak Loops (map — page 152)

Squak has a big classic and a pair of little classics, offering the same variety of forests and the same intriguing wanderings. The difference is that these loops are not within the park-as-is but the park-as-it-must-become.

Ascend the West Face Road (see Central Peak-Northeast Face Loop) from Highway 900, 425 feet, to the second switchback, at 1¼ miles, 1220 feet. Go straight off the end on the Chybinski Trail, a 1920s logging road that hasn't seen wheels since. The grade runs to the edge of a deep ravine and seems to end. Stringer logs of the old bridge span the gap, sprouting hemlocks. Admire. Then backtrack to the bypass trail down over an admirable trickle-creek and up again to the grade. Gently climb by holly and trillium, then contour the steep mountain wall in columbine, selfheal, and coltsfoot. At Choices Junction, 1¾ miles, 1525 feet, a decision must be made between two loops.

Chybinski Loop

Turn right, down a steep, washed-out cat track. In ¼ mile it gentles at 1070 feet. The cat track also completes a loop but the much better option is to turn right, up the bank, onto an old grade with a few logs to cross over but not so many to mar pleasure in alder, fir, and hemlock, the trickle of a creek, the windows (in winter) out on Cougar Mountain. At ⅓ mile from Choices Junction the grade obscurely joins the West Face Road at 1025 feet, a scant 1 mile from the highway.

Loop trip 3 miles, allow 2 hours
High point 1525 feet, elevation gain 1100 feet

West Peak Loop

From Choices Junction continue on the road as it starts south, bends north, steadily climbing. At a Y switchback right, up, to the summit plateau, 1750 feet; the lower subsummit, 1785 feet, lies to the left. Pass a short spur road to the Block House and continue to a saddle at a scant 2½ miles. To the right, with no trail access and no views but much green solitude is West Peak, 1950 feet. Stick with the road as it drops steeply to hit the North Ridge Road at 2¾ miles, 1575 feet. Proceed downhill to the West Face Road and go left to square one.

Loop trip 4 miles, allow 3 hours
High point 1750 feet, elevation gain 1350 feet

ISSAQUAH: THE TRAILHEAD CITY

Half-ringed by Grand Ridge, Tiger Mountain, Squak Mountain, and Cougar Mountain, coursed by the three forks of Issaquah Creek and by Tibbetts Creek, fronting on Lake Sammamish, the Squak Plain sets the foot of any pedestrian itching. "Let's climb a mountain!" cries one toe. "Let's head for the lake!" demands another. "A creek, a creek!" insists a third. "Let's just *go!*" chorus the others.

As of 1988, Issaquah Parks is developing a City Walkways and Trails Plan which will give pedestrians and bicycles machine-free routes from one end of the city to the other and provide connections to trails that exist, or will, on lands of King County Parks, the State Department of Natural Resources, State Parks, and the City of Bellevue. Because Issaquah lies on I-90 — and more importantly for the future, on the Metro 210 bus line — the trail system radiating from Issaquah will be hitched to every person in Puget Sound City who can afford bus fare. Issaquah is destined to become the most important of regional trailheads, a paradigm for America.

The city walkways (descendants of the sidewalks of older cities) will make good strolling in themselves, along creeks and always in broad views to the Issaquah Alps.

On the west the city system will lead to entries to the Cougar Mountain Regional Wildland Park — trails from Goode's Corner, Big Tree Ridge, Summerhill Ridge, the Military Road, The Precipice Trail, West Tibbetts trail, Bear Ridge trail. The Issaquah system also will connect to the Bellevue system.

On the south there will be trails down both Issaquah Creek and Tibbetts Creek to trailheads for Cougar Mountain, Squak Mountain State Park, and Tiger Mountain State Forest.

The trails on Cougar will connect across Tibbetts Creek to those of Squak, and those of Squak across Issaquah Creek to those of Tiger, thus linking Lake Washington to Tiger Mountain; very significantly, these connections will ensure the wildlife travel corridors from Lake Washington to the Cascades.

On the north a "rails & trails" use of the Burlington Northern right-of-way will lead to Lake Sammamish State Park and via a to-be-built Lake Sammamish Trail to Marymoor Park and the Sammamish River Trail.

To the east lie the city's de facto park on the Tradition Lake Plateau and Tiger Mountain State Forest. Also in that direction is the route to Preston, Snoqualmie Falls, and Independence, Missouri.

Issaquah–Snoqualmie Falls Trail

On the Fourth of July of 1890 Daniel Gilman celebrated completion of his railroad from Seattle to Woodinville to Issaquah (then called "Gilman," as was only just) to Snoqualmie Falls by running an excursion train to the falls. The line, later that year completed to Salal Prairie, east of North Bend, was successful for a time, hauling coal to Seattle and serving a farmland whose prosperity is suggested by the fact the trains killed 198 farm animals in a single year. However, in the 1920s passenger service was discontinued and several decades later the Northern Pacific, by then the owner, stopped the trains altogether.

The grade would have found its way into private hands had not King County Parks alertly come forth with a plan for a hiking-biking-horse (no machines)

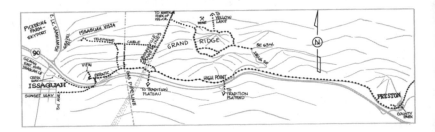

trail from Issaquah to Snoqualmie Falls, connecting (ultimately) at either end to other segments of a county-wide system. Using Forward Thrust funds, the county acquired most of the grade from Preston to Snoqualmie Falls; the State Highway Department bought the route west to Issaquah (see below).

As of 1988 the several segments are in various conditions; the whole way is negotiable but parts are not strollable. However, perhaps in the 1990s there will be a formal Grand Opening and another masterpiece will join the Burke-Gilman Trail and the Sammamish River Trail. Come now and watch the egg in the hatching.

Issaquah to High Point (map — page 156)

The State Highway Department, in building I-90, bought the abandoned rail grade to satisfy a Congressional requirement that it maintain a non-freeway connection between Issaquah and High Point. The intent of Congress is that the state should build a foot-bicycle-horse path and turn it over to King County Parks. The highwaymen have not done this but say they will, when they get around to it.

Go off I-90 on Exit 17, drive Front Street south to the stoplight on Sunset Way, turn left to where Sunset is about to become an on-ramp to I-90, and park on the residential streets, elevation 100 feet. Walk east on the north side of Sunset on a divider-protected walkway provided by the State Highway Department, past a city sign, "Snoqualmie Falls Trail," to a highway fence. Just past the fence is the East Fork, easily crossed on a footbridge built by volunteers.

Scramble over the blocks of rock heaped beneath the freeway bridge to a grassy slope and ascend to the old rail grade, attained at an elevation of 250 feet, ¼ mile from Sunset Way.

From High Point the starting is much simpler. Go off I-90 on Exit 20, turn left, and immediately upon leaving the interchange go left off Preston Way to a parking space on the rail grade, elevation 450 feet. Begin on the bridge (gated) over East Fork Issaquah Creek.

Between the two trailheads run 2¼ miles of the happiest strolling for many a mile around. No hills to huff up. No brush to soak the pants and socks. Creeks in cool ravines. Artifacts of an old coal mine. In spring, a hundred species of flowers in bloom. In winter, kingfishers and herons and eagles and whatever else on two wings or four feet that fancies spawned-out salmon.

Round trip from Issaquah or High Point about 6 miles, allow 4 hours
High point 450 feet, elevation gain 350 feet
Bus: Metro 210 to Issaquah or High Point

Issaquah–High Point Variations and Embellishments (map — page 156)

The trail is so rich in possibilities it amounts to a system in itself. Starting from the west, following are a few of the ingenuities:

Issaquah (Low) Vista. From the west end of the old rail grade (where the timber trestle used to span the valley to the slopes below the Tradition Plateau) go west, past one of the two most enormous erratics known in the Alps, a chunk of granite that Canada ought to bill us for. Ascend and descend across the freeway-remodeled hillside, following well-beaten paths to an erratic relocated by the Highway Department and subsequently kept well-painted by Issaquah youth. Enjoy views of the Little Town of Issaquah.

Issaquah (High) Vista. At about ⅓ mile from the west end of the rail grade turn steeply uphill on an obscure woods road through old gravel pits. At 525 feet the road tops out on the glacial-lake delta-plateau. At ⅓ mile from the railroad is a T with a telephone-cable road. Turn left to an enormous clearing, preparation for ultimate expansion of the Lakeside Gravel Mine. Continue some ½ mile to the brink, Issaquah Vista, the area's finest views of Issaquah, Squak Plain, and Lake Sammamish.

Tradition-Issaquah Loop. At a scant 1 mile note, below, a massive I-90 bridge over the East Fork Issaquah Creek. Descend near a freeway fence to the creek and there be amazed to discover a wildlife route between Grand Ridge and Tiger Mountain, a much-trampled slope of dry dirt sheltered by the

Nurse stump on Grand Ridge trail

enormous concrete roof. Emerging from beneath the modern bridge, cross the East Fork on the quaint little 1920s bridge of the Sunset Highway, amply wide for two Model Ts doing 20 mph. Ascend freeway grassery on animal paths which lead west to the swath of the Northwest Natural Gas Pipeline and thence via the Waterworks Trail or Big Tree Trail (see Tradition Plateau) to Issaquah.

Grand Ridge Rambles. At 1 mile turn uphill on a woods road that switchbacks through coal mine artifacts to the Bonneville powerline, ultimately to the brink at 700 feet, with views over East Fork Issaquah Creek to West Tiger and Squak. The powerline service road leads north to intersect the telephone-cable road, which connects to the gas line. There also are connections to the Hour Trail (which see).

High Point-Tradition-Issaquah Loop. Walk the High Point interchange under I-90 and loop back to Issaquah via Tradition Lake.

High Point to Preston (map — page 156)

The State Highway Department swore upon its honor to the surveyor of this here book that in building I-90 it would provide a foot trail all the way from Issaquah to Preston. It has not yet done so from Issaquah to High Point. From High Point to Preston it simply said the heck with the surveyor of this here book. Most of the way from High Point to Preston there is no trail — the highwaymen obliterated as much of the rail grade as suited their convenience and left the rest to grow up in hellberries. Even so, narrow old Preston Way — much of it none other than the veritable Sunset Highway of the 1920s — is a pleasant stroll, so little traveled and mostly so distant from I-90 as to give the feeling of still being in the 1920s.

The ending (the last stretch is on King County trail — see below) in the hamlet of Preston has a serendipity — a Metro 210 bus stop. A favorite hike for anti-fans of the private automobile is to use the bus as a connecting link for round trips which are walked only one way: get on the bus in Issaquah, get off in Preston, and walk the 6 miles back to downtown Issaquah; or get on the bus in High Point, get off in Preston, and walk the 3 miles back.

Round trip 6 miles, allow 4 hours
High point 500 feet, elevation gain 50 feet
Bus: Metro 210 to High Point or Preston

Preston to Snoqualmie Falls Vista (map — page 160)

Popular among the knowing few for years, the rail grade eastward from Preston emerged from obscurity into growing fame when the asphalt was laid for bikes. Cool forests and splashing creeks, flowers and birds and views, and the peace of a machine-free landscape reward the short-stroller on a summer evening or the long rambler on a winter Sunday.

Go off I-90 on Exit 22 (Fall City-Preston) and drive the short bit east and north to Preston County Park, elevation 500 feet.

Walk by the community building and up a path to the rail grade and turn right on the trail. (It begins ¼ mile to the west, beside the High Point-Preston Road, an alternative starting point.) Beyond a few houses the mood becomes totally woodsy-secluded. Now and then glimpse barns and houses down by the Raging River. Pass a fine wild creek with a path to the cool babble, and a powerline swath with a path inviting a long exploration up slopes of Mitchell Hill — also ascended by ancient woods roads become game trails.

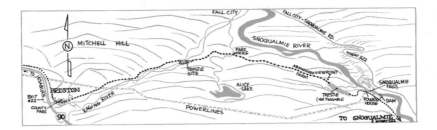

At 2 miles a handsome timber trestle used to span the Raging River Valley. Even as King County was preparing plans to plank-and-guardrail the historic monument the railroad perversely sold it for scrap. Hikers thus must backtrack from the vista point, descend a detour trail to the highway, follow it downvalley, and switchback up to the (former) other end of the trestle.

Back on grade, the trail bends east, passing a window to the Raging River quarry, then leaves the Raging for the Snoqualmie. At the old Fall City Siding, the way crosses the Lake Alice county road (alternate start for a walk), 380 feet, 3½ miles. Remember, only the right-of-way is public; logging has savaged much of the once-lush second-growth forest and for a stretch there now are homes and barking dogs. However, wildness resumes, tangled gorges are crossed on fills and trestles, and powerline-horse path is passed that leads to miles of roaming on Lake Alice plateau. Watch for an old farm, the foundation of the house hidden on the right by a tall hedge, the barn and fields sloping down left.

At 5 miles a long, high trestle spans a deep gorge. A few steps before it is a knoll on the left, logged in the 1970s; find an overgrown logging track out to the brink, push through the screen of young alders, and gaze over valley pastures to the white tumult of Snoqualmie Falls, Mt. Si towering in the background.

Round trip to airy trestle 10 miles, allow 6 hours
High point 500 feet, elevation gain 300 feet
Bus: Metro 210 to Preston

Trestle to Snoqualmie Falls (map — page 160)

The final 1 mile cannot be done by a hands-in-pockets pedestrian until the airy trestle, an architectural treasure (owned by King County Parks) is planked. Then, a route will have to be obtained onward from its far end. Puget Power owns the old rail grade and is planning a convention center, hotel, and whatnot. The owner of adjacent lands through which a bypass might be built is Weyerhaeuser, which is planning a championship golf course. As of 1988 the situation is treacherous.

It would be a crime against humanity were a private fence to forbid completion of the trail from Issaquah, preventing it from proceeding beyond the falls to Snoqualmie and North Bend, hooking to the Snoqualmie River Trail (see *Footsore 2*), and connecting to the rail trail between Rattlesnake Lake and the tunnel under Snoqualmie Pass.

At present (1988) a doughty scrambler can find a rude path down under the airy trestle and onward to regain the rail grade, which slices along the rock wall of the falls scarp. A scramble-path plummets to the Snoqualmie River at the

Snoqualmie Falls

base of the falls. (Beware!) A perilous brink a few steps off the grade gives straight-down looks to the plunge basin. (Watch it!) Beyond a Puget Power installation the grade touches Highway 522, elevation 400 feet.

For description of the route continuing east to Niblock Spur and the Puget Sound Railroad Historical Museum, the town of Snoqualmie (known until Gilman's railroad arrived as the "Hop Farm"), headquarters of the steam trains of the Snoqualmie Valley Railroad (the spirit of Daniel Gilman lives!), and North Bend, see *Footsore 2*.

Round trip 2 miles, allow (1987) 3 hours
High point 400 feet, no elevation gain

TIGER MOUNTAIN STATE FOREST

The "tiger" may have been: the cougar, mountain lion, catamount; the tiger lily which blooms so gaudily in late spring; a Scots word, "taggart," meaning rocky; or a rocky Scot named Taggart. In Issaquah it used to be called Issaquah Mountain; in Preston, Preston Hill.

During the last third of the 19th century bullteam loggers cut the giant cedars and Douglas firs of the lower slopes. Their careless fires and those of settlers clearing land to grow hops and cows ran wild up the mountain. In the 1920s railroad loggers arrived, based at three mills. From the Hobart mill they built a trail of rails angling upward across the west slopes to Fifteenmile Creek and ascending its valley to the summit ridge. From the High Point mill they engineered the famous "Wooden Pacific Railroad," a tramway that went straight up the fall line to the 1900-foot level, where a rail grade was gouged on the contour around the jut of West Tiger Mountain, through Many Creek Valley, to a deadend at Poo Poo Creek. From the Preston mill a series of switchbacks climbed to the summit ridge. The "lokies" began to quit the mountain in the Crash year of 1929 and by the middle 1930s had moved elsewhere, picking up their rails and ties to carry away with them. Tiger was abandoned to the new-growing forests, the wild creatures, the occasional hunter, and a scattering of moonshiners. The sole human structures on high were a state fire-lookout tower atop East Tiger and an airway beacon on West Tiger.

But there were hikers. The rail grades provided a network of routes to nearly every corner of the mountain. The boots of local folk pounded out accesses from their homes to the high country. The state trail to the fire lookout was walked by city folk who knew nothing more of the trail system; when the trail was replaced by a service road, they accepted that as equally serviceable for feet. Recreationally speaking, modern times came to Tiger — with a jolt — in 1966, when The Mountaineers put the service road in their epochal book, *100 Hikes in Western Washington.* Thousands upon thousands of urbanites learned to their delighted surprise that within minutes of their homes they could set out on a hike that would take them to a wild and alpine-like experience. The flood of hikers shared the road amicably with horses, with the few sturdy family cars ascending slowly (lest something get busted) to a picnic, and with the motorcycles of civil riders who chose that vehicle for the open-air freedom.

In the mid-1970s the idyll went sour. The family cars and the view-seeking motorcyclists were driven out by the 4x4s with roll bar and winch whose sport is "mud-running" and "snow-catting" and just plain slamming through the brush; the dirtbikes, sans muffler, sans spark arrester, sans an appreciation of nature, whose sport is churning soil, muddying creeks, scaring the wits out of family-car drivers and hikers; the three-wheel and four-wheel ATVs, machines whose redeeming virtue is that they are so dangerous they kill more of their drivers than they do hikers.

Further, in the mid-1970s the Weyerhaeuser Company, which in 1900 had acquired better than half the mountain from the Northern Pacific Land Grant, paying James J. Hill $6 an acre, or about $500,000 for its entire Tiger holdings, and had banked at least 25 times that through the first-round clearcutting, returned for a second feast. The state Department of Natural Resources, trustee-manager of nearly half the mountain, acting for a number of public-agency trusts (the largest being King County), prepared to follow suit. As the

Above a sea of clouds on West Tiger 2 (Photo by Harvey Manning)

two commenced harvesting the virgin forests left by the railroad loggers, they opened new roads which instantly were taken over by the wheel-crazies and the gun-crazies.

By 1980 Tiger Mountain resembled a war zone. Bullets flew in every direction, despite the only legal shooting being during hunting season, and that with shotguns. To walk the roads was to risk being mugged or raped. The police rarely could be talked into answering reports of crimes, saying the only force that might safely venture onto the heights was a platoon of Marines. Weyerhaeuser refused to act. So did the state DNR.

But in 1980 the tide turned. A new State Land Commissioner (head of the DNR) was elected, Brian Boyle. He came to the mountain, he saw, and in due time arranged a land exchange which got Weyerhaeuser off the mountain (*except* for the summit ridge of West Tiger, where it retains the tower colonies). In time, too, the DNR managed to put law officers on the mountain, beginning a taming process which still has some way to go.

Finally, Commissioner Boyle established a Tiger Mountain State Forest, "a working forest in an urban environment," to provide a continued flow of forest products while serving as a laboratory to perfect new forestry techniques compatible with the contiguity of Puget Sound City. As of 1989 the management plan for the state forest is being implemented, even as it is being refined and revised in the light of new knowledge and changing social needs.

The Issaquah Alps Trails Club, original proponent of an "urban tree farm" on Tiger where ways might be found to preserve the forest industry from its self-destructive urges, agrees with the DNR that large expanses of the mountain have soils and slopes ideal for farming. Here is where the DNR should lead the industry out of the frontier past into a civilized future.

However, in the West Tiger area the "tree farm" must be evaluated alongside the "recreation forest," as described by Lars Kardell, professor at Sweden's University of Uppsala:

Recreation forests should be given an imaginative kind of care, or in the best of cases, no care at all. We have to get away from the dominant production philosophy based on rotation schedules and clear-felling. In addition, I believe it is important to let the forest remain forest, rather than to urbanize or civilize it. There is a real risk that some new technical gadgetry will inspire demands to put the consumption-focused recreation of the computer age into our forests. If this happens, the forests will become only backdrops for something foreign to their nature. Our constant hunt for new sensations should stop at the edge of the forest. Within the forest we should learn that there are plenty of exciting things to discover, experience, and understand.

The entirety of the Tiger Mountain State Forest must give consideration to wildlife habitat, pure water for fisheries and domestic consumption, preservation of the history of the forest industry, teaching of environmental sciences in the schools, research into forest sciences — and civil recreation, both on the roads and on the near-city quiet trails — "wilderness on the Metro 210."

These other values grow so important in the West Tiger area that an output of forest products is by comparison miniscule — and too destructive of the other values to be prudent. The Tradition Lake vicinity has long since been a de facto park. Private and parochial schools have been using the trails as outdoor classrooms for years and are expressing ever greater need for the kind of educational opportunity presented.

To be kept in mind: In 1987 the state legislature empowered the DNR to set lands aside from income-producing purposes as "conservation areas," more park-like than tree farm-like. Among the initial dedications was the Mount Si Conservation Area. Hmmm...

Trailheads

Downtown Issaquah Trailhead
Go off I-90 on Exit 17, drive south on Front Street, turn east on Sunset Way to where it bends left to become a freeway on-ramp. Park anywhere on Sunset or adjacent residential streets — or hop off the Metro 210 bus. Elevation, 150 feet.

Mount Rainier from Tiger Mountain

Walk Sunset a short bit east of the bend and spot the trail passing through a portal in the highway fence and ascending steeply to the grade of the old Gilman railroad.

High Point Trailhead
Go off I-90 on Exit 20, signed "High Point." Turn right to the frontage road; SE 79 Street. Turn right on SE 79th for 0.4 mile to the turnaround and gate. Elevation, 450 feet. Walk past the gate on the powerline service road.

Issaquah High School Trailhead
Go off I-90 on Exit 17, drive south on Front Street to Sunset Way, turn left to Second Avenue, and turn right on it 0.7 mile, passing Issaquah High School, to just short of Second Avenue's junction with Front Street (here become the Issaquah-Hobart Road). Park on the shoulder. Elevation, 175 feet.

This spot is the apex of the Issaquah Switchback, where the railroad made a sweeping turn from a southerly to a northerly direction, to begin gaining elevation for the crossing of the "high point" between Issaquah Creek and the Raging River. From the Second Avenue sidewalk turn left on the grade and follow its curve around the football field. Where it establishes itself on a northward heading, go off right on a mucky woods road and follow it uphill, right, to a Puget Power gate closing the road to public vehicles.

Tiger Mountain Road Trailheads

The three forest roads emanating from Highway 18 (Tiger Mountain Road, West Side Road, East Side Road) were popular walking routes when they were first built, in the late 1960s and early 1970s. However, they were discovered and preempted by the crazies. In the mid-1980s the law came to Tiger and a semblance of civilization has been restored — at least while the heavily armed police officers are on patrol. As more hikers exert their political presence, on the trails and in letters to King County and the state Department of Natural Resources, progress toward peace will continue to be made.

Even without the crazies, the roads have become so popular among view-seekers and family picnickers that foot travel is not recommended except on weekdays. On the right days, at the right hours, they provide walks unsurpassed for forests and creeks and views. Additionally, when all the world's brush is soaking wet, the road-walker remains dry. Further, the routefinding is simplicity itself. The sociability quotient is high, what with three-abreast formation no problem and five-abreast usually possible.

Drive Highway 18 westerly 4.2 miles from I-90 or 3.4 miles easterly from Issaquah-Hobart Road, to the summit of Holder Gap, 1350 feet. Go off north through an old borrow pit to a reader board announcing "Tiger Mountain State Forest." Two roads go into the woods side by side.

The one on the right, the Tiger Mountain Road, ascends unremittingly to the head of Holder Creek valley and a split at 2.9 miles, 2400 feet.

The right fork climbs giddily along the side of East Tiger Mountain, in 0.6 mile meeting the East Side Road (see below), 2670 feet. The way switchbacks left a final 0.8 mile to the summit of East Tiger, 3004 feet. Family cars often rebel, demanding a halt at the 2400-foot junction, leaving the rest of the ascent to the leg machines. All vehicles must halt at the 2670-foot junction because a gate requires them to do so. How sweet it is! A summit ascent reserved for feet! Moreover, the devastation by decades of wheels is being cleared up and it's getting to be a pleasant summit.

The left fork winds along the summit ridge, drops sharply, passes the sideroad to Middle Tiger Mountain, traverses Fifteenmile Pass, 2060 feet, at 1.9 miles from the split, then ascends to Issaquah Gap, the saddle between West Tiger 2 and West Tiger 1, 2530 feet, 4.1 miles from the split. At some point it normally becomes unattractive to family vehicles. Trailheads are passed at a number of points, some of them noted in these pages, all of them in *Guide to Trails of Tiger Mountain.*

West Side Road Trailheads. From Holder Gap, 1350 feet, take the left road into the woods. The way follows close along Holder Creek, passing a sideroad to South Tiger Mountain and just beyond (at a roadside cedar across from Little Otter Lake), at 2.1 miles, 1500 feet, the 1988 south end of the Tiger Mountain Trail. (Ultimately the south trailhead will be at or near Highway 18.)

West Tiger Mountain trail

The road crosses the spur ridge between Holder Creek and Fifteenmile Creek (2.4 miles, 1675 feet) and in climax clearcut vistas switchbacks steeply down to the valley. At 3.6 miles, 1200 feet, is the trailhead, to the right in a brushy ravine, for Middle Tiger Mountain and the Middle Tiger Railroad. Bottoming out, or nearly, at 5 miles, 800 feet, the road passes the obscure Mine Road trailhead. In a short bit more, at 5.2 miles, 725 feet, it crosses Fifteenmile Creek and commences a steep and steady climb through the enormous clearcuts made by Weyerhaeuser as its farewell gesture. Most of the forests here were virgin, grown up since forest fires of the late or early 19th century — the largest expanse of virgin forest so near Puget Sound City.

At 7.5 miles, 1775 feet, is Poo Poo Point. A short bit down the closed-off road is the trailhead to the West Tiger Railroad.

East Side Road Trailheads. Drive Highway 18 to 3.1 miles west of I-90, 1.2 miles east of Holder Gap, and carefully make a treacherous turn off to the start of a narrow road, elevation 1100 feet. It climbs to the Bonneville powerline (great views east over the Raging River to the Cascades), contours through a last-gasp Weyerhaeuser clearcut, and ascends northerly along the slopes, largely following old logging railroad grades refurbished for logging trucks. The walking is choice on weekday mornings, or even afternoons — before the schools let out. Creek after creek tumbles through fine old forest grown up since the railroad logging of the 1920s.

At 1420 feet, 2.4 miles from Highway 18, is the lower trailhead for Silent Swamp, hard to spot while driving, obvious when afoot.

At 1468 feet, 3.2 miles, the East Side Road makes a sharp reverse turn left, from a spur road which continues straight ahead. Climbing, then leveling out on another old rail grade, at 1960 feet, 4.3 miles, the way passes the upper trailhead for Silent Swamp, identifiable by the undrivable sideroad whch goes down left, serving as the first few yards of the trail.

A few feet beyond, the East Side Road starts uphill. Just here is the Beaver Valley trailhead, the way beginning on the old rail grade.

At 2670 feet, 6.1 miles, the East Side Road comes to the junction with the Tiger Mountain Road.

Walkable all year, except in occasional spells of deep snow, November to March. East Side Road and West Side Road may be impassable in winter.

Tradition Plateau (De Facto) Park: Waterworks Trail–Big Tree Trail–Tradition Lake Loop (maps — pages 170 and 174)

No other municipality of metropolitan King County has more wildland within city limits than Issaquah. Though broad swaths of powerlines and a gas line cut through the trees, on either side are enclaves of deep woods. Two lakes nestle in bowls and several swamps hide in secret glooms. Bands of elk tramp the trails, bald eagles roost in snags. This is the quintessential "wilderness on the Metro 210," a place to spend winter afternoons or summer evenings or full days in any season, the wildness counterpointed by history — old logging, old homesteads, old waterworks, old golly-knows mysteries.

The easiest entry in terms of energy output is from the east, via the High Point trailhead (which see). The turnaround at the gate has an elevation of 450 feet, a quantum leap higher than downtown Issaquah, and that's why this is the entry preferred by toddlers and saunterers. Walk the service road, barred to every sort of public vehicle, ¼ mile to the powerline. Directly across is the woods road that leads to West Tiger 3, West Tiger Caves, and other wanderings. A short way to the west on the powerline is the woods road that is the eastern end of the Tradition Lake Loop. A scant 1 mile from the gate is Three-Way Junction, hub of routes discussed in following paragraphs.

The neatest entry is from the Downtown Issaquah trailhead, elevation 90 feet. From Sunset Way a gravel track climbs to the old Northern Pacific (older Gilman) Railroad grade at 200 feet, exactly where the trestle used to cross the valley.

Immediately turn sharp left on what seems an extension of the grade but actually is the remnant of a road to the old Issaquah Waterworks. In several steps a trail strikes directly up the forest slope. Here, at a very scant ¼ mile from Sunset, is Waterworks Junction.

Waterworks Trail-The Springs

Continue on the road remnant to the first Springs and a pair of reservoir tanks, an ancient one below the grade and a merely old one above. The service road which used to proceed onward to The Springs had a chunk bitten out by freeway construction. There is absolutely no reason for not building a trail to span the gap. Until then, the walker can easily improvise, such as by following the bicycle path east on the freeway shoulder from Sunset and ascending along the top of the concrete retaining wall to resumption of the service road.

The service road hasn't seen a wheel in decades. The joy of the walker reigns supreme — supremer, in summer, if nettle sticks are in hand to fight off the stingers. Down left is East Fork Issaquah Creek, where all year the water ouzels dip and in winter the salmon spawn and die, to be eaten by eagles. Up right is a wonder of a virgin forest steeply climbing hundreds of wild feet. And there are The Springs...

In Pleistocene time, as the Canadian glacier receded, a great lake formed at the Cascade front where now is North Bend. At a certain period the water overtopped High Point and flowed into another lake, a predecessor of Lake Sammamish, dammed by the glacier at a level much higher than the lake of today. An enormous delta was built, hundreds of feet deep, with layers of sand, gravel, and clay. In the post-glacial period the East Fork of Issaquah Creek sliced through the delta. On the north side of I-90 the sand and gravel have been mined for many years. On the south side the delta is intact; the Tradition Plateau is none other than the old lakebed, as modified by subsequent erosion. The abundant rainfall and snowmelt from West Tiger Mountain flow to the delta. Some feeds surface streams and the two kettle lakes (Tradition and Round). Most sinks in, filling a vast underground reservoir which was Issaquah's water supply until construction of I-90.

The reservoir empties out through an underground aquifer (or two) capped top and bottom by impervious layers of clay-rich sediments. At the scarp cut by the East Fork they seep out, trickle out, and gush out — one Spring after another for half a mile. The larger of them pass through concrete collection-filtration boxes formerly connected to the city's main water tank. Issaquah oldtimers — and kids with an attachment to historical roots — come here on pilgrimage to drink the waters, especially on hot summer days, declaring "You just don't get water like that anymore, not from city pipes."

At ¾ mile from the railroad grade is the last collection box and the end of the service road-trail. A somewhat rude animal trail continues up and down a scant ¼ mile to the gas line. Better, however, is to turn off before the gas line, very steeply uphill on a mean but brief stretch of path to the brink of the Lower Plateau, 425 feet. Turn left on the ill-maintained Brink Trail the short way to the gas line. At ⅓ mile from the last collection box is the eastern entry to the Big Tree Trail.

One way from Sunset Way to Big Tree Trail 1¾ miles, allow 1½ hours
High point 425 feet, elevation gain 600 feet

Round trip to the last collection box 2 miles, allow 2 hours
High point 200 feet, elevation gain 150 feet

Lower Plateau-Big Tree Trail

At Waterworks Junction take the trail steeply uphill in glorious forest logged so long ago, and so sparingly, it seems perfectly virgin. The way passes splendid large Douglas firs, skirts the ravine of a Spring, and joins a gravel path from the railroad. At 425 feet, a scant ¼ mile from Waterworks Junction, is the lip of the Lower Plateau, a magnificent viewpoint. Many folks climb here in sunset or twilight for the Christmas-card vistas over the little town of Issaquah, what's left of the green Squak Plain, and Lake Sammamish.

Walk the service road east a scant ¼ mile, to where it begins to climb to the Upper Plateau, and turn left into the woods on a well-beaten path. In several hundred feet is Big Tree Junction. The Brink Trail goes straight ahead, meandering along the plateau brink with looks down ravines of The Springs, at length emerging on the gas line.

For the sylvan spectacularity, turn right on Big Tree Trail. Though less than ¾ mile long, an afternoon is not enough. Examine the path for tracks and sign of coyote, cougar, deer, elk, bear, raccoon. Sit on a mossy log beside the luscious swamp, through which water moves ever so slowly and quietly, enjoy the blossoms of lily-of-the-valley, and fill lungs with skunk cabbage. See eight species of fern and scores of mosses and lichens and liverworts. Hear the winter wren and varied thrush. The wildland arboretum has two unique features, as well. A stretch of cedar puncheon dating from the 1880s is the area's only known surviving bullteam skidroad, along which oxen dragged the "big

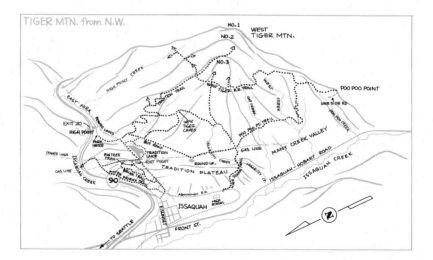

sticks." So much time has elapsed since then that trees too small to interest the loggers have grown to noble dimensions, a rain-forest mix of Douglas fir, Sitka spruce, hemlock, cedar, and fern-hung maple. Some Douglas firs were too large for the bullteams — one measures 24 feet in circumference and has been found by coring to be 1100 years old!

Emerge on the gas line — and perhaps turn around and do it all again. To the left on the swath are the outlets of Brink Trail and Waterworks Trail. To the right ¼ mile is the lip of the Upper Plateau, 500 feet, and the intersection of north-south gas line, north-south powerline, and east-west powerline — Three-Way Junction. Just to the west are concrete ramparts of Fort Puget.

One way from Sunset Way to Three-Way Junction 1¼ miles, allow 1½ hours
High point 500 feet, elevation gain 300 feet

Tradition Lake Loop

Tradition Lake is a body of water to dismay trout fishermen and other water purists, to delight bass fishermen, frogs, and birders. Fed by surface and subsurface flow from West Tiger and draining underground to swamps of the Lower Plateau, its level rises in winter to the edge of superb fir forest, drops in summer to expose acres of marsh grass, and more in fall to permit fields of mint to flourish, providing a most aromatic walk.

Both ends of the loop trail start from the east-west powerline. One, a path, enters the woods by a power pole a few steps east of Three-Way Junction; the other, a woods road, a few steps east of the lake and a few steps west of the woods road opposite the High Point entry road. Beaten out originally by beasts and birders and fishermen, latterly improved by volunteer work parties, the path goes up and down, sometimes on the shore through creek dogwood and ninebark, usually up the slope in forest of fir or alder. In winter-spring look for bald eagles perched in snags. In any season walk softly and sneak up on the ducks. In summer admire the green pads and yellow flowers of pond lily. When the water is low, spot remains of two lodges abandoned by the beaver colony in the early 1970s or so; see their ubiquitous chewings of stumps and logs. Hook the two ends of the loop together by walking the powerline road, which provides fine views over the lake to West Tiger.

Round trip from High Point trailhead 2¼ miles, allow 1½ hours
High point 500 feet, elevation gain 100 feet

Round trip from Sunset Way (Big Tree Trail and Tradition Loop combined) 4 miles, allow 3 hours
High point 500 feet, elevation gain 400 feet

West Tiger 3 (maps — pages 170 and 174)

The views from West Tiger are unreal as an aerial photograph, a surpassing lesson in the geography of Whulj country, spread out like an enormous relief map all around. Virtually the entire *Footsore* world is in sight, from Black Hills, Rainier, and the remnant of St. Helens south, to Olympics west, to San Juan Islands, Baker, and Shuksan north, and Cascades east. There is salt water from The Narrows to Elliott Bay to Admiralty Inlet to Skagit Bay, and cities from Tacoma to Bremerton to Seattle to Everett.

Of the West Tiger peaks, 3 is the lowest — and the best. It juts out farthest, seeming to hang in air over downtown Issaquah a swandive away from blue waters of Lake Sammamish. As of 1988 it has no over-communication towers and — though a Boeing bulldozer ran amok here in 1980, burying a power cable that could just as well have come from another direction—no permanent tracks touch the summit, which thus is razzer-free even on loud summer Sundays. Burned naked by the fires of many decades ago, blasted by cold storms in winter and hot sun in summer and vicious winds the year around, the thin soil barely covers andesite slabs and supports only a skimpy crop of trees stunted to a pseudo-alpine look; spring brings a mountain-meadow-like coloring of spring gold, lupine, tiger lily, and ox eye daisy.

Though it may truly be said, "all trails lead to West Tiger 3," the simplest is the Tradition Trail, ascending from the plateau near the lake. The two simplest approaches to the trail are from the Downtown Issaquah and High Point trailheads.

For the latter, walk past the gate, elevation 450 feet, ¼ mile to the powerline.

For the former, climb from Sunset Way, elevation 90 feet, to the Tradition Plateau, walk east on the powerline service road past Fort Puget, Three-Way Junction, and both ends of the Tradition Lake Loop Trail, reaching the same place in 1½ miles.

Directly across the powerline swath from the High Point entry road, go into the forest on an old woods road. In ¼ mile is a Y. The right (straight ahead) is the Greyhound Scenicruiser Bus Road. Go left, soon leaving the plateau flat and turning steeply up in mixed forest. The way winds and switchbacks, passes spurs left and right; the rule is, stay with the most-used and steadiest-up way. The only really confusing spot is a switchback just beyond a crossing of Tradition Creek, which runs most of the summer; take the switchback left, recrossing the creek.

At 1370 feet, a scant 1½ miles from Bus Road Junction, the old logging road ends. Constructed trail turns straight up the fall line. Shortly the grade relents and in a long ½ mile attains West Tiger Railroad Grade, 1900 feet.

The trail crosses the grade and continues up, emerging from forest into views over Grand Ridge and the Snoqualmie valley to the Cascades, and then proceeding through shrubs, over andesite rubble (or when winter winds blow from the North Pole, in drifted snow) up the ridge crest, at ½ mile from the railroad grade reaching the summit, 2522 feet.

For a special treat, stay for the sunset over Puget Sound and the Olympics. And then for the city lights.

Round trip from High Point gate 6 miles, allow 5 hours
High point 2522 feet, elevation gain 2100 feet
Bus: Metro 210

Round trip from downtown Issaquah 8¼ miles, allow 7 hours
Elevation gain 2500 feet
Bus: Metro 210

West Tiger Railroad–Many Creek Valley
(maps — pages 170 and 174)

Between the era of logging that used oxen and horses as pulling power, and modern logging with trucks, for several decades the railroad dominated the industry and tracks were laid throughout lowlands and foothills. Most grades have been converted to truck roads or otherwise obliterated. The longest remaining unmolested near Seattle is the West Tiger Railroad Grade, running 4 miles — the entire distance at an elevation of 1900 feet — from the north side of West Tiger Mountain around to the west, then south, in and out of the enormous amphitheater of Many Creek Valley. Logging concluded here in 1929. When hikers arrived in large numbers in the late 1970s they found the clearcuts grown up in handsome large alder and maple or mixed conifers, interspersed with patches of virgin forest ignored by the loggers. Moreover, they found that except for fallen bridges the grades were just as they were when the rails and ties were pulled up for use elsewhere. The West Tiger Grade is proposed for preservation as an Historical Landmark, a chapter in the history of the forest industry — and a delightful stroll, winter and summer.

A glory in itself, the grade is central to the looping for which West Tiger is famous. Trails go off both ends, climb from below, and climb above. Hikers doing West Tiger 3 or Poo Poo Point and finding themselves with extra time and energy commonly give the day a serendipitous conclusion, a loop return through Many Creek Valley. The number of possible loops approaches infinity. The following end-to-end description will stimulate the imagination.

The south end is the ravine of Poo Poo Creek. A trail connects to Poo Poo Point, the quickest, easiest access to the grade, via the West Side Road. Very near the terminus is the top of the High School Trail from Issaquah's 2nd Avenue. From here the grade rounds a ridge into Many Creek Valley on steep sidehill that gentles out in the squishier, creekier center of the amphitheater.

Whenever the grade runs out in empty air, backtrack to find the path down and up to a resumption. Note stringers of old bridges, mostly broken-backed and fallen, a few still intact, nurse-bridges growing ferns and hemlocks and candyflower in midair. Watch for railroad ironware, logging ironware — rusting history.

Having crossed West Creek at 1 mile and Gap Creek in ¼ mile more — the two largest of the eight or so (many) creeks — the grade curves onto steep south slopes of West Tiger. Now for something completely different: virgin forest of nobly large and tall Douglas firs, too small to interest loggers of the 1920s but such that 1980s loggers carry towels to sop up their drooling. These trees are on public land, owned by King County, managed by the state DNR. Can the public afford to preserve not only an historic logging railroad but a stand of historic left-behinds?

A sidetrail up to West Tiger 3 and the Tiger Mountain Trail is passed, and then the Section Line Trail down to the Tradition Plateau and up to West Tiger 3. At 2¼ miles is the intersection with the lovely and easy Tradition Trail that drops left to the lake vicinity and climbs right to West Tiger 3.

The grade bends around the ridge to the north side, at 3¼ miles joining the Tiger Mountain Trail where it descends from West Tiger 2. The united way crosses headwaters of High Point Creek, then splits at 3¾ miles, the TMT descending left, the grade contouring on to a powerline swath. This swath goes straight up to the summit of West Tiger 1, gaining 1000 feet in less than ½

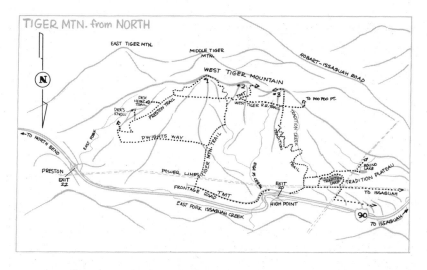

TIGER MTN. from NORTH

mile — a genuine mountaineering experience when under a foot of snow! A much nicer way to climb the peak is to follow the grade a short bit to its end at 4 miles, still at an elevation of 1900 feet; a trail continues to the Preston Trail.

One thing mightily puzzled the discovering hikers of the late 1970s. The railroad connected to nothing. At both ends, deadends. The mystery was explained by Professor Fred Rounds, who told how the "Wooden Pacific Railroad" connected the lumber mill at High Point, elevation 450 feet (all remains obliterated by I-90), to the upper railroad. Steam donkeys lifted rails and railroad cars and locomotives and loggers up this tramway, and lowered tramcars loaded with the "big sticks" whose stumps are gaped at by hikers of today.

One way 4 miles, allow 2½ hours
High point 1900 feet, elevation gain (missing bridges) 300 feet
Bus: Metro 210 to Issaquah or High Point

Sample loop combining Tradition Trail and High School Trail, 10 miles from High Point gate, allow 7 hours
Elevation gain 1800 feet

West Tiger Caves (map — page 170)

There are limestone caves, there are lava-tube caves, there are ice caves, and there are "talus caves." This last variety, formed when blocks of rock tumble together and leave spaces between, is the least interesting. Nevertheless, a cave is a cave, and everybody's great-great grandfolks used to feel cozy therein. Since their 1980 rediscovery (local kids had known where they were all along but organized cavers had misplaced them) the West Tiger Caves, described by the recognized archivist, Dr. William Halliday, as the "largest known talus caves in the state," have become exceedingly popular. Why, the

West Tiger Caves

claustrophobic wonders — but while refusing to follow Tom Sawyer and Becky Thatcher underground, he finds esthetic pleasure in the giant chunks of andesite that tumbled from glacier-oversteepened slopes and now lie so still and mossy-green beneath the big trees.

Of the many good ways to get there, the least energy expenditure and most greenland variety are provided by a start from the western High Point trailhead, elevation 450 feet.

Walk the service road ¼ mile to the powerline and cross to a woods road. In ¼ mile along it is a Y. The right is the Bus Road. Follow it over Tradition Creek and in about ½ mile turn sharp left, gently uphill, on a signed path through alder-maple forest, wending up an ancient logging road on a ridge between Tradition Creek and Cave Creek. At 1 long mile from the slope base at 550 feet, the way abruptly steepens to the big blocks, elevation 1250 feet.

Between the blocks are chasms with walls of cascading ferns. Atop are mossy old trees. All around are tall Douglas firs filtering the sunshine or fog. Walk softly! Stay on the marked paths! Spare the liverworts!

Don's Cave is a walk-in, large enough for a hundred hikers at once. If you forgot your flashlight you'll never get halfway to the end, where the wild things bring their dinners to eat them up, leaving only tiny bits of bones. O'Brian's Cave, discovered by a family of lost O'Brians in 1980, requires a short squeeze down a rabbit hole into a great room. The human bones here are thought to have been placed by a prankster.

For the looper, a trail connects north from the caves to the Tradition Trail, and another south to the Section Line Trail.

Round trip from High Point Gate 4 miles, allow 3 hours
High point 1250 feet, elevation gain 800 feet
Bus: Metro 210

Tiger Mountain Trail (maps — pages 174 and 177)

On October 13, 1979, was held the official opening of the Tiger Mountain Trail, by then 7½ years in the thinking and 3½ in construction, occupying close to 300 person-days, costing a total in public funds of $0.00, and resulting in a 10⅓-mile route that subsequently was acclaimed by a foundation-sponsored group engaged in a tour of inspection from coast to coast as "the greatest near-city wildland trail in the nation." A subsequent relocation of the north trailhead lengthened the distance to 11.1 miles; a projected relocation of the south trailhead on Highway 18 would bring the total to perhaps 13 miles. Along the way are broad and varied views, plant communities ranging from virgin fir to alder-maple to pseudo-alpine andesite barrens — a rich sampling of the good and great things of Tiger Mountain. The idea for this masterpiece of a trail may be said to have been hatched at a Mountaineers meeting in 1972. However, the fledgling never would have gotten out of the nest had it not been taken under the wing of Bill Longwell, who chose the route and led hundreds of work parties — Mountaineers, Volunteers of Washington, Issaquah Alps Trails Club, youth groups, students at Hazen High School — and went out himself on countless solo "parties."

The supreme hike of the Issaquah Alps is the TMT end-to-end, doing the entire 11.1 miles and 1200 feet of elevation gain (from the south trailhead) in a day, a good bit of exercise but in ordinary conditions (spring to fall) not overly taxing. The favorite method is a two-car switch, placing a car at the north trailhead, then driving to the south trailhead, which is 1000 feet higher and saves that much elevation gain.

The condition of the trail improves year by year. Longwell's Rangers go partying regularly to whack down the new-growing brush and cut through the new-fallen trees. The growing volume of hikers helps keep the bracken and nettles trampled; the early years of the trail saw only the occasional boots, compared to thousands now and steadily more as the good news gets around.

(Sorry to say, horses, too, have been coming in numbers. THEY MUST NOT. The tread is durable enough for people but not tough enough for beasts. THIS IS NOT A HORSE TRAIL.)

For all the improvement, the trip is not recommended for every casual stroller to do on his own. An experienced wildland navigator can find his way readily by consulting *Guide to Trails of Tiger Mountain* by (who else?) Bill Longwell, Chief Ranger of the Issaquah Alps. The inexperienced would do best to go along on a trip guided by the Issaquah Alps Trails Club or The Mountaineers or other group. All hikers must recognize that in winter the snow may pile deep on the trail and in any season the clouds may blow wildly by. Fortunately, all along the route are escape hatches to lower and safer elevations; see the trail guide.

The most used sections of the trail are the two ends: the north part provides both a splendid several-hour forest walk and a popular route to the summits of West Tiger; the south part, also with superb deep woods, offers the nicest way up Middle Tiger. For directions to the two trailheads, see Trailheads earlier in these pages.

Bill's guidebook has a very full description of the TMT route which not only makes sure a person can stay on it but adds immensely to enjoyment of sights seen along the way. Following is a brief summary, from south to north.

From the south trailhead, elevation 1500 feet, the TMT (so marked by small signs on trees) alternates between constructed tread and railroad grades of 1920s logging, wandering through a splendid mix of forests 1¾ miles to intersect the Middle Tiger Trail, 2120 feet, which drops left to Middle Tiger Railroad Grade and the West Side Road, climbs right to Middle Tiger.

The TMT rounds open, broad-view slopes of Middle Tiger and swings into the valley of Tiger's major stream, Fifteenmile Creek. At 1960 feet, 2½ miles, watch for an obscure sidepath left to Denny's Bulge, a fine viewpoint over the valley. A short bit beyond is a flagged route down to Middle Tiger Railroad Grade. At 3¾ miles, 2000 feet, the TMT crosses Fifteenmile Creek on a bridge and climbs to Fifteenmile Railroad Grade, which connects up right to Tiger

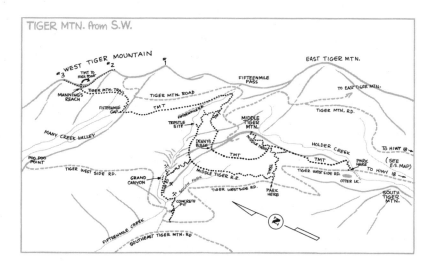

East Tiger Mountain from Middle Tiger

Mountain Road and Fifteenmile Pass, down left to Hidden Estates Trail. The TMT continues climbing to Lone Rock, 4½ miles, 2160 feet, then winds in and out of gullies, up and down to a ridge saddle and brief views at 2200 feet, 5¼ miles. In another ¼ mile the way intersects Hidden Estates Trail, which climbs right to the Tiger Mountain Road, a route to summits of West Tiger.

The way wends onward through woods, over West Tiger Creek and Issaquah Gap Creek high in the amphitheater of Many Creek Valley, then at Rick's Rock emerges into a magnificent alpine-like traverse in dream-like vistas of intermingling civilization and wilderness, climaxing at Manning's Reach, 6¾ miles, 2600 feet, highest point of the TMT.

A path climbs right to West Tiger 2, another drops left to West Tiger 3 and the West Tiger Railroad Grade. Views end in dark woods leading to West Gap, 7 miles, 2500 feet. The way descends and climbs to a final scenic spectacularity on the open north ridge of West Tiger 2 at 7¼ miles, 2570 feet.

Thence the way is down through shrub into forest, intricately and deviously switchbacking to the West Tiger Railroad Grade at 8 miles, 1900 feet. At 8¼ miles is a junction where one trail climbs straight-up right to West Tiger 1, another goes straight ahead to the Preston Trail, and the TMT descends left to briefly join the old route of the "Wooden Pacific Railway," the tramline that connected the West Tiger Railroad to the High Point mill. In a few steps the TMT quits the "Wooden Pacific," following new trail built in 1982 up onto a spur ridge which descends parallel to and just to the east of High Point Creek. This stretch of 1982 trail is the favorite of many TMT fans and an extremely popular short trip from the north trailhead; in a recent half-year period, a trail register was signed by people representing some 2000 individuals — probably out-numbered at least two to one by those who habitually do not sign registers. There are delightful wet glades, such as Ruth's Cove at 8¾ miles. There are cathedral stands of fir, hemlock, cedar, maple, and cottonwood — Tiger Mountain's largest old-tree forest.

At 9½ miles, 1130 feet, Dwight's Way traverses off right 1 mile to the Preston Trail, the best route to West Tiger 1.

At 10 miles, 920 feet, the TMT abruptly emerges from twilight to bright day on the Puget Power swath. Formerly it dropped to an old road paralleling I-90 and proceeded to the High Point interchange. *However,* private property owners have closed off this access. As of 1989 a new stretch of trail is being built from the Tradition Plateau to intersect the old route.

**One way from Otter Lake (south) trailhead to High Point (north) trailhead
11.1 miles, allow 8 hours
High point 2600 feet, elevation gain (ups and downs) 1200 feet
Bus: Metro 210 to High Point**

West Tiger 1 (map — page 174)

Highest of the three peaks, West Tiger 1 is worth going to only on the way to someplace else. The summit is cluttered with sky-trashing towers; WT 3 has better views and is more pristine and serene — and will stay that way if Weyerhaeuser is prevented from squeezing a dirty dollar from it as it has from the two higher peaks. However, WT 1 has the Preston Trail, crafted over the years by Dick Heinz, so plush that hikers usually suppose the government did

**Mount Rainier from Middle Tiger after a late October snowstorm
(Photo by Harvey Manning)**

the job and wonder when and why. Further, it fits neatly into any number of ingenious loop trips.

The bottom 1¼ miles of the Preston Trail have succumbed to residential development and no longer are open to the public. Until such time as a new route entirely on public lands may be devised, the access is via the Tiger Mountain Trail and Dwight's Way.

Starting at the north Tiger Mountain trailhead, elevation 450 feet, take the Tiger Mountain Trail (which see) 1½ miles, to 1130 feet.

Turn left on Dwight's Way, built by Dwight Riggs, a stalwart of the Issaquah Alps Rangers, specifically to salvage the Preston Trail. An up-and-down traverse crosses several small streams, rounds a spur ridge, and crosses a noisy creek to intersect the Preston Trail at 1150 feet, ¾ mile from the Tiger Mountain Trail.

Dick Heinz pieced together the Preston Trail from this and that logging railroad grade. Local residents have beaten many of these grades into accesses from their homes. Consequently a hiker must pay attention in order to keep proceeding upward and not be sidetracked on interesting explorations to golly knows where. The rule at the early junctions is to keep right; the feeder trails emanate from Preston, which is to the left and below. When the way has ascended nearly to the crest of the north ridge of Tiger, at 2000 feet, ¾ mile from Dwight's Way, it turns sharply (and obviously) left. The big old firs on the crest are visible from afar west, backlighted by the sunrise sky. Watch for the sidepath to Dick's Knoll, a rubbly andesite knob with remains of an old cabin and the hike's first views.

The trail follows on and near the crest of the ridge to a junction at 2150 feet; a newer Dick Heinz Trail goes off left 1½ miles to Fifteenmile Pass, a segment of the Grand Tiger Traverse from the Grand Canyon to High Point. In ¼ mile more, 2250 feet, a trail goes right to the West Tiger Railroad Grade and Tiger Mountain Trail (which see).

The way swings from the ridge over a slope of alder forest with winter views to the Cascades, enters dense small-conifer woods (blueberries in season), and at 2¼ miles from Dwight's Way attains the summit ridge and the first of the blabbermouth towers. A mucky service road leads ¼ mile along the flat to the main scene of electronic pollution and the views.

Round trip from High Point (Tiger Mountain Trail) trailhead 9½ miles, allow 6 hours
High point 2948 feet, elevation gain 2500 feet
Bus: Metro 210

Poo Poo Point (map — page 170)

In the winter of 1976-77 there was heard in downtown Issaquah the haunting call of the Yellow-Shafted Talkie Tooter, the "poo! poo!" and "poo-poo-poo-poo-poo" by which the choker-setter talks to the yarder. Thus was ushered in the Second Wave of clearcutting, the cleanup of patches of virgin forest ignored by the First Wave of the 1920s. The loggers proudly declare that mowing down the ancient trees on Poo Poo Point opened one of Tiger's finest views. Well, give Weyerhaeuser (then in charge around here) *that*. However,

Poo Poo Point from West Tiger Mountain

this was not merely virgin forest, it was old-growth. One observer commented, "If the company owned Seward Park, it would log that, too." Soon thereafter, the stumps of the old-growth trees mysteriously disappeared, evidently considered too embarrassing to be left for photographers to document and place in the dossier. The company has no shame.

Of the many routes, that from the Issaquah High School trailhead (elevation, 160 feet) has the richest sequence of woods and creeks. Ascend from behind the High School on the service road (the Old State Road), gated against public wheels. Follow it left around the sidehill, across Issabitty Creek, and at a long 1 mile from 2nd Avenue intersect the powerline. Climb andesite slabs to cross both powerline and gas line to the forest edge, 510 feet.

Two side-by-side roads take off from the gas line, diverging. Take the right, the High School Trail; the start of the grade is totally eroded away to naked rock. Ascend steadily into wondrous Many Creek Valley. At 1200 feet, 2½ miles, the way in quick succession crosses a summer creek, all-year Gap Creek, and the deep, richly forested ravine of West Creek. A jumble of rotted logs tells of the one-time logging-truck bridge. Sit beside the sparkling waters under marvelous big cedars and think of many things, of log exports and subdivision, and whether pigs have wings. Many folk escape here from city madness on hot summer afternoons and eat a picnic supper in the wildness and the cool.

A bit beyond still another ooze of a creek the old road ends, at 1280 feet, and a trail sets out straight up the slope, going through a stand of old-growth

Fifteenmile Creek

Douglas fir at 1500 feet. In a long ½ mile from the road-end, having gained 700 feet, the trail intersects West Tiger Railroad Grade, 1900 feet, 3¼ miles. Turn right a short bit to the end of the grade and follow a trail down across Poo Poo Creek, up, then steeply down to near the end of West Side Road at 1720 feet, 3½ miles.

Walk the road a long ¼ mile left and up to Poo Poo Point, 1775 feet. When school is in session there is peace and solitude here, in views straight down to green pastures of Issaquah Creek and the row of yellow schoolbuses by the high school, south to May Valley and Rainier and Renton, west over Squak and Cougar to Seattle and the Olympics, north to Issaquah, Lake Sammamish, and Baker.

Round trip from 2nd Avenue 7½ miles, allow 5 hours
High point 1900 feet, elevation gain 1900 feet
Bus: Metro 210

Middle Tiger Mountain (map — page 177)

Located way out in the middle of the air between the deep valleys of Fifteenmile and Holder Creeks, equidistant from the hulking ridges of West Tiger and East Tiger, Middle Tiger is the best vantage for studying the architecture of the "Tiger Range."

Of the several ways to the summit, the shortest and easiest is via the Middle Tiger spur from the Tiger Mountain Road, gated against vehicles, and then a short path — actually a gully dug by illegal motorcycles.

Most popular, requiring the least energy of the respectable routes and providing the most deep woods, is the ascent via the Tiger Mountain Trail (which see). From the Otter Lake trailhead, 1500 feet, walk 1¾ miles to intersect the Middle Tiger Trail and turn right ½ mile to the top.

Also well liked, owing to its looping potential, is the start directly from the West Side Road, on the remnant of a trail that used to ascend from the homes of Mirrormont before Weyerhaeuser clearcut that side of the mountain. Drive the West Side Road 3.6 miles from Highway 18. Park on a shoulder where the road crosses a deep gully, elevation 1200 feet.

The gully is so choked with alders the trail cannot be seen from the road. It is definitely there, however, starting with a scramble straight up the ravine wall from babbling creek and fallen timbers of a railroad trestle to hit the old trail. As the grade relents in the woods, at 1300 feet, spot the Middle Tiger Railroad going off left from the trestle site. The way ascends steeply in (mainly) alder forest to ¾ mile, 1760 feet, where a sidetrail goes off right to hit the Tiger Mountain Trail; at 1 mile, 2120 feet, is the intersection with the Tiger Mountain Trail. Continue up into patches of bracken and stands of young firs, pass windows out on lowlands; pause to admire lichen-green granite erratics dropped by the glacier from Canada. The way switchbacks from a gully to a sky-open ridge and the summit, 2607 feet, 1½ miles.

Burned bare by fires, new growth discouraged by cold of winter and heat of summer and loud winds that blow the year around, the half-naked, mountain-meadow-like summit is bright in season with lupine and spring gold, paintbrush and daisy and goldenrod. Or used to be. Now, however, the young forest is leaping skyward and the views and flowers are disappearing.

For flowers and views do the climb on a sunny day of spring or summer. For mystery do it in a soft autumn fog that mayhap settles into valleys to become a shining cloudsea. For arctic adventure come in winter when billions of flakes swirl around the summit — or billions of sun-sparkling crystals are flung in your eyes by a northerly gale. Ascend (carefully!) when dramatic cloud castles are drifting, drifting nearer, nearer, slanting gray rainlines to earth — and suddenly zapping each other and shaking the mountain and impelling your feet hastily downward. And don't forget the light show at night.

Round trip from West Side Road via Tiger Mountain Trail 4½ miles, allow 3 hours
High point 2607 feet, elevation gain 1100 feet

Round trip from West Side Road via Middle Tiger Trail 3 miles, allow 3 hours
Elevation gain 1400 feet
West Side Road may be impassable in winter

Grand Canyon of Fifteenmile Creek–Middle Tiger Railroad (map — page 177)

Rising in the broad saddle of Fifteenmile Pass, which separates the bulks of West Tiger and East Tiger, Fifteenmile Creek is the central watercourse of the mountain, the longest and largest completely *within* the mountain. Beautiful and wild and exciting for all its deep-forested miles, the stream scenically climaxes in the Grand Canyon, where falls tumble down a slot steeply and gaudily walled by green trees and shrubs, gray and brown and yellow sandstone and shale, and black coal. Poking about old mines and searching for yellow amber add interest.

Walkers wanting a bit more exercise commonly do a loop combining the Grand Canyon with the Middle Tiger Railroad Grade, proposed to be designated as an Historic Site and preserved from modern bulldozers and trucks.

Drive the West Side Road 5 miles from Highway 18 and look sharp. If you find yourself crossing Fifteenmile Creek, you didn't look sharp enough. Before the drop to the creek, note an unused, gated, private road joining from the left — the Tiger Mountain Mine Road. In a short bit, where the West Side Road bends left, the Mine Road goes off obscurely straight ahead, through a borrow pit into the forest. Park hereabouts, elevation 800 feet.

At ½ mile is a large field; wander off left to peer down into a concrete pit formerly containing a device with large steel teeth that were meant to chew up the coal that wasn't mined by a stock operation of the early 1960s. The road returns to forest and gently ascends along the sidehill of a splendid green valley, the creek roaring far below. At ¾ mile, 950 feet, the road bends in and out of the ravine of the South Fork, a delicious creek; look for a hole in the bank, either a coal prospect or an amber-miner's dig.

Around a corner at 1 mile is a Y, 980 feet. For the picnic trip take the left fork, contouring to concrete artifacts and rotten timbers and the end of the mining railroad; dating from around World War I and sporadically active in the 1930s, this operation produced little coal. A slippery path leads to the slot of the Grand Canyon, where water sluices through trenches in the rock and swirls in potholes and splashes hikers' hot faces. In winter the slot is totally occupied by raging furies; in late summer a person can scramble and slither in, startling the water ouzels as they flit by.

The right fork passes the mine (rusty algae ooze out, maidenhair fern hangs over the black mouth), sternly climbs past the slot, then levels out at creek level and at 1½ miles, 1200 feet, deadends. Note timber footings of the vanished bridge; in low water hop across and investigate ironware and the collapsed tunnel, which was timbered only with alder poles and went in just far enough to extract cash from the investors.

Round trip 3 miles, allow 2 hours
High point 1200 feet, elevation gain 400 feet
West Side Road may be impassable in winter

Now for the loop return.

From the deadend scramble strenuously up the bank past a large stump. Steep but easy flagged path ascends 300 feet in ¼ mile to the Middle Tiger Railroad Grade, 1500 feet. Though not as long as the West Tiger Railroad Grade, this survival is just as superbly historic and scenic. Professor Fred

Rounds tells us the grade came from the lumber mill at Hobart (where the millpond still can be seen beside the road), crossed Fifteenmile Creek valley on the famous Horseshoe Trestle, and via a switchback continued up the valley to Fifteenmile Pass. He and fellow loggers, based at the bunkhouse in Hobart, rode a speeder to work each morning. The logging ended with the crash in 1929.

Before doing the loop, turn left on the grade ½ mile to Fifteenmile Creek, 1780 feet, a bully site for a picnic in the wildwoods beside the splashing stream, watching the dippers dip. On the way note where the ¼-mile Horseshoe Trestle spanned the valley; a few of the uprights still are. Note the 2-inch cable, the skyline that was rigged between spar trees to carry the big sticks high in the air over the valley for loading on rail cars.

(To do a variant loop, near the creek a flagged path climbs 200 feet in a scant ¼ mile to the Tiger Mountain Trail, which leads to the Middle Tiger Trail.)

Returned from the sidetrip, follow the grade 1 mile in peaceful woods to the Middle Tiger Trail at 1300 feet. At several spots the trail detours around vanished bridges. This rail line was built by "Trestle" Johnson, noted for his fanatic devotion to trestle bridges. By contrast, that other self-taught Swede engineer who with double-bitted ax and jawful of snoose laid out the West Tiger Railroad Grade was equally devoted to stringer bridges. Whatever the comparative merits, it must be said that trying to bridge Fifteenmile Creek with a stringer design would've demanded the ingenuity of more than one Swede — maybe even of a Norwegian.

Descend the Middle Tiger Trail a short bit to the West Side Road at 1200 feet; in the gully of the large creek at the trailhead note fallen timbers of another of "Trestle's" masterpieces. Complete the loop by walking the West Side Road 1 mile back to the car.

Loop trip plus sidetrip 5 miles, allow 4 hours
High point 1500 feet, elevation gain 1000 feet

Silent Swamp–East Tiger Mountain (map — page 188)

East (Main) Tiger used to be hikers' most popular peak by far, and the standard "trail" was the service road that led to the fire-lookout tower and, when that was removed in the mid-1960s, to the blabber towers. Even now the views are so different from those on other peaks that the ascent can be warmly recommended — but only on weekdays before school lets out.

On the razzer-loudest Sundays the Silent Swamp is a gorgeous walk by itself — and combines beautifully with another wheelfree haven, Beaver Valley (which see).

Drive the East Side Road 2.4 miles from Highway 18 to the lower end of the Silent Swamp trail, elevation 1420 feet.

Ascend a short bit to a railroad grade. To the left it meets the East Side Road (for a reason to be explained below). Turn right on the grade, which makes a sweeping U-turn around the end of a low ridge, goes through a wide saddle at 1550 feet, and enters the valley of Silent Swamp. Hark! What is that new sensation that smites the ears? It is the sound of silence. The ridge has blocked out the din of I-90. Listen now to frogs and wrens. Gape at huge

Trout Hatchery Creek

stumps of cedar and fir. Admire devils club and skunk cabbage of the lovely swamp, headwaters of North Fork Trout Hatchery Creek.

The grade sidehills from the swamp to a junction at 1 mile, 1700 feet, and a lesson in railroad history—and the reason this railroad grade, as well as those of West Tiger and Middle Tiger, is proposed for preservation as an Historic Site.

Whereas the Hobart mill engineered its rail approach to Middle Tiger forests with a long, gradual sidehill ascent, and the High Point mill built a tramway up West Tiger, the Preston mill that operated on East Tiger employed switchbacks in this manner: A stretch of grade angled up a slope to a deadend. At the distance of one locomotive and a train of cars back from the deadend, the next stretch of grade took off uphill at an acute angle in the opposite direction. A train climbing the mountain proceeded past the junction to the deadend, pulled by the locomotive. A switch was thrown and the train went into reverse and backed up the next stretch, pushed to another deadend by the locomotive, which on the next switchback again took the lead.

On the route thus far, the Silent Swamp trail where first intersected had just completed a switchback from the stretch of grade now occupied by the East

Side Road. The sweeping U-turn was used to obviate the need for one switchback. Here at 1700 feet is the next switch.

The grade reverse-turning to the right leads ¼ mile in lovely woods to the East Side Road at 1850 feet — and another switchback. For the best walking, though, continue straight ahead to the deadend at the deep-woods ravine of South Fork Trout Hatchery Creek, 1¼ miles, 1720 feet. Why go on? No dandier spot for a picnic than by the splash of the creek. Watch dippers flit from boulder to boulder.

Round trip 2½ miles, allow 1½ hours
High point 1720 feet, elevation gain 300 feet
East Side Road may be impassable in winter

To continue to higher destinations, follow meager trail along and across the creek, then up the fall line to the deadend of an old logging road. Turn right, back over the creek, to the East Side Road at 1950 feet, 1¾ miles.

Note: A few steps up the road is the turnoff to Beaver Valley (which see).

For the summit, stick with the road all the way, nice sociable side-by-side walking, with rarely a vehicle on weekdays. The road climbs steadily, swinging around the side of the 2786-foot satellite peak of East Tiger; views begin to open through young firs whose crowns are leaping up to block views. The road tops the saddle between the peaks and drops a bit to join an offshoot of the Tiger Mountain Road at 2670 feet, 1½ road miles (3½ miles from the start of this walk). A gate now halts all wheels. Oh joy! Even on Sunday!

The final ¾ mile is packed with entertainment. One item is the interesting Spring, source of the Spring Fork of Raging River; ponder where it gets its year-round flow, here so near the summit. The other is the sky, which now grows enormously as trees shorten. Though there is never a single 360° panorama, views extend in every direction as the road winds south, west, north, west, and south again — so confusingly that a hiker needs a compass to avoid mistaking Duvall for Seattle. At one time or other there are views over the Raging River to Rattlesnake Mountain and the Cascades, views over I-90 to Lake Alice Plateau, Snoqualmie Valley, Glacier Peak, and Baker, views south to Rainier and the ruins of St. Helens, and over Middle Tiger to Seattle and Whulj.

At 4½ miles, 3004 feet, the road flattens on the bulldozer-leveled summit. The sky is trashed with metalwork. However, the tower people are cleaning up the summit, revegetating and generally beautifying the scar. A forest of huddled hemlocks blocks views north and east but horizons are open a hundred miles south and west.

Round trip 9 miles, allow 6 hours
High point 3004 feet, elevation gain 1580 feet

Beaver Valley (map — page 188)

A tiny blue dot on the USGS map caught the surveyor's eye and drew his feet — to a scene that made him feel as did those explorers prowling jungles of Yucatan who stumbled upon ruins of the Old Empire of the Mayans. Inspecting with the archeologist's eye, he speculated that soon after the loggers moved out in the late 1920s, the beaver colony moved in to harvest the second-growth salads springing up green and sweet, and that over a half-century they dammed not merely the single blue dot seen by the GS camera in the sky but the 20-odd others, building dams as tall as a hiker and up to 50 feet long. Some of the ponds are silted in and meadowed over, others are open water, their dams showing signs of repair quite recently. However, the teeth marks on large conifers, which aren't a beaver's notion of holiday feasting, tell of the hunger that led them to migrate, probably in the late or middle 1970s, in search of lettuce and tomatoes. The surveyor inspected evidences of a half-century of residence and saw they had so remodeled this headwater valley of North Fork Trout Hatchery Creek as to fashion an ecosystem unique in the Alps; contributing to the uniqueness is the unusual microclimate here in a nook of wind-swirls and sunshine-and-shadows between "Beaver Hill" and the main mass of East Tiger.

When the surveyor reported his discovery to the scientific world, it was investigated by specialists who confirmed and elaborated the specialness of the place. However, they added that the beaver residency dating from the 1920s was only the latest in a cycle of periodic occupancies-and-abandonments dating back perhaps centuries. Some of the dam remnants the hiker sees today are as old as George Washington, maybe Pocahontas.

Drive the East Side Road 4.3 miles from Highway 18 to just past the upper Silent Swamp trailhead and park carefully on the side of the road, elevation 1960 feet.

The East Side Road turns sharply uphill right. The old railroad grade goes straight ahead on the flat, in season so overgrown by salmonberry the start has to be found by the feet and the power of prayer. Once in the woods, though, the route opens out obviously.

At a flat below the grade, and also above, the curious can find artifacts of an ancient booze factory that probably lacked a federal license. In ¼ mile, 2000 feet, is the lip of the ravine of North Fork Trout Hatchery Creek.

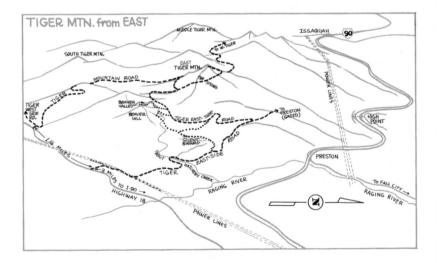

Here, at a landing with much evidence of donkey and yarder and railroad, look across the gap to resumption of the grade. Look down to tumbled ruins of the trestle and to the first beaver dam.

Turn right, uphill, on a non-rail road. Log-hauling in this vicinity apparently was by a peculiar combination of lokie and truck — rusty chunks of truck are scattered along the many roads that radiate from rail landings. The ingenuity of those Swede engineers knew no bounds.

In a short bit cross the creek on remnants of a fill and battle upward through devils club and other evils. The flagged path turns off the road, right, through dense, choked forest and down to the creek and the first of the big dams, ½ mile, 2080 feet.

Downstream there is only one major dam; most of the action was upstream. Allow hours for exploration and inspection and musing. The dams are a study in themselves, the way the sticks are woven together, the way sedimentation by the creek gradually made them watertight, then filled in ponds, requiring new dams elsewhere. See if you can find where the beaver lived, in lodges or perhaps creek-bank burrows.

The insect community is outstanding, waterskates skating, mosquitoes whining, spiders lying in ambush. The varied thrush nests hereabouts, and possibly the golden eagle.

Classified as an ecotone, a transitional plant community, the forest features an unusual combination of Sitka spruce, here near its far-east limit, and Pacific silver fir, here near its closest approach to Seattle. Other conifers mingle, and old snags — one or more may have been sparpoles during the logging. Shrubs include fool's huckleberry, Alaska huckleberry, bearberry. Flowers include queen's cup and St. Olav's candlestick. Mosses, lichens, and liverworts are various and profuse. Please walk softly, stay on paths established since discovery of the valley in 1980, don't stomp the scene to death.

At a long ¾ mile from the East Side Road is Salamander Lake, 2140 feet, in the saddle where the creek heads. The loggers seem to have had a landing here. The beavers did themselves proud, damming a pond that caught the eye of the GS in the sky. In spring the pond is a mass of egg sacs of frogs and rough-skinned newts, who for months put on a gaudy show.

Round trip 1½ miles, allow 1½ years
High point 2140 feet, elevation gain 200 feet
East Side Road may be impassable in winter

CEDAR RIVER

The Cedar is the most useful river in Puget Sound City. Rising on the Cascade Crest, it brings clean mountain water to Landsburg, where more or less of the flow, depending on the season, is diverted into the pipeline that empties into a reservoir, Lake Youngs, which fills the bathtubs and swimming pools, greens the lawns and washes the dishes of the south sector of Seattle and neighboring communities. The waters not so diverted enter Lake Washington, where they provide the flushing action without which the celebrated Metro sewage cleanup wouldn't have done the job of cleaning up Lake Washington. Exiting through the Ship Canal to Lake Union and Whulj, the river gives sockeye salmon a route from the ocean to spawning grounds.

Less known is the role of the 103,000-acre, closed-to-the-public Cedar River Watershed upstream from Landsburg as a reservoir of wildlife that constantly replenishes the populations of birds and beasts in the Snoqualmie valley, the Issaquah Alps, and the entire Lake Washington-Lake Sammamish-Cedar River-Green River area. The Washington State Department of Wildlife (formerly, Game) correctly reminds that controlled recreation can coexist with potable water. However, that excellent agency has a traditional and powerful clientele for which "wildlife" means something to eat. If hunting were permitted in the watershed — now completely closed to all forms of recreation — the number of animals shot dead would be a small fraction of those well-warned to be warier. Becoming warier, they would stop wandering out into the suburban areas which have become No Shooting zones and thus game sanctuaries.

Seattle City Water is considering a limited opening of the watershed. If this means guns, the quality of hiking — and living — in the Issaquah Alps and adjacent areas will be diminished. The watershed is the reason there are cougar and lynx and bobcat and bear and elk ranging near the shores of Lake Washington and Lake Sammamish; no matter how thoughtful a "harvest," it is bound to be discouraging to the "harvested."

Granted, City Water fences may be unnecessarily blocking off lands where recreation of some sorts could do no harm. Rattlesnake Ledge (see *Footsore 2*) used to be behind the fence; one of this surveyor's early ascents cost him and a companion $100 in fines and attorney fees. Subsequently the fences were moved back and the Ledge became legal; City Water has not reimbursed the surveyor a sum that in constant dollars, plus interest, would amount to perhaps $1000.

The fence easily could be drawn back to allow the currently illegal — yet highly popular — ascents of the East Peak of Rattlesnake Mountain and Herpicide Spire. Possibly, too, the railroad from Landsburg to Rattlesnake Lake could be opened to hikers, permitting what is now a Moonlight Sneak. However, if letting in boots means letting in guns, wildlife-loving pedestrians will prefer to maintain the status quo. Boots have other places they can go. The wild creatures are running out of escapes.

USGS maps: Mercer Island, Renton, Maple Valley, Black Diamond, Hobart
Walkable all year

Gene Coulon Memorial Beach Park

Gene Coulon Memorial Beach Park (map — page 194)

What man has put asunder, man may sometimes have a chance to put back together. Renton Parks has done so here. It started with 57 acres of Lake Washington shore hemmed in by railroad tracks, uglified by generations of industrial mucking about. Working from a Jones & Jones design it created a multi-use park that on fine weekends swarms with swimmers, sunbathers, fishermen, canoeists, stinkpotters, sailboaters, and little kids yelling — but on weekdays is as peaceful and lovely a lakeshore for walking as one could wish, only the goslings and ducklings making a racket. Named for a former head of Renton Parks, this longest stretch of public waterfront south of Seward Park does his memory proud.

Go off I-405 on Exit 5, signed "Park Avenue," turn right on Park, then right on Lake Washington Boulevard, then left into the park, elevation 25 feet.

In an air distance of 1 mile are 1½ miles of in-and-out shore path. For the full trip park at the south end in the lot serving South Beach. Walk to the water, passing the Shuffleton Power Plant, with which Puget Power used to make electricity from steam generated by burning coal. The little Nature Island is often closed at the bridge to let the birds rest between scoffing fish and chips. Views are impressive of the gaping maws from which issue Boeing jets; the panorama includes the mouth of the Cedar River, Beacon Hill, a glimpse of Mt. Selig, and the south end of Mercer Island.

Shore paths lead northward past the kids' playground, the bathing beach (enclosed by a concrete walkaround excellent for out-in-the-lake viewpoints), coots, duck, and geese to a bridge over the marsh estuary of John's Creek. Across the bridge is a second parking lot, serving the boat-launch and boat harbor. Past the harbor is the lagoon enclosed by the 1000-foot floating boardwalk of the Picnic Gallery. The Gazebo, the Pavilion, the Ivar's Eatery all are in turn-of-the-century architecture poignantly recalling the waterfront amusement parks of Seattle's past. *Interface,* a bronze sculpture by Phillip Levine, demands a pause. The shore continues along the largest enclosure, Log Boom Pond, which has logs moored at the outer edge to keep razzer-boats away. The narrow strip of land between water and railroad tracks has been intensively landscaped, provided with The Mount, a hummock that adds topographical interest, and a profusion of plantings of trees and shrubs, native and exotic, that by the turn of the century will give the park innumerable sylvan nooks. In all, some 15,000 trees and 90,000 shrubs and water plants have been set out.

At an entry road from Lake Washington Boulevard is the third and final parking area, serving the Canoe Launch and the North Park, ½ mile of pathway with no vehicle intrusion. Granite boulders have been installed on the shore, as well as old timbers seen to be handsome and thus rescued from the dump. The concrete piers and rotting pilings of an old booming ground remain; here the railroad used to dump logs for rafting to mills. A bridge crosses Trestle Marsh (cattails and blackbirds). A fishing pier lets a person walk on the water. The park ends at the residences of Colman Point.

Round trip 3 miles, allow 2 hours
High point 25 feet, no elevation gain
Bus: Metro 110

Renton-to-Bellevue trail passing through Gene Coulon Memorial Beach Park

Renton-to-Bellevue Trail

For *Footloose,* predecessor to *Footsore,* Janice Krenmayr walked the railroad from Ballard to Bothell and proclaimed it "oughter be" a trail. And so it is, now, the Burke-Gilman, probably as busy as any urban trail in the nation. The trains still are running from Renton to Bellevue and long may they do so, but trains and walkers have coexisted for a century and a half. There is no reason pedestrians cannot walk, now, from Renton to Bellevue, so long as they keep an eye to the rear.

For short stretches there are alternatives on the Lake Washington Bikeway, provided by the state Highway Department at places where it obliterated the ancient and honorable Lake Washington Boulevard for I-405. However, these bikeways are beside the freeway, loud and gassy and inferior to the rail route.

Much of the railway passes through residential areas, resembling the Burke-Gilman. Parts are off in secluded woods. All in all, the route is better for neighborhood strolling — or long-distance walking — than for nature walks. But the same can be said of the B-G and see how the folks throng *there.*

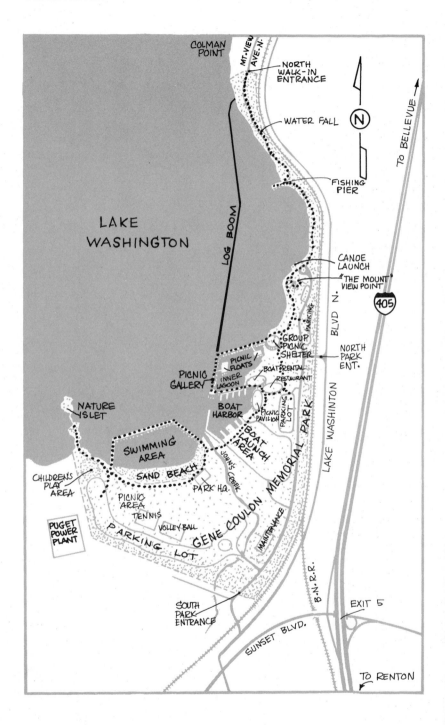

South 1¼ miles from Gene Coulon Park the railroad intersects the Cedar River Trail (which see), a connection east through Maple Valley to Landsburg and ultimately to Snoqualmie Pass, as well as west to the outlet of the Cedar River into Lake Washington. The rails continue, for some distance near and then absolutely *on* the route of the Seattle & Walla Walla Railroad, Seattle's first railroad, which extended from Elliott Bay to the Newcastle mines; the line is now proposed as a National Historic Landmark.

Presently, however, the walking south from Coulon Park is mainly of historic interest, so the route will be described from that point (elevation, 25 feet) north. The mileages given below are *driving* miles, on Lake Washington Boulevard and associated roads, to indicate places the car can be parked in order to start walking.

At 1 mile from the north end of Coulon Park, round Colman Point to Kennydale Snappy Mart. Access from boulevard to tracks. Across the water is the South Point of Mercer Island. The old Seattle & Walla Walla left the shore near here to climb to the high country of May Creek.

1.2 miles, Kennydale Beach Park. The public is permitted to touch the lake.

1.6 miles, Barbee Mill, recalling when shores of lakes and Whulj were lined with mills and rafted logs.

Cedar River and Renton Airport

1.8 miles, cross May Creek. A rude path goes up the north bank toward May Creek County Park.

2 miles. At a fork, Ripley Lane goes left and then north 0.25 mile to railroad access at the end of the log sea of a piling-treatment company. Ripley shortly ends and a stretch of Lake Washington Bikeway begins.

4 miles. Having crossed I-405, recross to the west side on Exit 9, to a T. To the left, south, is Pleasure Point, where a tramway used to lower coals from Newcastle to barges on the lake. In 0.7 mile the road ends and bikeway begins. To the right from Pleasure Point Interchange, Lakehurst Lane goes north 0.5 mile to the road-end and start of bikeway.

Walk from the road-end down to the tracks. The road forks, both left and right going to private homes. Between them, however, is Newcastle Beach Park. Very interesting. To the birds and the muskrats. This last piece of the Coal Creek delta that has not been preempted for fancy houses and noisy stinkpots is (1987) entirely a wetland jungle, not so much as a mushroomer's path into the brambles and the groves of cottonwoods and the ooky black-as-coal muck. Bellevue Parks is doing something (1988) with the 28 acres, but not very much. A bit of beach for wading. A view dock. One thing it is doing is very great, however. William Way, who specializes in taking water out of ditches and transforming it into wildland creeks, is creating "Newcastle Creek," with gravel for fish to spawn in, ponds for ducks to float in. Nature will take over from Mr. Way and in a year nobody will realize he was at all involved.

5 miles. Having gone onto I-405 at Exit 9, go off on Exit 10, turn left on Coal Creek Parkway to Lake Washington Boulevard, just where it goes under the railroad and just where the Lake Washington Bikeway comes in from the south.

6.7 miles. Bellefields Nature Park trailhead. Access is easy from here to railroad, now up on the hillside at an elevation of 100 feet.

North from here the railroad goes through Bellevue and Kirkland, drops to the Sammamish Valley, and connects to much of the world.

One way (by rail) from Coulon Park to Bellefields Park 7 miles, allow 5 hours
High point 100 feet, elevation gain 75 feet

Cedar River Trail (map — page 201)

From points at or near one end, three partly potential and partly existing trails lead to beautiful logic: a walking route along the line of the historic Seattle & Walla Walla Railroad to Elliott Bay; another up and along Beacon Hill, then down to the Skid Road and Elliott Bay; a third north beside Lake Washington to Bellevue, with offshoots up May Creek and Coal Creek to the Issaquah Alps.

From points on the way to the other end, walking routes to Lake Wilderness and Black Diamond; to Big Soos Park and Auburn; and to Snoqualmie Pass.

—And on the trail itself, any number of choice spots to observe the windings of the river through a city, through the countryside, and through wildland.

Lake Washington to Cedar River Park (map — page 201)

In this age when Growth is coming to be seen as not worth it if it adds only flesh, no spirit, many a community is engaged in a quest for identity, a search for soul. Renton found part of its soul in the heart of town — the Cedar River — and built a splendid trail where citizens can walk and jog close to home, and where visitors can learn what Renton is all about.

Drive Logan Avenue North from the city center north past Renton Stadium to the entry of Boeing Renton Plant. Turn left on North 6 Street, signed "Cedar River Trail," and proceed to a deadend at Lake Washington, elevation less than 25 feet.

A Boeing fence unnecessarily blocks access to the absolute mouth, a few feet distant, but doesn't shut off views to Mercer Island, Beacon Ridge, Queen Anne Hill, and Cougar Mountain.

The wide trail — blacktop, then cinders — parallels the channelized river in lawns amid new-planted trees and shrubs. The water floats fleets of ducks and gulls; thickets shelter flitter-birds. On every side are big tin pots sicklied o'er with the pale cast of watercolor — Boeing jets built on the trail side of the river and trundled across a bridge to Renton Airport to make maiden flights from which they never return because the field is too short for jets to land.

Listening to the thundering present, ponder the wild past. Primevally, the Black River drained from the lake hereabouts and flowed close beneath the steep slopes of Beacon Ridge to join the Green River; on the way, somewhere in the middle of the plain that until recently became part of the lake during the rainy season, the Black was joined by the Cedar River, which later was diverted into Lake Washington.

Note the future opportunity — the Seattle City Light powerlines descending Beacon Ridge, the potential link to Seattle and the Whulj Trail.

The park lane passes Renton Stadium, crosses under Logan Avenue, goes by a massive pier of the long-gone railroad bridge, and passes Renton Senior Center. The path enters a residential section, crosses under Williams Avenue, Wells Avenue, and Bronson Way to Renton Public Library — whose structure bridges the river!

Past the baseball field, by the swimming pool, cross the street and go under the railroad and I-405 to Cedar River Park, mainly noted for Carco Theater. Here the river debouches from Maple Valley onto the Renton Plain, part of the Big Valley. At 1¾ miles from the lake, Stoneway Concrete presently halts progress.

Round trip 3½ miles, allow 2 hours
High point 25-odd feet, insignificant elevation gain
Bus: many Metro lines to downtown Renton, 110 to Renton Library

Cedar River Park to Maplewood Golf Course (map — page 201)

Renton plans to extend its trail to the golf course, 4½ miles from the lake. Sidewalks already follow Maple Valley Highway the entire distance. However, one hopes the official trail will start on the other side of the river — quieter, greener.

Drive Highway 169 (signed "Enumclaw") from Renton under the railroad and I-405 to Carco Theater-Cedar River Park. Park on the west edge, elevation 25 feet.

Ascend the embankment to the railroad, cross the bridge over the Cedar, and at the junction turn left, leaving the Big Valley for Maple Valley. Industry and cars are quickly left behind. The rusty, silent rails cut the foot of the valley wall, green and rugged and wild for 350 steep feet.

CEDAR RIVER

At 1 mile from the junction, just past a gaudy cliff of sedimentary strata, is a long, broad river terrace, once inhabited, but by 1987 become wild and lonesome, the quiet fields lined by tall poplars and cottonwoods, man's vanished residence recalled by mountains of lilacs and the blossoms of garden escapes. The surveyor had fondly hoped the joyous spot had been obtained by Renton for a park. Almost that was true. The city did get a bit of riverbank for a "natural section" of the Cedar River Trail. The rest of the terrace is fated for houses. A new bridge will replace the old plank structure that crosses the river at SE 5 Street. The trackwalker likely will wish to sidetrip to the parklet, then resume the rail route. At ⅓ mile more as the tracks go (past a swamp and lily pond) and ½ mile as the river runs, railroad bridge #1 makes a logical turnaround. The parklet on the upstream side has public parking and a sandy beach for wading.

Round trip 3 miles, allow 1½ hours
High point 350 feet, elevation gain 325 feet
Bus: Metro 110 to Renton Library

Maplewood Golf Course to Maple Valley Junction (map — page 201)

The bad news for a hiker is that folks hereabouts are so tired of fishermen tromping through their petunias and agitating their dogs that they've fenced, posted, signed, and almost totally privatized the Cedar, both along the Maple Valley Highway and on Jones Road, across the river. The so-so news is that the railroad tracks continue straight through, but are mostly beside the noisy highway, rarely by the river. The good news is that King County Parks owns several large, undeveloped chunks of floodplain and floodway fields and forests where vehicles and guns are prohibited but feet can romp as they please.

Maplewood Wildwood (map — page 201)

At railroad bridge #2 commences a gloryland of an old farm acquired by King County Parks.

Drive Maple Valley Highway 0.4 mile east from bridge #2 at the end of Maplewood Golf Course. Note on the right a two-storey, mossy-roofed, white farmhouse (very handsome). Just beyond, on the left, spot a gate barring a lane out into the field. Parking space for several cars, elevation 75 feet.

The entry lane winds to the river through fields that grow only grass, broom, tansy, and hellberry — toured by hawks, so something lives there, scurrying around in the weeds. The width of the fields so softens highway noise that the river readily drowns it out. From the far bank steeply rises a 325-foot wildwood wall. Peace.

The lane turns downstream on a short stretch of dike to a place where the state Department of Fisheries annually, October-November, installs a weir in the river to divert spawning sockeye salmon to a holding pond where eggs can be stripped — part of the Cedar River Enhancement Program, which has been so successful that in spawning months a person can hardly see the river bottom for the big red fish — and can hardly take a step along the banks without stirring up a gang of ducks, herons, gulls, and other fishers.

The downstream way enters a forest distinguished by monster cottonwoods; sidetrails lead out on gravel bars. Across the river are a magic grotto

Cedar River Trail in Renton

where a creek falls free into the green, and a tall wall of sandstones and shales with a seam of coal at the foot. In low water one can wade ...

The upstream way prowls through more cottonwoods to a river meadow with a look across the water to a sand wall pocked by swallow holes.

Round trip (upstream and down) 2½ miles, allow 2 hours

Elliot Jungle (map — page 201)

This chunk of King County parkland runs along 1 mile of river — with just about zero easy walking. However, you can't beat it for privacy.

CEDAR RIVER

Drive 0.4 mile east from the entrance to Aqua Barn Ranch and spot a wide turnout on the north side of the highway, at the railroad's Mile 16.

Walk the tracks back west toward Aqua Barn, looking for a chance to bust through the snowberry and wild rose (a colorful duet in autumn fruit) to the cottonwoods, onward to the river.

Then walk the tracks south. Beside a highway take the old road-path over a field, down to an ancient gravel mine, and to the river.

Round trip both ways 2 miles, allow 2 hours

Indian Forest (map — page 201)

Just east of a sprawl of buildings occupied by a roofing company, on the site of the old Indian Mine, park on a wide turnout on the north side of the highway.

Find a gated woods road into the columnar cottonwood, to a dike that runs ½ mile upstream. Paths continue on, steadily more obscure. Between railroad and river lies nearly a square half-mile of floodway sloughs and floodplain forest, a wild tangle, a grandeur.

Round trip 2 miles, allow 2 hours

Titanic Cliff (map — page 201)

From railroad bridge #3 to Maple Valley Junction the houses are too frequent and the river and highway too adjacent to please the walker. However, the Titanic Cliff cannot be ignored.

Just before reaching #3 from the Renton direction spot a tiny road going off right. Park on the highway shoulder and walk the gated road to the river, elevation 275 feet.

A riprap bulwark keeps the Cedar from undermining Titanic Cliff. Stroll ⅓ mile to the foot of the neckbending wall, naked and terrific and 200 feet to the impossible top. Goggle and retreat, because just beyond is the gulch that drains Lake Desire-Shady Lake-Otter Lake-Peterson Lake, and it surely is a wild magnificence, but you could sink into the ook and nevermore be seen.

Round trip ¾ mile, allow ½ hour

Maple Valley to Landsburg (map — page 201)

Now for something completely different — wild river flowing through lonesome wildwoods, beside gravel bars to delight and under gravel cliffs to astound.

The railroad distance from Maple Valley Junction to Landsburg is 5½ miles, a nice distance for an easy day's round trip. Park near the rail line, elevation 343 feet, and hit the tracks.

However, since the best of the trip is near Landsburg, the description will start at that end. Drive Issaquah-Hobart-Ravensdale Road 3 miles south of Hobart to the Landsburg Bridge over the Cedar River. Park near the railroad tracks, elevation 560 feet.

Fisherfeet have beaten a trackside path for 1 mile, and paths every few yards to overlooks of dippers and ducks, mossy nooks among the maples, and bars fit for a picnic. On the survey in early October there were a gull or heron on every boulder, squadrons of ducks patrolling the avenue, raptors circling

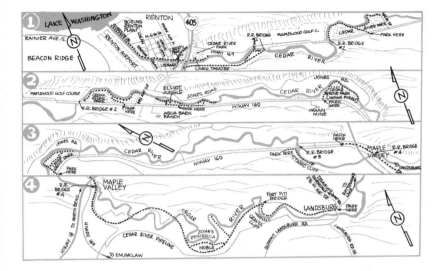

above, and backwaters and pools so full of sockeye salmon you could walk across and never get your feet wet.

Where the tracks enter an odd little valley, turn off on a riverside path that follows the river around a big loop for ⅔ mile (the railroad gets to the end in ⅓ mile). Enchantment! Virgin-looking forests of big old conifers. Groves of giant cottonwoods. Understory of vine maple in flame (in October). Camps on the gravel. And across the river the Great Gravel Cliff rising an absolutely vertical 150 feet from the gulls. At first the way follows what appears to be an ancient railroad grade, then becomes a mixture of mucky woods roads and fishing paths, a bit brushy at spots. The segment concludes at a bridge signed "Fort Pitt Bridge Works Pittsburgh PA 1908." It's a beauty and absolutely must be placed on the State Historical Register before B-N scraps it to earn a dirty nickel.

Across the bridge are more deep-shadowed wildwoods, more sunny bars, but this area is suggested as the turnaround for a neat little walk from Landsburg — what with all the sidetrips you easily could be the whole day at it, especially if the kids have anything to say.

Houses now enter the scene, across the river. And there are no more easy paths to the water. However, at a long ½ mile (as the rails run) from the first bridge is the Cedar River's most exciting moment, a pair of peninsula ridges enclosed by giant meanders. John's Peninsula, on the far side, only can be explored when the river is wadable. The one on the near side, a skinny ridge with cliffy walls, is strictly for the doughty.

Though wildwoods continue, excitement diminishes. At ⅓ mile from the start of the peninsulas is a crossing of SE 248 Street, entry to the hideaway homes of Noble. Public feet are pretty well excluded from the river. The survey stopped at the second bridge, 1 mile from the Noble road, because suburbia thickened. However, the long 2 miles (with two more bridges worth photographing) to Maple Valley Junction would be superb prelude to the climax upstream.

CEDAR RIVER

Round trip (with a few sidetrips) from Landsburg to first bridge 4 miles, allow 3 hours
High point 560 feet, minor elevation gain

Round trip (no sidetrips) from Maple Valley Junction to Landsburg 11 miles, allow 6 hours
Elevation gain 300 feet

Landsburg to Rattlesnake Lake (map — page 201)

At Landsburg begins the Seattle City Water Cedar River Watershed, in all the 25 air miles to the Cascade Crest closed to humans except a handful of city employees, several scientists, and a few thousand loggers, each of whom signs a pledge to drop chainsaw and run to the Sanikan in case of need, in order not to pollute the city's chlorinated, fluoridated, limed, asbestosized, pipe-eating water.

Rumor hath it that phantom hikers have walked the railroad east from Landsburg by the light of the moon, risking deportation to a penal colony, but meeting no vocal objection except from the coyotes. At something like a dozen

Cedar River and Titanic Cliff

miles from Landsburg they are said to have been picked up by confederates lurking in the shadow of Rattlesnake Ledge. They are reported to have been enraptured by the river, the railroad bridges, sites of vanished logging villages and sawmills, the broad delta flat of Green Valley, the creeks flowing from Taylor and Rattlesnake Mountains and nameless peaks of the Cascades front. However, these phantoms scofflaws must stand condemned by society.

Lake Wilderness Arboretum (map — page 204)

How many acres are in this wildland? Impertinent question! As well ask a person, "How big is your imagination?" Or ask the South King County Arboretum Foundation, "Does man have a soul?" Driving here on the pandemonic freeways and the frantic arterials, the philosopher may lean toward answering the last question in the negative. He may not even be softened by a summer Sunday in the antic Lake Wilderness County Park. But once a few steps onto the largest trail system in this vicinity, the balance of is body humors will swing from the choleric and melancholic to the sanguine.

Drive the Maple Valley-Black Diamond Road, Highway 169, south 1.2 miles from the center of the Maple Valley bridge over the Cedar River, turn right on Witte Road 0.8 mile, and turn left on 248th for 0.25 mile to a triple fork. The right leads 0.5 mile to the county park, the middle ("Private") to what used to be the University of Washington Continuing Education Center, and the left, gated shut ("Pedestrians Only") into the arboretum (which occupies county parkland). Park on the shoulder well back from the gate. Elevation, 470 feet.

For openers, walk around the gate to the kiosk to study the map of the trail system. Not that there's any danger of getting irretrievably lost, but you wouldn't want to miss anything. While in the kiosk area tour the Rhododendron Garden, the Alpine Garden, and the other works of imagination and soul being added by the year.

Return through the gate and spot a path going north into the woods, marked by a railing fence. Shortly a sign announces, "To the Nature Trails." But you are already there, in a forest of Douglas fir getting along toward the century mark. In some ⅛ mile is a Y. The right goes a long ¼ mile in excellent forest to the former Continuing Education Center and the shore of Lake Wilderness. But that's not the best way.

Take the left, up a few steps onto the abandoned rail grade (see Maple Valley-Lake Wilderness-Black Diamond Trail). On the far side is the Boundary Trail running the property line north, east, and south, in some ¾ mile emerging on the rail grade. But that's not the best way, either.

Walk a short bit east on the rail grade and go off north to the Self-Guiding Interpretive Trail, which with all its loops and side-alleys is something on the order of 1¼ miles. You won't believe all this is contained in 40 acres.

Complete tour about 3½ miles, allow 2 hours
High point 475 feet, minor elevation gain

Maple Valley to Lake Wilderness to Black Diamond Historical Museum (map — page 204)

Along this line the Pacific Coast Railroad hauled coal from the mines of Black Diamond (and Franklin, and Kummer) to Maple Valley, picked up more coal there, still more in Renton from the branchline to Newcastle, and hauled it all to the docks on Elliott Bay. Now, with rails and ties gone and motorcycles razzing free, walking the route over the height of land from the Cedar River to the Green cannot be recommended on any day at any hour when the children are not in school. On a February morning in a gray drizzle a person could be lonesome and quiet here, could break a sweat and walk away worries. The southernmost stretch, to Black Diamond, has a great deal more to offer than exercise.

For the exercise, drive to Lake Wilderness Arboretum (which see), elevation 470 feet. Take the nature trail ⅛ mile to the rail grade.

For Maple Valley turn left, in woods and then pastures, under and along highways and across the Seattle City Water pipeline. In 2½ miles is the gap where the railroad used to cross the Cedar River. The bridge is gone so transfer to the adjacent highway bridge to join the active (well, still with rails in place) railroad at Maple Valley Junction. Along the way are views of McDonald and the many peaks of Tiger.

For Black Diamond turn right and, mostly in woodland, passing large marshes, briefly near the highway but usually some distance off, follow the grade 5 miles to Black Diamond. Along the way are looks out to McDonald and Rainier, looks in to creatures of wildwoods and wildmarshes. Sorry to say, some parts of the route are hellberry — impassable, even to motorcycles. Improvise.

Round trips 5½ and 10 miles, allow 3 and 6 hours
High point 600 feet, elevation gain 200 feet

The memorable trip, giving just enough exercise to sharpen the appetite for the great deal more, and enough space to put that more in perspective, starts at SE 288th, a minor road which turns obscurely west off Highway 169 at 1.25 miles south of Four Corners, the junction with the Kent-Kangley Road. Elevation, 525 feet.

A few steps from the highway (shoulder parking there and on 288th) find the rail grade; backhoed piles of dirt meant to daunt wheels have not done so, have merely enhanced the sport. The grade diverges sharply from the highway and the rest of the way to Black Diamond is as distant as ½ mile from the noise. Table-flat topography, clearcuts, second-growth, stumpranches-cum-suburbia, marshes. Few external stimuli to interrupt introspection.

At 1½ miles from 288th, wake up! History lives! Heaps of black dirt, heaps of gaudy clinkers, heaps of shining coal! Towering above coal-black truckways, conveyor belts clank up and down a piece of industrial machinery closer to the

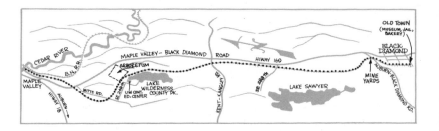

Lake Wilderness from the old railroad grade

19th century than the 21st. The last underground mine was closed in 1974 but the company lovingly renovated the 1930s washing house to process coal trucked here from the John Henry, a surface mine located somewhat to the east. Palmer Coking Coal Company ordinarily turns a blind eye on pedestrians who skulk quickly through the coalyards from the end of the rail grade onto Black Diamond streets. That is, an historian who stays out of harm's way may not be prosecuted for trespassing unless he gets hurt and files suit.

Beyond the mine the rail grade can be approximated on streets to Railroad Avenue and the Black Diamond Historical Museum. To drive here, go west from Highway 169 on Baker Street at the sign to "Old Town."

Stop in the Old Confectionary Art Gallery, the Old Saloon and the Old Pizzeria. Do not omit the legendary Bakery — tour buses feature it on their itineraries, bicycle clubs make it their destination, and the surveyor once saw half a hundred Harleys parked outside, the black leather jackets standing politely in line — bread, famous bread, is the great civilizer.

The center of Old Town is the depot, dating from the arrival of the railroad in 1884. Just four years earlier the Black Diamond Mining Company of Nortonville, California, had discovered the McKay Seam, the highest-quality coal ever found on the Pacific Coast. By 1895 Black Diamond had grown from a tent village to a town of 3000, the biggest producer of coal in King County. After coal's decline in the 1920s, construction of the highway from Maple Valley to Enumclaw saved the settlement from the extinction which was the fate of Franklin, Bayne, Durham, Hyde, and companion mining centers. Palmer Coking Coal bought the mines in the 1940s and sporadically since then has operated, underground or on the surface.

In 1976 the brandnew Black Diamond Historical Society undertook restoration of the railroad depot, abandoned for that purpose since the 1930s. In 1982 the museum opened. Days and hours are Thursday, 9 A.M. to 3 P.M., and weekends, noon to 3 P.M. Thursdays are work days, when society members are on hand to continue the refurbishing. The visitor may then find them with free time to explain the adjoining jail, wash house, "model mine" with mine cars and electric locomotive, and other displays, inside and outside the depot. They may tell tales of the "bumps" that killed miners in the mile-deep No. 11 Seam, of the strike of 1921 when locked-out miners moved a short way west to found Morganville, named for the hospitable farmer who let them squat on his land, and of the product which gave Black Diamond a new fame in the Prohibition, not necessarily because it was so much better than could be obtained in

Cedar River near Maple Valley

Seattle but because it was sold so openly, the law knowing better than to mess with these miners.

To tour the museum at leisure — and to buy bread — come any time except the weekend of the second Sunday in June. However, by all means come then for Black Diamond Day.

Round trip 4 miles, allow all day
High point 600 feet, elevation gain 100 feet

Lake Youngs Perimeter Trail (map — page 208)

The fourth-largest lake in lowland King County never will have swimming beaches or hydroplane races, rarely will even be seen by the general public — except from Tiger Mountain. Yet most everybody in the south half of Seattle takes a bath in it now and then because this is the holding reservoir between the Cedar River and Seattle City Water mains. The shores are not for recreation, nor are the forests that cover three-quarters of the 4 square miles of Lake Youngs Reservation. But outside the fence is the Lake Youngs Perimeter Trail, built by King County Parks on a City of Seattle 25-foot-wide dedication.

For many years the 9-mile Fence Run was popular with joggers, who didn't mind traffic on arterials. Walkers and horsemen preferred the several stretches where the fence diverges from roads, making possible a quiet and delightful and deeply green route, kept so because the city protects the inside-fence lands and because the outside-fence folks live there specifically to be neighbors to a wildland. Then, at the end of the 1980s, King County Parks linked up the trail stretches with a continuous pathway. The entire perimeter thus can be enjoyably walked now on a single trip. However, the route is also attractive for short strolls. The "wild segments" (those most distant from roads) are the favorites.

Trailheads are readily recognizable by King County Parks signs and the gates barring vehicles, signed "No Motorcycles" and citing the statute under which violators may be stripped of their leather jackets, given forty lashes, and deported to Australia.

Segment 1
Drive SE Petrovitsky Road (the main Renton-Maple Valley speedway) to where Old Petrovitsky Road loops off to the fence, elevation 500 feet.

Walk east. This is the least-wild segment since it several times jogs to parallel the road. However, these are brief intrusions in 1¼ miles of peace.

Round trip 2½ miles, allow 1½ hours
High point 670 feet, elevation gain 400 feet

Segment 2
From the same place walk west. How quiet it is. How green. How tall is the green. The way drops to a bog aromatic with Labrador tea, then climbs a bit and goes onward to pass 148 Avenue SE in ¾ mile.

Round trip 1½ miles, allow 1 hour
High point 533 feet, elevation gain 150 feet

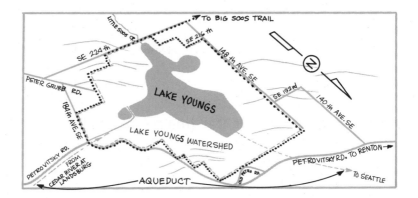

Segment 3
Drive 148 Avenue SE to SE 216 Street, elevation 500 feet.

The trail drops a bit to a wetland — note the large Sitka spruce. Then the large hemlock. Admire the tall Douglas fir. In October be dazzled by the vine maple. Humanity intrudes, but gently, at a creek dammed to be a duck pond. At a fence corner look sharp for a glimpse of the lake near its overflow outlet, Little Soos Creek. The 1¼ woodland miles end at SE 224 Street.

Round trip 2½ miles, allow 1½ hours
High point 500 feet, elevation gain 150 feet

Segment 4
Drive SE 224 Street east from the vale of Little Soos to still another gated lane, elevation 555 feet.

The ups and downs, zigs and zags, proceed 1½ miles to SE 184 Avenue.

Round trip 3 miles, allow 2 hours
High point 600 feet, elevation gain 250 feet

Perimeter loop trip 9 miles, allow 5 hours
High point 670 feet, elevation gain about 900 feet
Bus: Metro 155 to 140th and Petrovitsky

The equestrian (human feet allowed) section of Big Soos Park Trail (which see) follows SE 224th ¾ mile to join the Perimeter Trail.

A plan has been booted about to build a trail similar to the Tolt Pipeline Trail on the pipeline swath from Lake Youngs to Landsburg. From the lake to Maple Valley the pipeline mainly is beside Petrovitsky Road, excellent for horses and potentally bicycles, less interesting to walkers. From Maple Valley to Landsburg the pipeline is mostly in wildwoods, sociable and peaceful strolling, though not as exciting as the railroad (see Cedar River Trail).

Green River in Auburn

DUWAMISH-GREEN RIVER

On the far side of the bridge, Tukwila Commerce Park provides paths along the riverbank. On the near side, Allentown (King County Parks) Pea Patch announces the farming frontier and permits riverbank walking.
of water from the Frog People and while at it dug a sneaky hole in the dam and the water ran out into rivers and lakes and everybody forever after could drink as much as they liked without paying.

The White River used to flow from Mt. Rainier to Elliott Bay, joined at Auburn by the Green River. Actually, Elliott Bay then extended south to Tukwila and wrapped around the south end of Beacon Ridge and filled the valley north of

Renton, where the Cedar River flowed into the tidewater. Old Coyote thought the area needed a lake, so he had the three rivers silt in and push Elliott Bay around to where it belonged. His new Lake Washington emptied through the Black River, which on its way to enter the White at Tukwila was joined by the Cedar. Next thing, Old Coyote thought it would be fun for Tacoma to be able to say that Rainier (Tahoma) was none of Seattle's business, so he dug a ditch that carried the White south to the Puyallup. Then he decided Kirkland might enjoy being a port for ocean-going ships, so he dug a ditch west from Lake Washington that in a WHOOSH lowered it to the level of Lake Union and dried up the Black River. Finally, Old Coyote felt Metro would need help in cleaning up Lake Washington, so he diverted the Cedar up the abandoned channel of the Black to give the lake a regular supply of pure mountain water. Old Coyote, he was a crazy guy.

He played these pranks in the Big Valley, the heavy-throbbing (if frenetically, erratically) heart of Puget Sound City. Where once the Big River flowed from Canada's Big Glacier, trying to escape south around the Olympics to the ocean, freeways now rumble over the unfruited plain and thunder up the valley walls, jets rocket cloudward like so many Flash Gordons headed for Mongo and plummet forestward like so many gaudy baubles seeking Christmas trees. A person may pray for Someone to stop the music, so everybody would have to stay where they are and settle down to grow corn.

Year by year the industry and commerce of Puget Sound City bulldoze south from Elliott Bay and north from Commencement Bay. The brown-black alluvium that once fed Tacoma and Seattle garden truck and dairy products now produces a crop of concrete and prefab and fumes and noise. And yet, contradiction though it may seem, the Duwamish-Green River never has been so footful as now, and the pedestrianism of today is nothing compared to what's coming. Walking routes are planned the full length of the Duwamish River from Elliott Bay — actually, from Duwamish Head, connecting there to the Whulj Trail. The grand scheme for a "River of Green" Trail will in the fulfillment rank with the supreme long-distance walks in the region. In the nation. As for the Green River Gorge, when the magnificence is fully preserved and given appropriate public entries it will have to have a book of its own.

Other possibilities abound. With the Seattle & Walla Walla Railroad route made an Historic Site and provided a trail, walkers could hoof it from Elliott Bay to the Issaquah Alps and Snoqualmie Falls and the Cascades. The Cedar River through Renton and Maple Valley would be another way to the mountains. Finally, in Auburn the Green and the White Rivers flow close where they used to flow together; the Green readily could be linked to a Commencement Bay-to-Mt. Rainier Trail along the White River (and/or the Puyallup and Carbon Rivers — see *Footsore 4*) so that pedestrians could walk from the Elliott Bay arm of Whulj to the glaciers of Mt. Rainier National Park — to make it again Seattle's business.

For the present the only mountain hike in this chapter is on the Cascade front. Mt. McDonald gives panoramas over the lowlands and long looks up the Green toward Howard Hanson Dam, whose reservoir waters Tacoma and helps the dikes de-water the Big Valley.

USGS maps: Renton, Maple Valley, Black Diamond, Cumberland, Eagle Gorge, Auburn, Des Moines, Poverty Bay
Walkable all year

DUWAMISH RIVER TRAIL

For quite a long while folks have been having a dream about the Duwamish River. In 1983 some of them got together as the Friends of the Duwamish and soon had the City of Seattle, Port of Seattle, and Metro dancing (more or less gracefully) to their tune, backed by a chorus line of just about every other government in the region. Plainly, someday there will be a trail from Elliott Bay to the Cascades.

The Duwamish section is the most difficult to establish because here is the industrial heart of the region, base of the shipping that gives Seattle a maritime character, source of a substantial share of the paychecks and taxes which keep the show going.

Metro has one solution. It is now building a secondary-treatment plant in Renton, a stone's throw from where the Duwamish begins, and plans a 12-mile pipeline along Interurban Avenue, West Marginal Way, and Harbor Avenue to Duwamish Head, where a new outfall will flush our secondarily treated toilet output into Puget Sound, eliminating the presently primarily treated flushings into the Duwamish. Whatever may be the other merits of the project, the 12-mile trail will be an amelioration of the glaring faults.

The Metro trail will only partially satisfy the appetite for close views of heavy-industrial America. To obtain these, the City of Seattle had to sit down at the card table with the Port of Seattle. The Port and its allies had all the heavy money. But the City was not destitute. Many public street-ends had been illegally closed off by industry and the Port and were being used for illegal dumping and general immoral corruption. Further, the state Shorelines Act gave the City the whip on any changes in shorelines wanted by the Port. As of this edition, the City has agreed to vacate seven public streets and grant 17 shoreline permits. Some critics say the City was swindled by the Port—again. But the voyeur won't remember that as he revels in the close looks at big ships, big machines, really big business, at the viewpoints conceded by the Port.

Elliott Bay: Duwamish Head to Salty's (map — page 212)

The northern terminus of the Metro Trail will be Duwamish Head, where the outfall pipe will plunge deep beneath the bay floor. The northern portion of the trail, along Elliott Bay, is open now, and no thanks to Metro or the Port.

Drive Harbor Avenue to the Duwamish Head parklet at the northwest end of Alki Beach Park (which see). The views out to Bainbridge Island and the Olympics, across the bay to Magnolia Bluff and Queen Anne Hill, and the high follies of downtown Seattle fill the day sufficiently for many a visitor. Not to mention the ferries. However, for closer views of the industrial turmoil of the Duwamish, walk south.

At proper tide one can set out on the veritable beach. Soon the route must climb atop the seawall, where the path passes the parking lot, viewpoints, and boat-launch of Don Armeni Park and then the new Seacrest Park, with boathouse, fishing piers, moorages, and restored shorelines, none of which existed at the time of survey.

In ¾ mile the parks and the shore walk end at the projection of Salty's on Alki.

In less than ¼ mile more is the start of the railroad tracks and the big noise. A dogged enough walker could follow the steel up the Duwamish and onward to Chicago, if that seemed desirable.

Round trip 2 miles, allow 1½ hours
Bus: Metro 37

The Industrial Duwamish (map — page 212)

It's a mad mad mad mad bad bad world, along the two Duwamish Waterways and on Harbor Island between them. Why does it make a person sigh nostalgically? Because in certain of the New Industrial Centers, such as east of Lake Washington, enormous tracts of land are covered up with buildings which make no sound except at quitting time, when the workers come out and rev up their BMWs. One doesn't know what is made in those buildings or whether it is necessary or desirable. The Duwamish neither doubts itself nor leaves any question in the minds of viewers. This is the Industrial Revolution still going strong, bangetty-clangetty ding-dong crash-smash. A person worries how many of those itty-bitty East Side chips the world can afford. He believes absolutely in the bright-orange, sky-ranging, 40-ton cargo cranes of the Port.

The fences and "Hard Hat" signs will not readily let a birder to the water. However, the Port has conceded eight viewpoints. The surveyor found another, not strictly illegal, that suggests the City has been too timid and the Port too belligerent.

KJR Vista

The City doesn't claim it and the Port doesn't mention it, but there it is, a spit away from where the West Waterway enters Elliott Bay.

From Harbor Avenue-West Marginal Way turn east on SW Florida Street. When trains block the way as the switch engine pulls and pushes freight back and forth on sidings, profit by watching the names on the cars. The surveyor collected a rarity, "Elgin Joliet & Eastern Ry." To his knowledge this is the first report in our area.

Follow Florida as it turns south to become 26 Avenue SW and at 0.4 mile from Harbor deadends. Turn left into the enormous parking lot beneath the KJR towers. Put on your hardhat and take your salami in hand and brazen out to the edge of the parking lot. All around, on both sides of the waterway, Lockheed builds ships, when not on strike or lockout.

West Duwamish Waterway with Kellogg Island on left

Terminal 30
On the east shore of the East Waterway, just where it opens into Elliott Bay. Boat-launch, fishing piers, picnic areas.
Access from Alaskan Way S via S Massachusetts Street.

Terminal 18
On Harbor Island, on the west shore of the East Waterway.
Access via 11 Avenue SW north of Spokane Street.

Diagonal Way South
On the east bank of the Duwamish Waterway upstream from the split into East and West Waterways. Picnic areas, boat-launch, and beach access. View across to Kellogg Island.
Access from East Marginal Way (Highway 99) via the deadend of Diagonal Way S.

Terminal 105
On the west bank of the Duwamish Waterway.
Access from West Marginal Way at SW Idaho.

Kellogg Island Vista/Terminal 107

In the 1850s the estimated 365 Duwamish people still surviving were "removed" and Europeans began raising "apples more than 16 inches in circumference." Half a century later it was the European farmers who were removed to make room for manifest destiny. Beginning in 1913, 16 miles of meandering river was straightened to 18 miles, and 20 million cubic yards of dirt were relocated from Denny Hill and Beacon Hill to dry up the tidal mudflats and fill the beds of the closed-off meanders.

Kellogg Island was caught in the middle of history. In the early 19th century it was some 100 acres in size — except at very high tides, when it had no acres above the salt surface. Here was where mudflats and saltmarsh met and where since approximately A.D. 670 the Duwamish people had lived on a site across the river from the island, harvesting the clams and oysters, the salmon runs, and hunting elk and deer on the ridge of West Seattle and harbor seal in Elliott Bay.

The modern Kellogg Island is only some 30 acres — of fill dirt heaped high above the tides. The Port saw no reason not to finish the destruction while building a new Terminal 107. But the poker game was played out and the Port will build Terminal 107 in such a way as to let the shrunken, remodeled island alone as a wildlife refuge. It is so much a refuge that human visitors are forbidden. Kayaks can float by, but mustn't touch. As for pedestrians, all they can do is look. And muse. It is enough.

Access is from West Marginal Way at SW Hudson Street.

Terminal 115

On the west bank of the Duwamish Waterway. Boat-launch and picnic areas.
Access from West Marginal Way a bit north of 1st Avenue S Bridge.

1st Avenue S Boat Ramp

On the east bank of the Duwamish Waterway.
Access from East Marginal Way south of 1st Avenue S Bridge.

South Portland-8th Avenue S Access

On the west bank of Duwamish Waterway. Picnic areas.
Access from West Marginal Way via S Portland Street.

The Meandering Duwamish (map — page 214)

The bends of the river were filled. Harbor Island was created. Upstream, the Duwamish became a line-straight "Waterway" ditch. Had the pork barrel held out, and the appetite for places to dock ocean-going ships, the straightening might have proceeded to the glaciers of Mt. Rainier.

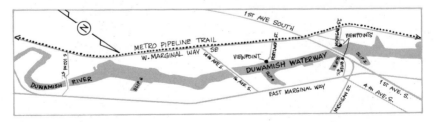

Duwamish River and First Avenue South Bridge

However, at 6 air miles from the bay the blue lane on the map narrows and meanders and the map hails the transformation by changing the name from "Waterway" to "River." Industry by no means ceases but the intervals grow wider, room for happy little anachronistic houses, startling farms, and even parks.

Mt. Motorcycle (map — page 216)
The supreme vantage for the transition from Waterway to River is the summit of Mt. Motorcycle, 110 feet, what's left of a larger mass of basalt after quarrying.

Park on the shoulder of S 115 Street where it turns east from E Marginal Way, elevation 15 feet. Follow wheel ruts up the abandoned quarry to the bald summit. Gaze north along the industrial Duwamish to the tall orange cranes of the working waterfront and Mt. Selig thrusting high above downtown Seattle. Gaze south along the tree-lined Duwamish to Rainier. Listen to the roar of I-5 and Old 99 and 599 and 181 and 900 and, in the sky, Route 666, where the beasts bellow as they plummet into forests of Riverton Heights.

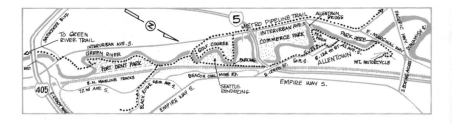

Eventually the quarry will be developed, probably condo-ized. On the other side of the mountain a twisty little road winds to the summit, passing through a community of affordable houses of the sort America no longer can afford to build. The passerby poignantly realizes there are individuals inside these houses, not assembly-line clones.

Round trip ½ mile, allow 1 hour
Elevation gain 100 feet
Bus: Metro 123

Mt. Motorcycle to Allentown Pea Patch

Descended from the mount, walk out on the Marginal Way bridge to look down to (but not through) olive-green waters flowing between steep mud "beaches" (the river here is still tidal). Ponder rotten pilings and bulkheads, slimy riprap, and ducks. The marvel is how much swimming, and floating, and diving, and flying continues.

Now commences the upstream march. It must be on the road shoulder, but views are continuous up and down the water corridor framed by tall trees and across to homes of folks whose lives are quieter and more rural than out in the suburbs.

Allentown Bridge gives more views of the water, and of fisherpeople, some of whom slide cockleshells in the river and paddle about. One ponders the possibility (and wisdom) of a rubber-raft float to Elliott Bay.

On the far side of the bridge, Tukwila Commerce Park provides paths along the riverbank. On the near side, Allentown (King County Parks) Pea Patch announces the farming frontier and permits riverbank walking.

One way 1¼ miles
Bus: Metro 154

Allentown to Black River (map — page 216)

From the P Patch the river route continues on 124 Street. (A jog onto 125th gives a view across the water to a mudbank from which fishers wade, and also their dogs, and also cows from the glebe.) The river road changes to 50 Place S, passes under viaducts of S 129 Street and I-5 and becomes single-lane. Off right, 56 Avenue comes in from a new bridge whch destroyed the neighbor-hood. The public road ends at the Seattle Rendering Works, where over-aged fish, horses, dogs, and cats are made into soap or something. A bit short of the plant entrance is a turnout-parking area beside the railroad tracks. In the next stretch the pedestrian has no competition from automobiles — but must keep an eye to the rear, lest Amtrak's annual passenger train come through.

The rendering works flavor the start of the walk. Across the tracks is a fine, large marsh, splendidly birdy, vividly contrasting with the violence of Empire Way, high above on the side of Beacon Ridge. The marsh also is accessible via S 129 Street viaduct and little old Beacon Coal Mine Road, a 19th-century survival worth a visit in its own right.

Across the river sprawls a greensward that would gratify a Whig lord of the reign of good Queen Anne, and one considers taking up golf in order to walk there. Then the greensward is beside the tracks, and paths through the hellberries tell that non-golfers *do* walk there, at such season and hours and in such weather as not to disturb the game. In fact, canny non-golfers have beaten paths down from fairways to mudbars to compete with herons and gulls and ducks. A graceful footbridge connects the two sections of the Foster Golf Course (public links, City of Tukwila), which with all the meanders runs along nearly 2 miles of riverbank — the greenest and quietest remnant of the Old Duwamish. A walker who chooses stormy days is unlikely to meet another soul. Stick to the weedy rough. Perhaps carry an old golf club.

"Black River Junction," says the railroad sign. And there it is, by golly, a drainage ditch beneath the bridges.

One way 2 miles, not counting the golf game

BLACK RIVER

It was the outlet of Lake Washington and thus carried the waters of the Sammamish River, May Creek, Coal Creek, Kelsey Creek, Juanita Creek, Thornton Creek, Issaquah Creek, and scores more. Less than a mile from the lake it accepted the Cedar River and thus snowmelt from the Cascade Crest. It was a substantial stream, indeed, when it met the White River (later transformed into the Green River) to form the Duwamish River. Of course, it couldn't match the White for volume and during spring floods from Mt. Rainier would be so backed up that it reversed flow and emptied Rainier water into the lake; "Mox La Push," or "two mouths," the local folks called it. In 1912 the Cedar was diverted into Lake Washington—to exit again in the Black. But in 1916 the lake was lowered 9 feet and provided a new outlet, the Lake Washington Ship Canal, and the Black went out of the river business.

It lived on as a seepage, though, and memories of its days of glory were kept alive by the railroads, who put it on their maps as "Black River Junction," mightily puzzling the new arrivals who look in vain for a river. The experienced landscape detective who persists in the search will not be disappointed. The Black River lives!

Discovering the Black (map — page 218)

From Empire Way-Dunlap Canyon Road (Highway 900) drive south on 68 Avenue S to a crossing of railroad tracks and then the Black River. A short bit beyond the bridge, park in the lot on the west side of King County Public Works Pump Station No. 1, elevation 20 feet.

DUWAMISH-GREEN RIVER

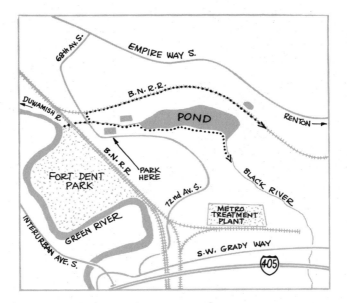

Two walks sample the Black. For the first, follow the service road down beside the riprapped ditch in which the river flows, when it has any water, to the Momentous Spot, the confluence with the Green (formerly White) River, the start of the Duwamish River. Let the eye drift into way-back focus. See the Duwamish people paddling or poling dugout canoes, taking the all-water route from Elliott Bay to Issaquah. See the barges carrying coals from Newcastle, the paddlewheel steamers bringing garden truck to market. See the ladies with parasols being paddled or rowed by their swains on Sunday voyages from Georgetown to Renton.

For the second walk, enjoy the parklet on the east side of the pump station, then follow the mowed lane down the slope to the enormous stormwater retention pond. The reason for this pond and the pumping station is that, though Tacoma's Howard Hanson Dam holds back mountain floods and dikes keep the Green to its channel, often the river flows so high that drainage from valley walls can't get into the river. Without pumping stations the floodplain still would regularly flood. Once man starts messing around with Mother Nature's arrangements there's no end of it.

Never mind. Though the Earlington Golf Course is becoming a business park, the mowed lane is on a terrace secluded below on the bank of the pond. Trees have been planted that in time will provide shade. Find a patch and sit down and get out the binoculars. On a day in late June four separate, large families of Canada geese were observed. Ducks took off from the water, flopped in the water, quacked. Swallows swooped low over the surface, snapping up bugs. Killdeer ran about, squealing piteously. Mysterious splashings testified to creatures diving — or surfacing and pulling their heads back under before the binoculars could swing around. Who knows what secrets lurk in that opaque water? A chain of islets is brilliant yellow in summer with the bloom of deervetch. The far shore is a brooding jungle of tall cottonwood swaying in the breeze. Beware the "GARK! GARK!" of the dreaded GBH!

In a scant ½ mile the pond bends to the south, to the entry ditch of a south branch of the Black that drains the plain beside and south of Longacres Race Track. When the business park is completed it may have paths along this ditch and perhaps elsewhere in the former golf course.

The big thrill is looking to the far east edge of the pond, spotting a narrow bayou emerging from the cottonwood forest, and realizing this is the shrunken remnant of the Black as it came primevally from the lake.

Round trips 1¾ miles, allow 1½ hours

Seattle & Walla Walla Railroad (map — page 218)

Rails first reached the Black River in 1877, when the Seattle & Walla Walla Railroad arrived from Georgetown, headed for Renton and ultimately the Newcastle mines. In 1883 the Northern Pacific linked the Black River to Tacoma and the East. By 1909, when the Milwaukee came through, there were five lines at the Junction. (So Paul Dorpat tells us in *Seattle: Now and Then II.*) There still is a north-south mainline and, taking off easterly toward Renton, the former Milwaukee line, kept minimally alive by the Burlington Northern.

The view across the pond to the cottonwood forest and the bayou forces the detective to investigate the line east. The old Seattle & Walla Walla ran parallel a few yards to the south; from Renton to Newcastle the exact grade largely survives and indeed is regularly walked on scheduled hikes of the Issaquah Alps Trails Club, which proposes that the rail route from the mines to Elliott Bay be declared a National/State/King County Historic Site.

Sadly, the cottonwood forest which from the pond seemed so immense is now seen to have been narrowed in 1987 to a thin fringe; the cottonwood logs lay stacked in decks when the surveyor came by, wringing his hands and moaning at the thought of all the murdered morels. This is to be Blackriver Corporate Park, "a 150-acre corporate research and office park." Incredibly, a considerable stretch of the old Black survived this late, until the 1987 arrival of the corporate loggers and blacktoppers who utterly extinguished the last visible memories. One suspects this destruction of the Black was illegal, the violation winked at by the City of Renton, and no river-protector on hand to prevent the crime. The rewards of eternal vigilance are demonstrated by the fact the cottonwood forest is 660 feet wide rather than the 250 feet the developer intended and the city approved because Marty Murphy found a great blue heron nest in the doomed strip.

Yet the walk has rewards. Above the tracks to the north rises the mile-long green wall of the south end of Beacon Ridge, potentially a splendid wildland trail. Hemmed by the rail grade against the green wall is a wild pond concealed by thickets of willow and brambles. One ventures to say things live in and around that pond.

The chief reward — magnificent — lies near the start of this jaunt. Spared from the dredging for the storage pond, sitting off to one side like a cutoff meander, is a stretch of oxbow marsh — a bit of the very course of the ancient river! The Black lives!

Round trip to end of green bluff 2 miles, allow 1 hour

GREEN RIVER TRAIL

Tukwila, Kent, Auburn, and King County are working toward the end that pedestrians may someday walk continuous trail from the Black River to the Green River Gorge. Bikers do the entire route now, but bikers are different from thee and me — they have wheels. No pedestrian in his senses will wish to walk every step of the Green River, not in 1988. The time will come. Already there are sections, short and long, of excellent footing. Here we distinguish: (1) trail decently apart from roads, highly recommended; (2) roads where the traffic is so slow and sparse and the riverside so nice that walking might be considered; (3) roads not recommended for walking but offering sidetrips to riverbank seclusion; (4) and junk country, such as the west side of Kent.

Fort Dent (King County) Park (map — page 218)

One searches in vain for an historical marker explaining which war. Perhaps it is the one in progress, between the armies of children togged out for soccer, football, baseball, and whatnotball. The contemplative pedestrian will want to shun the scene on weekends and all summer. In quiet hours, however, the park has the present distinction of lying where the Green, Black, and Duwamish meet and the future distinction of being the place where the Duwamish River Trail and Green River Trail will meet. Aside from that, it's a pleasant little stroll.

Cross Interurban Avenue on Southcenter Boulevard to the bridge over the Green River, elevation 30 feet.

Mill Creek in Kent City Park

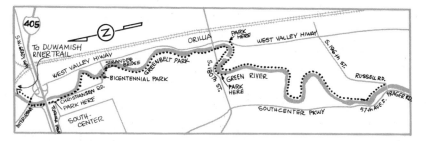

Park near the bridge and walk lawns to the thickets hedging the river. Paths trench through for close looks at birds and canoes and condos. Views in the other direction are to the Black River Quarry, engaged in dismantling Beacon Ridge stone by stone. A path circles a Storm Water Retention Pond, signed "Ducks Only," lest the children go wading and get eaten up by the geese, who are irritated by the sign's speciesism. The path leads to the mouth of the Black River for a moment of revery at the Confluence.

Loop trip 1½ miles, allow 1 hour
Bus: Metro 150

Tukwila (map — page 221)

Tukwila (more commonly known as Southcenter) has completed its civic duty by the Green, and very handsomely. Though ultimately a ¾-mile path must be provided along Southcenter Boulevard to connect to Fort Dent, from I-405 south to the city limits the trail is in, the shade trees planted, the benches and picnic tables installed. This may be the most used river path in the region, thronged on nice noons by lunchers from offices and factories and shops of Southcenter, busy morning and night with joggers and bikers.

Parking opportunities and trail accesses are too many to note. Driving south on Andover Park E or Industry Drive, a person needs but head east on almost any sidestreet and find an office park bounded by river and trail. The north end is just south of the I-405 bridge over the Green, near the intersection of Christiansen Road and Tukwila Parkway, elevation 20 feet.

Office park on one side, river on the other, the path bends this way and that with the river to Bicentennial Park, featuring a little log-cabin picnic shelter. In a long ½ mile it passes under Strander Boulevard and becomes Christiansen Greenbelt Park, greener by the year as the new-planted trees reach for the sky to join the old cottonwoods. The storage pond behind Pump Station No. 17 floats and feeds a goodly number of ducks, though nothing like the tens of thousands which wintered or nested in the vast marshes that were paved to become Southcenter — Tukwila, that is. The black alluvial soil then also fed Seattleites garden truck far tastier than the agribusiness products from California and Moses Lake.

At 1¾ miles the trail passes under S 180th and follows a river bend west and north ½ mile to "The End"; the dike continues but is gated. Never mind. A bit before "The End" a pretty footbridge arches from true left bank to true right bank, there meeting an entry trail coming in at a scant ¼ mile from a small parking area on Interurban-West Valley Highway-Highway 181.

In ¾ mile from the bridge the trail arrives at the city limits and Tukwila rests on its laurels, with a park bench.

One way from I-405 to city limits at 189th 2½ miles, allow 1½ hours
Bus: Metro 123, 145, 150, 155, and others

Kent (maps — pages 221 and 222)

The Tukwilization of the Southcenter floodplain is so nearly complete that office parks have come to seem as normal for the Green as the City of London for the Thames. The frontier country south of Southcenter is rather sad. Industrial and commercial blocks brood lonesomely in empty fields where the rich alluvium grows naught but tansy and mullein and thistle and survey ribbons fluttering forlornly in the breeze. Yet as one goes along, fields appear which still grow food and — thanks to King County's Farmlands Preservation Program — will continue to do so. At worst, always the river flows, bearing waterfowl, fish, and rubber rafts, and always there are views across the Big Valley to the Issaquah Alps, north to Beacon Ridge, and south to Rainier.

Both sides of the river have dikes that are walked. Access is by any number of huge parking lots at the ends of any number of sidestreets off West Valley Road-Interurban-68 Avenue-Highway 181 (the main artery is given many names on maps and signs). However, the route described here is the "official" one.

189th-194th

Tukwila yields to Kent at a prominent westerly meander of the Green; just about there, 190th leads west to the dikeside parking lot of Meteor Communications. The dike path provides a scant 1 mile of isolation from highways and a bit south of 194th runs out on Russell Road, close beside the river.

One way 1 mile on path, allow ½ hour

194th-228th

Russell Road is a narrow lane clinging to the riverbank, signed "Kent Recreational Corridor — Yield to Bikes and Pedestrians." Both forms of locomotion are common and walking can be very enjoyable on a weekday morning, when the Grand Prix drivers are in their office parks programming computers. (However, farm boys, too, now drive red roller skates that can take a corner like at Monaco.)

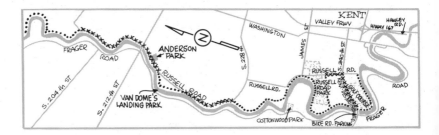

Mill Creek trail in Kent City Park

On any hour of any day the walker will be pleased by Van Dohns Landing, a park commemorating the site of an 1887 cable ferry. A scant ½ mile south of 212th, Russell Road swings away from the river and for ⅓ mile encloses the park and its riverbank path.

Driving, biking, or walking, whether on Russell Road or its across-the-river twin, Frager Road, the visitor will delight in America the rural beautiful, not yet subdivided for warehouses and stuff, and some of it definitely *not* to be. Yes, north of 212th there is one entire square mile of Boeing. (We've heard of rain dances. Is there a glacier dance?) But the western valley wall is near and wildly green. The air is fragrant with fresh manure. The camera feels compelled to record cows, barns, and farmhouses. In season one absolutely must stop and pick raspberries or buy fresh corn and cukes.

One way 2½ miles (⅓ mile on path, the rest on little slow Russell Road), allow 1½ hours

228th to Russell Road Park

Russell Road swings east, away from the river, to meet 228th, and the river trail takes the opportunity to occupy the bank, following the sinuous stream ¾ mile, then running again into Russell Road.

In a scant ¼ mile Russell Road crosses SE 240th and trail resumes, entering Russell Road Park, Kent's really big all-purpose park, room for millions of soccer rioters, a cityful of picnic lunchers. The dike path runs ½ mile and then, at a property line, must return ½ mile to Russell Road, which at this point is closed to through traffic, another thoughty act by the City of Kent.

Few walkers will care to go on. The route follows Russell Road a short bit to the Kent-Des Moines Road and turns west on sidewalks a scant ½ mile to the river bridge (where the bike path comes in from Frager Road). Dike path resumes for ½ mile, to where Russell Road ends at the river.

One way from 228th to Russell Road end at the river 3 miles (2¼ miles on path, ¾ mile on road), allow 2 hours

Downtown

The west end of Kent is what the Chamber of Commerce doesn't brag about, the city government wrings its hands about, and no recreationists frequent except photographers of the Ashcan School seeking to preserve for posterity scenes from AAA Auto Wrecking, Bison Auto Wrecking, Rock's Auto Wrecking, and Budget Auto Wrecking.

East of Central Way S (which crosses the Green River to become Auburn Way and various other names) is something else — the most popular walk in town. The dike from Central Way bridge passes Oakhurst Office Park, then apartments and other residences, some with canoes or truck innertubes for going right out in the middle of the kingfishers and the fish and the twitterbirds.

At the tip of a great meander the apartment houses end and so does the dike, at Green River Road S — exactly where North Green River Park begins.

One way 1 mile (on path), allow ½ hour
Bus: Metro 150

North Green River (King County) Park
(map — page 225)

Having come so far upstream, it is meet to pause and reflect on the changes in river and valley since Fort Dent and the Black River. The river is still rigidly channelized between dikes, frequently riprapped. But the water ... It's transparent! Not absolutely clear, yet boulders in the bed can be seen. There are rapids! And mudbanks of the tidal area have yielded to fine sand. The elevation of downtown Kent is something like 35 feet.

Often called "Kent Valley," at this point the Big Valley is more than 2 miles wide from forested scarp to scarp, largely occupied by freeways. The city is a mixture of the industrial and commercial, old-residential detached houses with yards, newer-residential trailer courts with communal asphalt, and new-new semi-high-rise condos that face their little lawns and minute decks out upon the Green River where wild things swim and fly, creep and crawl. From some condo windows, farms can be seen.

At North Green River Park the mood of the route undergoes a dramatic and permanent transformation. Largely this is because though Kent gives way almost immediately to Auburn and the cities are virtual twins, the river has

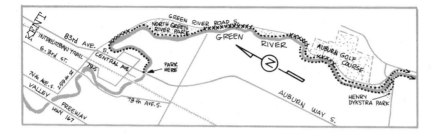

crossed the Big Valley to hug the east wall. Beyond the stream are Auburn and the 2 roaring miles to the west valley wall. Here there is King County Park, river, and river road that is almost walkable and genuinely is a "pleasure drive," and has many places to pull off on a shoulder and wander to the water. The subdivision of the Big Valley is at least half out of the mind because half the time the eye is on the wall of forests, as much as 400 feet tall. The houses lining the far bank aren't so bad because they are there and the public park is here, and people who choose to live beside a river can't be written off as a total loss.

The northernmost access is Kent; from Central Way S, S 259 Street turns off east and becomes Green River Road S. At the end of the apartment houses an unmarked path leads out across a field, drops to an old woods road, and spins off many paths to the river, where a low-water route along banks and bars connects south again to Green River Road.

Parking shoulders and paths are frequent. Playfields and a King County P Patch lie between road and valley wall, and then the Auburn Golf Course. On the river side of the road are cottonwood collonades, meanders isolated from the road, quiet bars for sunning, wading, picnicking.

A final river path swings away from the road into a stupendous grove of cottonwoods with a parking area and picnic grounds and a sandy bar where children swim and wade. Curiously, no sign announces that this is Henry Dykstra Park, City of Auburn, connected to the city by a delightful swinging footbridge.

One way from Kent to S 320th-8th Street NE 4¼ miles (1½ miles of riverbank path)
Bus: Metro 150

Auburn (map — page 226)

Auburn has the least of the river within its jurisdiction. Yet a body of opinion holds that Auburn is the best city-walking on the river.

From Auburn Way follow 22 Street E to Henry Dykstra Park. On this side of the river the park is tidy lawns, playground, and picnic tables. On the other side of the happy footbridge it is the unsigned and rather rude cottonwood forest noted above. With the two banks and the upstream-downstream, there are four separate walks.

This side, downstream. The dike is gated but not posted. (Throughout this section of town large signs announce, "Riverbanks closed to motorized vehicles and horses." What they mean to say is the dikes are freely open to human

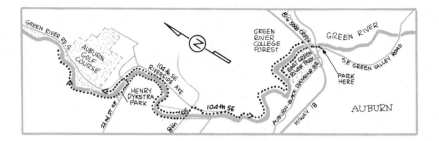

feet.) Lovely homes and landscaped yards line the riverside way. In 1½ miles the dike ends at Auburn city limits.

This side, upstream. The dike gate says "Public Fishing Easement." Be polite and quiet as you walk beside homes 1½ miles to the 8 Street NE bridge over the river.

The other side, downstream. To Kent.

The other side, upstream. Walk 1½ miles to 8 Street NE, cross, and proceed on 104 Avenue SE to Green River College Forest, described below.

One way north to dike's end 1½ miles, allow 1 hour

One way south to 8th Street NE 1½ miles, allow 1 hour
Bus: Metro 150

East Green River (King County) Park
(map — page 226)

A distinction must be made between the "Green River Valley" (Kent Valley, Kent-Auburn Valley, Big Valley) and the "Green Valley." The former is where the Really Big River used to flow from the snout of the Pleistocene glacier, and later the White River from the glaciers of Mt. Rainier. The Green River doesn't feel at home out there in the alien vastness of that 2-mile-wide expanse of floodplain made by far mightier floods than ever have been in its power. The Green River "belongs" to the homey little valley, the floodplain barely ½ mile wide at most, which extends some 7 air miles downstream from the exit of the Green River Gorge. A King County park upstream from the Big Valley lies within Green Valley coziness yet gives an outlook to the scariness.

For the neatest access to the park, drive east from Auburn on Highway 18 and just before its bridge over the Green River go off on the Black Diamond Road. Shortly, just before this road's bridge over the river, turn right on Green Valley Road and immediately pull off left to the fishermen's riverside parking area, elevation 75 feet.

Walk downstream beneath the Black Diamond Road bridge, the railroad bridge, and the Highway 18 bridge. Across the Green is the mouth of Big Soos Creek, babbling from the woods. Sit on the gravel bar and admire. Note that the river, at journey's start a pea soup, by Kent become a clouded limeade, now is clean and clear elixir — well, not for drinking, but inviting hot feet.

A broad dike guards the pasture to the left. In low water the hiker will prefer to walk gravel-sand bars, the river's width away from the valley wall rising from streambank willow-cottonwood to Douglas fir of the Green River College Forest (which see). Swallows flit, ducks quack, hawks circle, and pterodactyl-like herons implausibly lift off from the gravel and ponderously flop to treetops. Remote, peaceful, idyllic.

The dike road swings left and fades out in woodland paths between a murky pond and the river. At 1 mile from the start a path reaches railroad tracks, the park boundary. Along the tracks to the right a short bit another road leads right to another dike. More pastures and birds and river. Now, as the Green River is entering the Big Valley, hugging the foot of the bluff for comfort, houses begin and the hike is best ended, 2 miles from the start.

For another experience of the Green Valley mouth, cross the railroad bridge at Big Soos Creek and explore the other side of the river, as described in Green River College Forest, below.

Round trip to start of houses 4 miles, allow 2 hours

Green Valley (map — page 227)

Upstream from the Big Valley the valley of the Green River is as prettily pastoral as can be found so near Puget Sound City. When King County embarked on a Farmlands Preservation Program wherein owners would sell development rights to the county, thus getting the tax assessor and the developers off their backs so they could continue farming, the tragedy of the Big Valley was foremost in the preservers' minds. It had been a victim of the process which since World War II had gobbled up two-thirds of King County's farmlands, more than 100,000 acres, or 160 square miles, and was generally thought to be a lost cause. Happily, several in-the-nick coups in the Kent vicinity netted 989 acres on the banks of the Green, 1½ square miles which will remain green, growing good things to eat.

The protected acreage in the Green Valley is less — 926 acres — but in those cozy confines is sufficient to keep in permanent green virtually the entire distance from the valley mouth to the gorge exit, on both sides of the river. Further, adjoining the 926 acres on the south are 4476 protected acres on the Enumclaw Plateau, reaching south to and nearly encircling Enumclaw and guarding a great long stretch of the banks of the White River, treated in *Footsore 4.*

Grand news, indeed, that agriculture may prevail elsewhere than in California and on the Columbia Plateau, that the agonies of Tukwilization do not lie in store for us here.

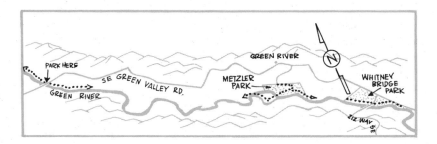

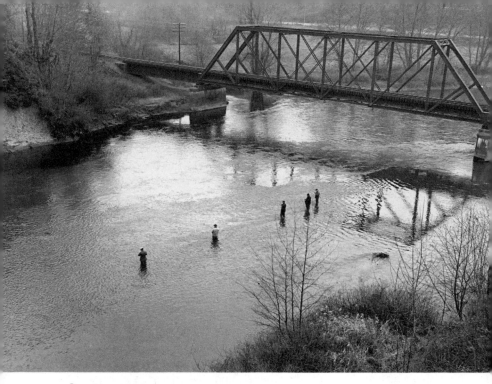

Steelhead fishing in Green River

But (you ask) must we enjoy it solely on wheels? May we walk? Not so much as one might wish, as on a trail of 10-odd river miles between Big Valley and Green River Gorge, savoring the close wildness of the valley-wall forests, the cows and the corn on the valley floor, and the river. That may come. Meanwhile, the State Wildlife Department has obtained streambank easements at several places: hikers who can't find them should ask the fishermen who tore down the signs in order to hog the fish. Our chief benefactor is King County Parks, which bit by bit is obtaining segments of an Upper Green River Park.

Lower Valley Bridge
Drive Green Valley Road 1.7 miles from the Black Diamond Road to a bridge and a parking shoulder, elevation 100 feet.

Note the obscure sign, "Use Stiles and Trails Provided." Downstream the river swings to the north side of its floodplain and cuts the green precipice of the valley wall. Upstream the farm edges and gravel bars might let a person hop and wade to the gorge.

Round trips perhaps 2 miles, allow 1½ hours

Metzler (King County) Park
Drive Green Valley Road 4 miles from the bridge to the valley delight, Metzler Park. Do not drive in haste. Go slow, to converse with the cows and

horses. Keep the window open; in early summer the entire valley reeks of strawberries, in fall of corn. Real strawberries, real corn, not the watery synthetics fabricated in California.

A lane leads off to the parking area, elevation 150 feet. The path strikes off upvalley at field's edge, bends right to cottonwood forest, and drops several feet to floodway terrace. The main route turns downvalley ⅓ mile to the riverbank; sidepaths go off upvalley to the bank. The cottonwood aroma overpowers the strawberries. The walker pauses to fill lungs.

Hark! What is this odd aural sensation? A person newly arrived from the rackety-bang of the Big Valley believes his ears have cut out. It is the sound of —no, not silence, but *quiet*. The green valley walls make no sound, nor do the green fields. Cars pass on the valley road only occasionally, muted by so much greenery. As many as a dozen minutes may pass without the brain being jellied by a jet. It is eerie to be able to hear dogs barking so far away. A distant horse whinnies and almost one yells, "Hold it *down*, willya?"

The river is not silent. It is politely loud, but so clear and cool it tempts even the thirsty Shelty usually too timorous to approach water that has a voice. The woods across the water are wild and green. The gravel bars and floodway forests invite the poking-about and wading foot.

Round trips many miles, allow many hours

Whitney Bridge (King County) Park

Drive Green Valley Road a scant 2 miles from Metzler Park, to a scant 1 mile from Flaming Geyser Park. Turn south on 212 Way SE to Whitney Bridge and a parking lot, elevation 200 feet.

The park extends ½ mile along the river, fields ending at the shrub thicket on the riverbank. There are few gravel bars except in low water and a cursory survey revealed no paths. But there it is.

Round trip 1 mile, allow 1 hour

GREEN RIVER GORGE

Immediately after issuing from the Cascade front the Green River enters a canyon slot whose walls rise as much as 300 feet, always steep and often vertical or overhanging. For 6 air miles, or 12 stream miles, its meanders are intrenched in solid rock, slicing through some 9000 feet of tilted strata of shale and sandstone, with interbedded coal seams and imbedded fossil imprints of shells and vegetation.

There is absolutely nothing in the region that compares. (There used to be but those other canyons were drowned to generate electricity.) From the time the miners arrived, a century and odd years ago, the gorge has been a major scenic attraction. Lacking any form of permanent protection, however, it was sure to be exploited eventually for private profit and public exclusion. Then, in the mid-1960s, Wolf Bauer undertook a detailed survey of the gorge on foot and in kayak and drew up a proposal for "a unique natural showcase of free-flowing wild river and primeval canyon." His lobbying stimulated the Legislature's creation of a Green River Gorge Conservation Area.

Youth-on-age

The primary concern of the administrating agency, Washington State Parks, is acquiring and preserving the gorge from rim to rim, including sufficient buffer strips to forestall "Canyon Rim Estates" and "Eagle's Perch Condos." Appropriation by appropriation, State Parks is working toward that goal. Though pristinity takes precedence, the hiker is served by trails equalled in richness and variety only by the Issaquah Alps. Three sections of the gorge have major public accesses. In the middle is the Green River Gorge Resort, where private owners maintain an extensive trail system in and around the gorge climax, the narrowest and most spectacular portion. State Parks has developed the gorge outlet and the gorge inlet and is holding for the future a number of other properties. As with the Alps, this book provides a sampling only, not an exhaustive inventory. The addicted hiker should buy the trails map published as a public service by Green River Gorge Resort, 29500 Green River Gorge Road, Enumclaw, WA 09022. Write for a copy or pick it up at the resort, for $2 (cheap). They don't make any money out of this, or indeed, out of running their funky resort. Someday State Parks will buy the resort; until then, it's a connection with the 1920s.

A trail has been talked about from one end of the gorge to the other. Someday such a trail may be built. Or maybe not. The route would have to stay mainly on the rim in order not to molest the isolation of the river, and such a route has less interest than the bottom of the gorge. For much of its length, this bottom is for floaters, not walkers, though there are a number of ways down to the water, and for varying distances beside it. In late summer and early fall, when Tacoma is drinking so much of the Green there's only enough left to float the fish, much longer hikes can be taken than are described here. Conceivably a water-level route could then be walked (and/or waded, maybe partly swum) the full 12 miles.

Flaming Geyser State Park (map — page 231)

At the downstream end of the gorge, where the bluffs, though still high and steep, retreat from the river, which thereafter flows over a floodplain ½ mile wide, is the site of an old resort now a state park with a full-fledged trail system.

East of Auburn, just before Highway 18 crosses the Green River, exit onto Auburn-Black Diamond Road and from that almost immediately exit right onto Green Valley Road. Drive 7 miles east to a Y and go right to the bridge over the river to the park. (Or, stay on the Auburn-Black Diamond Road to the Black Diamond-Enumclaw Road, follow it to 1 mile south of Black Diamond, turn west at the "Flaming Geyser" sign, and drive a scant 3 miles past the Lonely Red Schoolhouse of old Kummer to the bridge.) Parking is available at the park gates but the hikes are described here from a start at the far end of the park, 1¼ miles from the gate, elevation 225 feet.

Romping the Fields

But before doing *that,* park at any of several spots near the entry gate and strike off through the fields. Paths are mowed around the edges, by the river, and out in the middle. Strolling the "lawn" corridors through meadow grasses

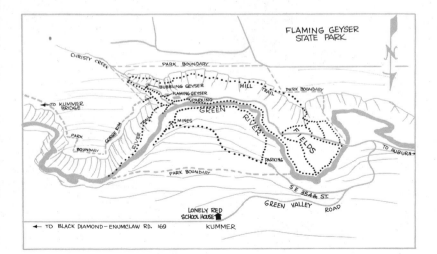

as high as an antelope's eye is an experience unique to this park, and the people love it. Some love it so much they don't even stay on the lawn strips.

Sample romp 1 mile, allow 2 hours
No elevation gain

Perimeter Loop, Hill Trail and Riverbank

Having driven to the picnic area parking lot, walk upriver past a series of concrete fish ponds. At the fence corner turn right up Christy Creek. Pass a pool bubbling with gas, the flow from a pipe ignited (sometimes) to form a flame 6-12 inches high. In 1911 a test hole probing coal seams was drilled 1403 feet down. At 900-1000 feet were showings of methane gas. In early days of the former private resort the "Geyser" was flaming many feet in the air; now it's pretty well pooped out.

Continue over a bridge and up the creek in mossy-ferny maple woods, the trail dividing and uniting, passing a bridge and stub trail to the gray mud of Bubbling Geyser. Up a short set of stairs and then again upstream, the main trail recrosses the creek and ascends the bluff and begins a long upsy-downsy contour along the sidehill in a green tangle of maple and cedar and alder and lichen and moss. Views (screened) down to the river. Sidepaths offer secluded nooks for lunch or rest or small adventures suitable for small folk. The way at length drops to the floodplain and road, the trail now a mowed strip (or strips) in pasture grass. Cross the road and walk out in the field to the park entry bridge. Turn right and follow the riverbank upstream to the picnic area, by sandy

Flaming Geyser in Flaming Geyser State Park

beaches, through patches of woods, meeting ducks and water ouzels, gulls and herons, and kayakers landing after voyages down the gorge.

Loop trip 3 miles, allow 2 hours
High point 425 feet, elevation gain 200 feet

River Trail to Gorge Outlet

Beginning as before, past the fence corner cross Christy Creek to a Y. Go straight on the right fork (the left quickly ends at the river) and then left (the right goes to the rim) up the old road-now-trail, climbing 100 feet above the river, contouring the sidehill, then dropping to a sandy flat in fine woods. The width of the floodplain dwindles to zero, the walls crowd the river, and as the trail enters the gorge it ends. Admire the 100-foot cliff of stratified rock, the river cutting the base. In low water a hiker can round the corner and proceed into the gorge.

Round trip 1½ miles, allow 1 hour
High point 325 feet, elevation gain 200 feet

Gorge Rim

The State Park Conservation Area protects the gorge rim all the way to the Kummer (Black Diamond) Bridge. The surveyor once walked the 3 miles — never on the rim and not often on public land, mainly in a bewilderment of logging roads. It wasn't really worth it and definitely is not recommended for the inexperienced. Indeed, even the doughty wildland navigator will have second thoughts as the 4x4s and dirtbikes kick dust in his face. However, the wily brush-buster can find a number of vantage points for impressive views straight down to the river. Moreover, by persistent snooping he can ferret out several paths beaten by the boots of insane fishermen and go slippetty-slide down into the wild gorge, visiting spots otherwise known only to kayakers.

Beginning as before, at the Y just past Christy Creek go straight on the right fork, then immediately right again on the traces of a road-trail whose brushy remnant climbs to the bluff top at 525 feet. Beyond that, lots of luck. Rangers say the only hikers ever lost in the park (and then found) have been attempting this route.

Round trip 6 miles, allow 4 hours (plus more for getting lost)
High point 525 feet, elevation gain 500 feet, not counting sidetrips to river

Across the River and Into the Trees

Half the park is across the river, offering the walker a combination of wildness and memories of a long human past.

To reach this part of the park, recross the river on the entry road, turn right, and in 0.4 mile up the hill toward Kummer turn right off the Green Valley Road onto SE 354 Street. Descend to the parking area on the valley floor, elevation 200 feet.

Pass the barn and keep left, crossing the green floodplain at the foot of the bluff. At ½ mile are an old orchard and Y. Take the road-path straight ahead and downhill into woods. In a short bit is another Y. The right fork goes ¼ mile

Green River in Flaming Geyser State Park

through forest to the river and a sandy beach for kiddies to safely wade, and a luscious pool of limeade for anybody to deliriously swim; a trail is planned downstream along the bank 1 mile, looping back to the parking area. The left fork goes a similar short way past interesting coal mine garbage to the river; a trail is planned upstream to the outlet of the gorge.

Complete tour 4 miles, allow 3 hours
High point 200 feet, minor elevation gain

Kummer (Black Diamond) Bridge (map — page 237)

The view of the gorge the best-known to the most people is from the Kummer (Black Diamond) Bridge, 2½ miles south of Black Diamond on Highway 169. A walkway offers thrilling views of the vasty deeps.

From the parking area on the north end of the bridge, elevation 450 feet, several paths dive to the river. The diving is mainly done by youths who have not yet attained sanity and trout fishermen and steelheaders doomed to go through life on the whacko side. The rewards of idiocy are that should a person arrive intact at the river, he would find paths downstream about ½ mile and a short distance upstream to the foot of a very fine sandstone cliff. In low water the walking can go much farther in both directions.

For advanced cases there is also a plummeting path on the south side of the bridge, also with upstream-downstream boulder-hopping. The surveyor once carried up this path a chunk of lignified tree weighing 50 pounds. (Well, his father carried it most of the way.)

South from the bridge ½ mile on the highway a woods road takes off to the right, gated and signed "No Tresspassing" (sic). Actually, the owners of the private property between the highway and the state land don't mind walkers, just wheelers, especially garbage-dumpers. However, caving-in mine workings make this one of the most dangerous areas of the gorge. Again, fishermen walk the road, bend right past the mines, and plummet down the gorge wall to a riverbank path that goes downstream to tumbled timbers of a mine structure and upstream ½ mile, nearly to the bridge; at low water the gravel bars extend the route.

If a person were to bluff out a route upstream on the gorge rim from Flaming Geyser, this is where he'd come out. Or where the search parties would start looking for him.

(Note: South from the bridge is a Department of Natural Resources campground signed "Green River Gorge Camp and Picnic Area." This is a splendid forest with a dandy ¾-mile nature trail but has no connection to the gorge.)

Hanging Gardens (Cedar Grove Point) (map — page 237)

The State Parks Conservation Area has nearly 3 miles of river and gorge rim on the northwest side here; for a sampling, see Franklin, below. It has half that much length on the southeast side. Short walks give tastes.

Drive Highway 169 south from the Kummer (Black Diamond) Bridge 1.5 miles and turn east on SE 385th-Enumclaw-Franklin Road.

At 1.7 miles see two gated roads on the left, nearly side by side. The first leads to a fish hatchery, with a connection to the second, which drops to the river. Neither route has been surveyed for this guide. Be surprised.

At 2.3 miles note, on the left, several dumped stumps, heaps of trash, and motorcycle tracks through and over all obstructions. Park here, elevation 680 feet.

Walk the road into the woods, shortly reaching the chainlink fence of the Black Diamond Watershed. Follow the fence to where it turns right; at a Y there, take the right fork down into lush mixed forest. The road soon yields to a trail plummeting down the bluff, following the crest of a finger ridge around which the river makes a sharp intrenched-meander bend. The point is distinguished by a grove of big cedar trees. It also features a sandy beach at the tip directly across from the Hanging Gardens, a vertical wall from which jut ledges sprouting shrubby trees and (in season) gaudy splashes of flowers — a phenomenon not unusual in the gorge but rather especially nice here.

Round trip 1½ miles, allow 1 hour
High point 680 feet, elevation gain 250 feet

Franklin (map — page 237)

The Johnson girl was born in 1896, died in 1897. Edey Standridge came to the world in 1892, left it in 1893, "Asleep in Jesus, blessed sleep, from which none ever wakes to weep." Mary Llewellyn's dates were 1890-1892. Francis Marie Myers lived from March 13 to May 24 of 1901. Alice Johnson knew six days in January of 1902. Something like half the headstones in the Franklin Cemetery are of infants; the recumbent lamb was the stonecutter's top seller.

The other half are for men in their twenties and thirties. On August 24, 1894, there died Luici Farro, 32; Rocco Tittara, 37; and Filippo Dimarino, 27; the three are memorialized by a single stone. Another stone states that on the same day James Gibson, 27, died. An historian poking through the hellberries and nettles, ivy and periwinkle, might find others who met their ends that day in the mines.

The location of the Franklin Cemetery will not be described here. However, it must be mentioned in order to urge the authorities (State Parks, King County, City of Black Diamond) to, first of all, continue their policy of gating all roads into the area; and second of all, to fortify those gates to keep out motorcycles. To be sure, the only legal four-wheelers on the service roads are public servants and that is why the Franklin Cemetery has survived intact. But two-wheelers sneak past the gates and in a single rowdy Saturday night could ravage a century.

History. That's the centerpiece of the banquet. The townsite. Relics of the old mines. The intact grade of the railroad. Yet there is also, always, the river, the gorge. And the forest, with deer and coyotes and bear running through. The miles aren't many but you can't do all of this feast in one day. The hiker's arterial is the railroad grade from Franklin to Black Diamond. This will be described first in one go, and then, in sequence, the sidetrips.

Franklin to Black Diamond Railroad

From Highway 169 in Black Diamond turn east on Green River Gorge Road 4 miles, to a few yards short of the Franklin Bridge (see Green River Gorge Resort). To the right see a park-like flat, the road into it barred (very partially) by a gate. Park outside the gate, elevation 608 feet.

The road inside the gate passes a trail down left, into the gorge, not surveyed for this guide. (There are so many!) A second gate, painted white in the State Parks style, is securely closed to four-wheelers — and used to be to two-wheelers and should be again. Two sideroad-trails go off left through the flats of "Lower Franklin" to the gorge; neither were they surveyed, we are so rich.

The road gains a bit of elevation and at a scant ½ mile from the highway switchbacks to a T with the Franklin-Black Diamond Railroad. The way to the right leads to Franklin, discussed below; go left.

In a few steps the road one has been walking turns uphill from the rail grade to the Big Hole, discussed below; go left on the level grade of the vanished rails, on a foot-only trail occasionally but sufficiently maintained by the excellent people of the Gorge Resort (on state land).

Remember as you walk — this railroad was built in 1884. Hasn't seen choo-choos since — when? — around about World War I? The grade is sliced

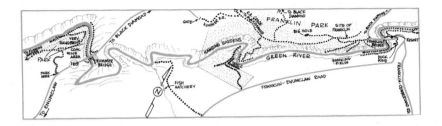

through a cut, then in sandstone walls of the gorge. A window opens in the superb mixed forest to a view across the gorge to the Smoking Fields. The river can be heard if not seen. The rock cliffs drip maidenhair fern and ivy. From under the boots comes the scent of crushed mint. A path into and out of a gully where the trestle has been missing for half a century crosses a cool ooze of water down mossy slabs.

At 1 mile the footpath-on-the-rail-grade becomes a road and comes to a Y. The right is the powerline road to Black Diamond, discussed below; continue straight ahead, left, on the rail grade, which cuts across the neck of a promontory ridge to the powerline swath and another Y. The left descends to the river, discussed below. Continue straight ahead on the rail grade.

In a long ½ mile from the powerline-swath Y, the drivable road turns off left; this is the rail grade to Kummer, discussed below. Continue right, on rail-grade-again-footpath. In a long ½ mile the path enters private property and the decent thing to do is turn back. If one doffs hat and humbly begs permission to pass, and is not torn to pieces by packs of dogs, in another ½ mile, where the grade used to be before driveways and houses obliterated it, the walker will reach Highway 169, cross it to find Railroad Avenue, and in ¼ mile arrive at the Black Diamond Bakery.

Round trip from Franklin to bakery 6 miles, allow 5 hours
High point 725 feet, elevation gain 150 feet

Franklin Townsite

At a scant ½ mile from the highway is the T with the rail grade. Turn right on it, over a flat bench where ivy climbs high in poplars, hellberries daunt the doughtiest pothunters, and white roses blooming in wild greenery grab at the heart.

A gash in the slope to the left can be recognized as a collapsed mine mouth. A hillock on the right reveals to the investigating boot that it is made of waste rock and clinkers. Three marvels of masonry testify to the craft of mine folk; slabs of cut sandstone are concreted together, brick-like, in Mayan-like temples. This is all there is of a town that early in the century had some 1200 residents.

The rail grade ends in a very scant ½ mile. The trail continues onward and up, some 2 miles to the Green River Gorge Road near Lake No. 12, of more interest to horses than hikers.

Sidetrip round trip to Franklin town limits ¾ mile, allow 1 hour

Big Hole

A few steps from the Franklin junction, the road takes off uphill from the rail grade. One wonders why there is such a road. In a long ¼ mile is the answer. Here, at 800 feet, the road ends abruptly at a Big Hole, a mine shaft, capped with a grate in 1987 by the federal Office of Surface Mining. The road is reverting gracefully to trail. Hikers come to gaze in awe at a black pit said to go straight down 1500 feet. Toss a rock and listen for a splash.

Sidetrip round trip to Big Hole ½ mile, allow 1 hour
High point 800 feet, elevation gain 75 feet

Black Diamond Reservoir

At 1 mile from the highway the rail grade is intersected by the powerline service road of the Black Diamond Water District. This road is firmly gated against public vehicles and thus may have some interest to hikers.

From Black Diamond drive Green River Gorge Road 0.6 mile to a narrow sideroad signed only "Diamond J Ranch." In 0.25 mile is a gate. Park here, elevation 800 feet.

The service road climbs to the new Black Diamond Water Reservoir, continues through clearcuts to a ridgetop at 1025 feet (look back north over Puget Sound lowlands to the summit of Mt. Selig), and descends to the Franklin Railroad at 700 feet, 1¾ miles from the gate.

Round trip from gate to railroad 3½ miles, allow 2 hours
High point 1025 feet, elevation gain 600 feet

To the Bottom of the Gorge

At a long 1 mile from the highway, shortly after the powerline service road has come down to the rail grade from the right, this latter proceeds down left, passes a City of Black Diamond pumphouse at the end of the powerline, and continues down in fine, cool forest of nicely big cedars to one of the very few sizable river terraces to be found in the gorge. At ¾ mile from the railroad is the river, 375 feet.

And how fascinating it is! What a lot of poking about to do in so little room!

The hiker's imagination is certain to have been inflamed by the "footbridge" shown on the USGS map. He is sure he'll find nothing more than naked cables. He is virtually consternated to find the bridge is intact — a genuine swinging bridge. Especially if accompanied by a pair of cowardly dogs, he will not cross the bridge, and that's just as well. It is a bridge to nowhere — to no trail. It is the pipeline (plus walkway for maintenance purposes) that brings water across from the Springs on the other side of the gorge (see Hanging Gardens), thence up to the pumphouse and onward to the reservoir.

A short bit upstream from the bridge are mossy masses of old concrete and a new grate over a pit of black water. In 1987 the Office of Surface Mining installed the grate after a horse fell in the mine airway and drowned.

Downstream the road-trail ends in a grove of great cottonwoods and a path drops to the gravel bar. On the other side of the river a creek tumbles whitely out of the greenery. Sandstone walls leap up. See the fishermen. Watch the kayaks slide by.

Kayaking in the Cedar River at Kanaskat-Palmer State Park

Sidetrip round trip from rail grade to bridge 1½ miles, allow 2 hours
High point 700 feet, elevation gain 350 feet

Kummer Railroad

At 1½ miles from the highway, where the grade continues ahead to Black Diamond, another grade, improved to a drivable (State Parks) service road, turns off left. This is the rail grade to Kummer.

At the turnoff, fields open out in the forest to the left, domain of the Black Diamond Gun Club, a good place not to be on weekends when ricochets may whine off into the fine forest. In ½ mile the road is absolutely barred to public wheels by a sturdy white gate of the State Parks variety. That's good, very good.

Also good is the fact that this gate can be reached from the other side. From Highway 169, where Green Valley Road turns off west, turn off east on a road signed "Black Diamond Gun Club Inc." In 0.3 mile the gun club road swings off right and the old rail grade proceeds straight ahead, arriving at the white gate at 0.6 mile from the highway. Park here, elevation 666 feet.

The old rail grade used to extend west of Highway 169 close to and partly on the modern Green Valley Road. In ½ mile is a little building with a school bell atop, prominently signed, "This is Kummer. Formerly School Dist. 123. Home of the Lonely Red Schoolhouse."

Round trip from Highway 169 to Franklin Railroad 2 miles, allow 1 hour

Green River Gorge Resort (map — page 240)

The history of the resort began in the 1880s. When King Coal was the dominant industry of King County, folks came not only from the mining towns but the coal-shipping cities to marvel at the wild depths. Later, when the nation was seized by a moral fit, folks came from faraway for the wild life in a free realm where Prohibition agents dared not intrude. From this period came the decline to a dark and seedy time when families shunned the resort as they did the Skid Road.

That's all in the past, and a colorful history book it would make. The present is an ownership whose principals have turned down offers from State Parks because they're having too much fun building and maintaining trails. The idea of fun among these entrepreneurs is busting brush and gouging tread, chopping hellberries and nettles, on their own land and on state land and on the lands of any timber companies and miners who'll stand still for it.

Before hiking at the resort or in the area, buy the resort's trail map.

From Highway 169 in Black Diamond turn east on Green River Gorge Road 4 miles to the Franklin Bridge. (Alternatively, from Highway 169 at 1.5 miles south of the Kummer Bridge take the Enumclaw-Franklin Road 4 miles to the bridge.) Park near the inn, elevation 580 feet.

Quintessential Gorge

The most important gorge hike of all is from the snackery down to the water. The trail fee is a modest contribution to maintenance of the area's trails.

From the snackery gate the way drops to a Y. To begin with the downstream route, turn left down a staircase-path over the brink of a waterfall to the river. There's too much to see to go fast and that's good; speed kills. Pass through dark clefts between huge mossy-green boulders, over slippery slabs by churning green pools of The Chute, under fern-and-moss cliffs where in season hikers can get a free shower from Rainbow Falls.

To go upstream from the Y, turn right, in ¼ mile descending a staircase to walk-in camps on a forest flat by the river. This is a loop trail — but only at low water because at high water a stretch of several hundred feet requires knee-deep wading. At seasons when the trail so enters deep water, turn back to the camp area and take a straight-up path to the gorge rim, reached in a picnic area. From the upstream end of this area find the other end of the loop trail and descend spectacularly on staircases to the river and a T. The left fork goes downstream (the loop way) to a high-water end at a wonderful great cave. The right fork, a delight every step, proceeds to exposed coal seams and — it is claimed — all the way to the Cinnabar Mine.

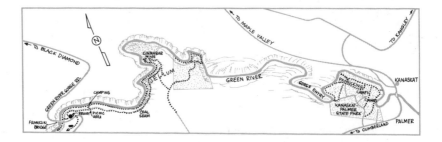

Complete roundtrip all trails 6-8 miles, allow 4-6 hours
High point 580 feet, elevation gain 500 feet or 1000 or more

The Rim

On a first visit to the resort a person definitely must walk out on the Franklin Bridge, built in 1914 to replace a wooden span that must have been a wonder of the world. The looks down to the gorge depths invite explorations there and along the rim.

From the resort's camping area across the road from the snackery, a trail leads downstream along the rim 1 mile and then drops to the river. The area of the Smoking Fields and Hot Springs has been fenced off for residential seclusion.

Upstream, the Mercury Mine Trail goes along on high 1 mile to the sidetrail down to the mine (see Jellum).

Round trip up and down the rim 4 miles, allow 2 hours

Jellum Site (Big Boulders and Cinnabar Mine) (map — page 240)

Two undeveloped park areas are called the "Jellum Site." One is a magnificent spot for the special gorge sport of creeping through cracks between huge mossy boulders. The other is notable for relics of the cinnabar (mercury) mine.

From the junction just uphill and east from Green River Gorge Resort, drive east on Green River Gorge Road 0.5 mile. At the top of a rise, in an enormous clearcut of the mid-1980s, spot a road left barred by a white gate. Park here, 789 feet.

Walk the road (in private property but on a public easement) over a plateau through the clearcut into forest, to a Y in a scant 1 mile.

For the bouldery place, go right a short bit to the bluff rim, down which the road sidehills to a broad bench, in ½ mile from the Y ending in a fir-grove camp, once the site of some complicated activity (mine-related?). From the bench a trail goes over the brink, instantly splitting in two pieces, left and right, the two ends of a loop demanding to be hiked in its entirety. It is, however, the left fork that leads directly to The Place, featuring one enormous boulder that has atop it 18-inch hemlocks whose roots reach 25 feet down the rock to find nutritious earth. Not so much a trail as a clambering route, the way proceeds downstream, dodging through clefts, passing under a great overhang sheltering a ramshackle cabin, crossing sandy beaches, to a high-water end ½ mile from Camp Flat.

Round trip 4 miles, allow 3 hours
High point 789 feet, elevation gain 200 feet

For the mine, go left at the Y to ruins of an old shack on a jutting point, then follow the switchbacking road-trail down to mine garbage and timbers. From here a path drops to the mine mouth (collapsed) and the waste rock sloping to the river. Mine artifacts and cinnabar ore mixed with coal are interesting, and the bouldery river, and the forest, displaying one 8-foot cedar. But the scene for soft summer days is the great sprawl of sand dipping into the slow flow of river,

Deer track along the Cedar River

a place that demands taking off shoes and rolling up pants and wading — if not taking it all off and thrashing around, crying "Evoe!"

Round trip from the Y 1 mile, allow 1 hour

Kanaskat-Palmer State Park (map — page 240)

If the two state parks located at the exit and the entry of the gorge have the least of gorge excitement to offer, they have the most of easy river walks. The paths in this one are thronged on fine summer weekends, as are the deep pools of cold limeade. In other seasons it's a grand place to be lonesome.

Drive via Enumclaw or Black Diamond to old Cumberland and thence to old Palmer. Alternatively, drive from Issaquah-Landsburg or Kent to old Georgetown (that is, the Ravensdale Market). Turn east 1 mile on Kent-Kangley Road to a Y. Keep right on Retreat-Kangley Road 3 miles and turn right on Cumberland-Kanaskat Road. Proceed 1.7 miles, passing through old Kanaskat and crossing the Green River to old Palmer and the entry to Kanaskat-Palmer State Park.

Trails take off from a number of points on the park's road system and all are excellent woods walks, totalling some 3 miles and lending themselves to any number of loops. To go straight for the best, at a Y in 0.6 mile, where the road right leads to campsites, keep left. In 0.2 mile more pass a sideroad left to the downstream boat put-in and take-out. In a final 0.2 mile is the turnaround at the picnic area and midway put-in and take-out. Elevation, 740 feet.

To the right, by the bulletin board giving boating information, a path enters the woods and leads upstream, keeping mostly at some distance from the river. Sidepaths go off inland to the camping area. A path goes off left to the upstream put-in and take-out. At 1 long mile the route intersects the entry road not far from the entry.

A deadend path starts from the garbage cans at the turnaround circle, passes picnic tables, and drops to a gravel bar — the put-in and take-out spot. Just upstream the river falls over sandstone slabs into a spacious swimming pool.

The major trail downstream takes off from this deadend path a few steps from the parking lot, passes a privy, a picnic shelter in a broad lawn, and dozens of picnic sites tucked into a forest new-growing after a semi-clearcut in 1976. Sidepaths from the tables go a few steps to the brink of a bank dropping steeply to the river. At the end of the picnic area the blacktop trail veers left to the entry road; the river trail, now plain earth, enters cool mixed forest in which the alders and vine maple are particularly fine. Frequent rude sidepaths demand sidetrips to choice spots to sit beside the river. In ¾ mile the trail ends at the downstream put-in and take-out. Walk from the path out onto sandstone slabs beveled flat at the base of sandstone cliffs — not high, but announcing what lies just ahead. Stand at the edge of the beveled slab and look down into the water. E-gad! Retreat! The bottom can barely be made out, perhaps 12 feet down. The water is quiet, twigs fallen onto the surface scarcely moving. It is impossible not to wish one were a good enough swimmer to dive in. But that's not necessary. One can be quite content gazing upstream to a picturesque jutting point of rock with a large fir whose roots clutch the rock, barely keeping the leaning tree from falling into the water, and downstream, where the beginnings of the true gorge can be guessed just around the horseshoe bend.

On the surveyor's first exploration here, before the park was developed, he found rude paths to the top of the cliffs of the incipient gorge and followed them along a bench in virgin forest of giant cedars, firs, and hemlocks. In ½ mile the terrace and trail ended at a lovely camp. The surveyor proceeded without trail toward Jellum and got so splendidly lost that his compass read 180 degrees wrong, no matter how hard he banged it. The vicinity has been so completely scalped in the last decade that the virgin forest probably has been moved to Japan. But a person could go look.

Loop trip upstream 2 miles, allow 1½ hours
High point 750 feet, minor elevation gain

Round trip or loop trip downstream 1½ miles, allow 1½ hours
High point 740 feet, no elevation gain

Nolte State Park (Deep Lake) (map — page 244)

Not in the gorge but nearby is 39-acre Deep Lake, owned by the Nolte family since 1883, operated as a private resort since 1913, and on her death in the late 1960s willed to the public by Minnie Nolte. Because during olden-day logging only the cream (the huge cedars) was skimmed, the forest of Douglas firs up to 6 feet in diameter feels virgin, giving a pristine quality to the quiet (no motorboats allowed) waters.

From Cumberland (see Kanaskat-Palmer State Park) drive south 1 mile to the park, elevation 770 feet.

DUWAMISH-GREEN RIVER

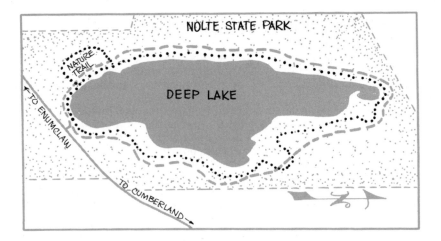

The trail loops 1 mile around the lake, through the big firs, plus 5-foot cedars and 3-foot cottonwoods, crosses the inlet, Deep Creek, passing a number of paths to the shore.

Loop and sidetrips 1½ miles, allow 1 hour
High point 770 feet, no elevation gain

Interurban Trail (maps — page 245)

Accentuate the positive. This is a very fine bicycle path, 10 feet wide and smoothly paved, the only legal motorized traffic being service vehicles. It's also a grand foot-stroll for railroad buffs, closely paralleling busy-working lines. And, amazingly, little pockets of wildness survive — drainage-ditch creeks a-swimming with ducks, bits of unfilled marsh with blackbirds a-nesting, pastures of as-yet-unsubdivided pastures with cows a-grazing. And views are long up, down, and across the Big Valley, from one forested bluff to the other.

Eliminate the negative. Forget if you can that until killed by the Pacific Highway in the late 1920s, for a quarter-century the Seattle-Tacoma Interurban Railway offered quick and convenient transit.

The old interurban right-of-way, owned by Puget Power and used for power-transmission lines, is now — through granting of permission by the company — a public trail. The city of Kent opened 6½ miles in 1972 and King County another 8½ miles in 1979, completing a route from Tukwila on the north to the Pierce County line.

Unlike locals, who can walk or bicycle from home, outsiders have a parking problem — unless they come by bus. For that reason, though there are many possible starting points for many different trips, a sample introductory trip is suggested which goes south from Orillia and returns.

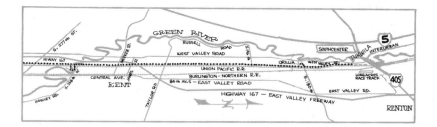

From Highway 405 at Tukwila, exit on the West Valley Road, then exit from that to the quaint little old hamlet of Orillia on S 180 Street (formerly a train station was a major reason for its existence) and park, elevation 50 feet. At the east town edge find the sign, "Interurban Trail Park. Open Daylight Hours. Bicycles Horses Hiking." Here, 1½ miles from the north end of the trail at Tukwila, begins the Kent-maintained segment.

Closely paralleling the Union Pacific and Burlington Northern tracks, the trail proceeds south, now in heavy industry, now in surviving fields. At 3¾ miles (from Tukwila) the way crosses 212 Street (parking possible) and at 5½ miles, just after crossing under Highway 167, is James Street, site of a Metro Park & Ride lot that provides good access. At 6½ miles is Meeker Street, in Kent; the downtown section east a block has handy parking and buses. At just short of 7 miles it is necessary to jog east to cross the Green River on a highway bridge (the interurban bridge long gone), then west to resume the trail. Parking is possible here. This is suggested as the turnaround for the sample introduction; enjoy the Green River, which has been nearby but unseen the whole way south.

At 277 Street, 8 miles, the Kent stretch of trail ends; parking is chancy here, though hikers can park at a distance with ease and walk the street to intersect trail. At 10 miles is Auburn's NW 15 Street, a crossing under freeways, and after a quiet rural stretch, increased industry. At 11 miles is the center of Auburn, with plentiful parking plus bus service. Having all the way to here followed a perfect north-south line, now the route turns southwest, passing Algona at 13 miles, Pacific at 14, and at 15 miles leaving the Big Valley and swinging west into the valley of Jovita Creek, ending (for now) at the county line.

Sample round trip (Orillia-Green River) 11 miles, allow 7 hours
High point 50 feet, no elevation gain
Bus: Metro 150 to Kent

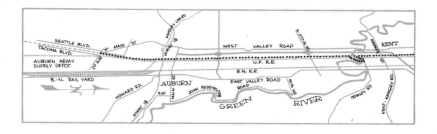

Mill Creek Canyon Park (map — page 246)

A green gash in the valley wall of the Green River, formerly a garbage dump, has been restored and preserved in a Kent city park, creek and forest running continuously the full length of the canyon from a gulch in the upland to debouchment on the floodplain of the Big Valley.

From Central Avenue on the east side of Kent turn east on Smith Street (Highway 516, the Kent-Kangley Road) to a stoplight. Turn south a few feet on E Titus Street (confusingly signed "Jason Avenue" at the light) to the parking area of 100-acre Mill Creek Park, elevation 50 feet.

In 1982 the place of debouchment, a mere four blocks from Kent City Hall, was transformed from a motorcycle-savaged meadow into an earthwork by the renowned Herbert Bayer; it serves at once as a stormwater-retention pond and as an under-the-summer-stars concert hall, also available for weddings and bar mitzvahs.

Two trails, one on either side of the creek, lead upstream. For an introductory tour, take the north-side trail.

Now down by the creek, deep in shadowed depths, now slicing the steep sidehill, now high on the rim, the path proceeds up a valley in forest of fine big cottonwoods and other hardwoods, then mixed forest with cedars, hemlocks, firs, and a rich understory and groundcover. Street noises fade. Glimpses of houses on the rim diminish. Feeder trails join from surrounding neighborhoods, sidetrails drop to creekside sitting spots, the main trail splits and unites, in a scant 2 miles ending at a paved road on the rim. However, by taking a sidetrail down to the creek and up to the opposite rim, the trip can be extended a bit to a field (and private property) where Mill Creek is no longer in a wide wild canyon but a narrow gulch fouled with farmers' garbage.

Round trip 4 miles, allow 3 hours
High point 350 feet, elevation gain 300 feet
Bus: Metro 150 to Kent, walk to park

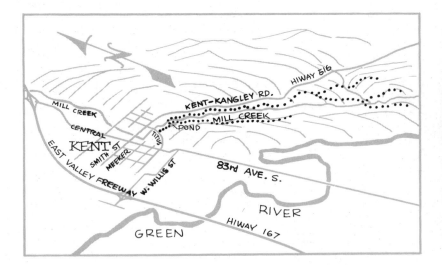

Green River College forest trail

Green River College Forest (map — page 248)

On the high promontory whose bluffs fall west to the Big Valley, south to the Green Valley, and east to Big Soos Valley lie the Green River College campus and its contiguous forest, the living laboratory for an instructional program that encompasses the planting and tending and harvesting of trees and the design and construction and maintenance of trails. Totalling some 4 miles in length, the trails sample big-tree wildlands on the plateau, forests on the steep bluffs, and tanglewoods of birdland sloughs along the Green River. In various conditions of repair from plush to overgrown, they offer a range of experiences from leisurely strolls to sweating, face-scratched, shin-bruised, boot-soaked adventures. While crashing around in the brush it's hard to believe the campus and forest cover only some 300 acres. The trails are unsigned, no problem when spending a full day poking about to see where every path goes.

Drive Highway 18 east from Auburn and shortly after crossing the Green River turn left and follow signs to the main campus entrance, elevation 425 feet. Buy an all-day parking permit at a vending machine and park in any unreserved space.

The map shows the route taken by the surveyor on his first long day's journey. However, the students are ever busy at their lessons, practicing the art of the clearcut and thereby erasing earlier trail projects. They are, meanwhile, building new trails, yet in their enthusiasm for fresh creation may neglect the old, letting the brush creep in. The surveyor has given up trying to keep up.

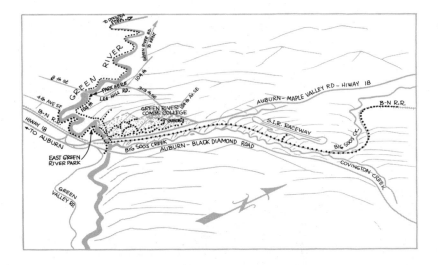

Begin by consulting one of the many locator maps placed around campus. So guided, navigate to the street bounding the south edge of the campus. Five or so trailheads lead into the woods. Any will do. The paths tour superb big-tree forest. They open into broad-view plantations of young trees. They go this way, they go that way, they go around and around. Do not rest content until you have tasted the two chief delights.

One is the bluff dropping to the Green River. Poke about and you will come upon a path that steeply follows the narrow crest of a ridge of stupendous forest poised above two tanglewood gulfs. Wilderness!

The second stellar attraction is the Green River. At least two paths (including Stupendous Forest Ridge) drop to the water. A path leads upstream to Big Soos Creek Trail (which see). The downstream direction is the main show. Across the water is East Green River Park (which see), an easy wade when Tacoma is watering all its lawns at once in the parching sun of late summer. No need to cross, though. This is the wild side. Proceed out of the college trail system onto an old road with more forest, many ways to riverside, gravel bars, and duck-watching spots. In about 1¼ miles the way ends at a public streetend (104 Avenue SE), an alternate access reached in 0.2 mile from Lea Hill Road-SE 320th, out of Auburn via 8th Street NE.

A person who wanted to be really systematic could do as the surveyor did — visit the college's Department of Forestry and ask for a current map; mapping, too, is part of the curriculum. The best plan, though, is to allot a day and count on getting lost. If after a reasonable time you can't find yourself, blow your whistle; the college also has courses in Search and Rescue.

Suggested round trip 5¾ miles (college forest loop 2¼ miles, off-campus sidetrip 3½ miles), allow 4 hours

High point 425 feet, elevation gain 800 feet

Bus: Metro 153 to campus (weekdays only); 150 to Auburn, walk Main, M, and 8th Streets 1½ miles to Green River bridge, on far side walk 104 Avenue E to campus

Big Soos Creek Rail Trail (map — page 250)

The Three Bears came in assorted sizes. So do these three valleys that also live together: the Big Valley (too big), the Green Valley (too many strawberries to be trampled), and the Big Soos valley (ju-ust right for walking). The Big Soos isn't really, except by comparison with the Little Soos. The pastures are miniaturized. The cool-shadowy wildwoods have scarcely enough pulp to justify firing up a chainsaw. The creek never roars, at most babbles.

Park as for East Green River Park (which see), elevation 75 feet. Walk downstream to the railroad bridge over the Green River. (Alternatively, especially if coming by bus, approach from Green River College, which see.) Most of the way paralleled by a walker-horse path, the tracks pass cows in pastures, fish in a hatchery, and soon swing away from Highway 18 into quiet forest. Note: This is a mainline railway so keep a sharp lookout for speeding trains.

A deep, nameless tributary valley is crossed on fill. Then, out of sight but on Sundays not out of sound, is passed the Seattle International Raceway. Farms are left behind for a remote-feeling wildland. At a scant 3 miles the tracks cross Big Soos at its junction with Covington Creek, along whose valley is a woods road. A path to the creek gives a look at the handsome old fern-draped masonry arch of the Soos culvert; they don't build 'em like that anymore. Subsequent paths give further access to gravel bars and rapids.

At 4 miles the tracks return to farms, the gorge dwindles to a mere gully, and Jenkins Creek, larger than Big Soos, enters. A sand-cliff swallows' apartment house is the last sight to see before turning around. From here the tracks leave Soos for Jenkins Creek and proceed to points east in less interesting country, though the long-distance walker would find it a much more stimulating route to the Cascade Crest and Chicago than I-90.

As for Big Soos Creek, in the next 2 miles upstream its course is blocked to feet by a succession of barb-wire fences. Then, however, begins Big Soos Park (which *definitely* see).

Round trip 8 miles, allow 5 hours
High point 300 feet, elevation gain 225 feet
Bus: see Green River College, East Green River Park for two approaches

Big Soos Park (map — page 250)

From its headwaters to the point south of Lake Meridian where it begins trenching down to enter the Green River, Big Soos Creek exemplifies the phenomenon, familiar throughout lowland King County, of being "undersized" — not big enough for its britches. The valley it follows was dug by a far mightier stream vanished these dozen millennia or so. Gravels of braided channels that once swung from valley wall to valley wall have been buried by peaty bogs, cattail marshes, willow swamps. The water scarcely flows, mostly oozes through tangled greenery.

The common fate of undersized creeks is to have their wetlands dried up — fill dirt heaped, water ditched, houses and shopping centers built. The Forward Thrust of the 1960s saved a marvelous long strip of Big Soos from all that — 5 air miles, up to ¼ mile wide. In the late 1980s King County Parks began building an end-to-end trail. Local folk instantly came walking and running, riding horses and bicycles and scooters, and, thanks to the smooth and mainly

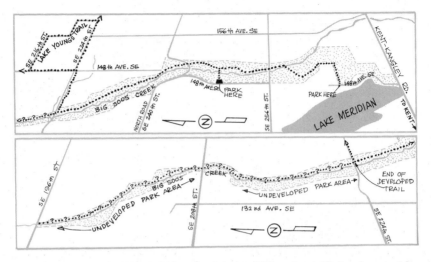

level blacktop, being pushed in wheelchairs. When the trail development is complete the fame will spread through the region. The county has nothing else like Big Soos. Not anymore.

To begin from the south, drive Kent-Kangley Road, Highway 516, to Lake Meridian County Park. Turn north on 148 Avenue SE 0.4 mile to 266th. Though the park actually continues south to Lake Meridian, and paths can be walked from there, the large parking area at 266th is the southernmost major trailhead. Elevation, 400 feet.

A blacktop lane serves bikes (and wheelchairs); a dirt lane, horses; hikers are welcome to both. The way swings away from houses onto the western valley wall, forested by tall firs, then drops to a willow woodland and crosses the creek on a handsome bridge; children wade here. The path emerges from woods to a powerline sky to a crossing of 256th, with shoulder-parking space for several cars, and ascends a bit to the eastern valley wall. At 1¼ miles a sidepath comes in from across the creek; this second major trailhead is reached by driving 148 Avenue SE to 249th.

The 2 miles north to SE 240th and SE 224th (two more accesses) will be complete by late 1988. The route is mostly on forest slopes secluded from houses, with morally uplifting pastoral vistas over boggy meadows and scattered horses.

The equestrian path (pedestrians allowed) turns east from Big Soos Park on 224th, then north on 148th, in a long 1 mile linking to Lake Youngs Perimeter Trail (which see).

The blacktop lane ultimately (1989?) will extend north 1½ more miles, crossing 208th to a northern trailhead at SE 192 Street, elevation 370 feet. The walker who has spent 5 miles in a valley of preserved wetlands will be edified by Forest Estates, north of 192nd, where the wet has been filled dry and Big Soos confined to a backyard ditch, no blackbirds and mighty few dragonflies.

The final development (1990?) will bring the regional fame. The trail has mostly been kept at a polite distance from the creek, where the wild things need their space. However, at carefully selected spots boardwalks over the squish will permit human visitors to pay their respects. As an example of how quickly creatures move in when granted a bit of secure water, the ponds that have been dredged to retain stormwaters do double duty. Already the reeds and cattails are filling in, the blackbirds are harassing hikers, and in season the ponds are alive with salmon fry leaping for mosquitoes.

Round trip (when complete) 10 miles, allow 7 hours
High point 400 feet, elevation gain 400 feet
Bus: Metro 158

Mount McDonald (map — page 251)

A supreme vantage for studying the geography of Whulj country. From the Cascade front between the Forbidden Valleys of the Cedar and Green Rivers, look across the upland sliced by the Green River Gorge to the Osceola Mudflow and The Mountain from which it gushed 5000 years ago. Look to the peninsula thrust of the Issaquah Alps touching shores of Lake Washington. See Seattle and the Olympics and smoke plumes rising from the pall customarily hiding Tacoma.

One of several ways to drive is via Georgetown, whose most notable surviving feature is the Ravensdale Market. From this junction of Kent-Kangley Road and Landsburg Road and Ravensdale-Black Diamond Road, turn east 1 mile on Kent-Kangley Road, go right at a Y for 3 miles on Cumberland-Kanaskat Road, passing Lake Retreat and the Bonneville Space Center (with a view of McDonald), coming to a dangerous Y where the right rises to a bridge over railroad tracks. Keep straight on Kanaskat-Kangley Road 0.7 mile to a lane on the right, SE Courtney Road. Park on the highway shoulder, not up the lane. Elevation, 874 feet.

Walk up Courtney Road a short bit through the barking dogs. Cross the grade which had railroad tracks until the late 1970s. Turn left on a woods road to a very firm gate which absolutely bars four-wheelers but is high enough above the ground to let walkers crawl under — and motorcycles, too, more's the pity.

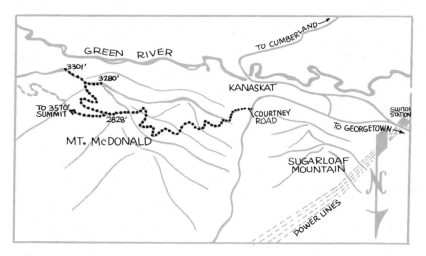

Mount Rainier from Mount McDonald

The road climbs steadily in mixed forest, lesser spurs going off left and right. In ½ mile a window opens to pastures below and out to the Olympics and Rainier. At 1 mile is a waterfall-creek. As the road twists and turns around the mountain, the forest changes to young conifers, mostly hemlocks, and views commence over treetops and through them. At 3 miles, 2828 feet, is a Y where both forks are major. Go right, climbing. The views on this trip are cafeteria-like — something of this here, a bit of that there, never everything all at once. In this stretch are the best views north, down to the Cedar River and out to Taylor and Tiger and Squak and Cougar, as well as to Rattlesnake and Si, Baker and Index and Three Fingers.

In a final 1 mile, with a couple more switchbacks, the road reaches a clearcut plateau atop McDonald Point, elevation 3280 feet. Here, formerly the site of a fire lookout, is a monster of a TV repeater powered by a noisy diesel generator. Gasp at the fumes and enjoy the grand view off the edge of the scarp. Then, for a variation, follow a sketchy road ¼ mile through small silver firs and western hemlocks to a 3301-foot point. See huge Rainier and distant St. Helens and nearby Grass. See the Enumclaw plain and silvery meanders of the Green River and hear the trains blow, boys, hear the trains blow.

Round trip 8 miles, allow 7 hours
High point 3301 feet, elevation gain 2400 feet

From Junction 2828, the left (straight ahead) fork goes on and on. The 3570-foot summit of McDonald ought to be accessible with some 6 more round-trip miles.

INDEX